CHALLENGES IN EDUCATIONAL MANAGEMENT
Principles into Practice

Challenges in Educational Management

Principles into Practice

BILL DENNISON and KEN SHENTON

CROOM HELM
London & Sydney
NICHOLS PUBLISHING COMPANY
New York

© 1987 W.F. Dennison and K. Shenton
Croom Helm Ltd, Provident House, Burrell Row,
Beckenham, Kent, BR3 1AT

Croom Helm Australia, 44-50 Waterloo Road,
North Ryde, 2113, New South Wales

British Library Cataloguing in Publication Data

Dennison, W.F.
 Challenges in educational management:
 principles into practice.
 1. School management and organization—
 Great Britain
 I. Title II. Shenton, Ken
 371.2'00941 LB2901
 ISBN 0-7099-0892-X

First published in the United States of America in 1987
by Nichols Publishing Company, Post Office Box 96,
New York, NY 10024

Library of Congress Cataloging-in-Publication Data

Dennison, W.F.
 Challenges in educational management.

 Bibliography: p.
 Includes index.
 1. School management and organization — Great Britain.
2. Teacher participation in administration — Great Britain.
3. Teacher-administrator relationships. I. Shenton, Ken.
II. Title.
LB2901.D45 1987   371.2'00941   86-23588
ISBN 0-89397-266-5

Printed and bound in Great Britain by
Biddles Ltd, Guildford and King's Lynn

FOREWORD

This is a book about the effective management of our schools. Its authors are widely experienced in the provision of management training: their practical experience is firmly underpinned by their extensive reading of management literature. Indeed, this book is a happy combination of the practical and the theoretical: of sound commonsense and relevance.

For practising teachers the literature on management is, as the authors imply in their introduction, so vast as to be daunting. As a headteacher for nearly twentyfive years I am well aware of the problems involved in trying to keep up with the spate of books relevant to the wide issues of school management. With so much dense wood around — dense in both content and presentation far too often — I would have found a book such as this invaluable. In the few years since I left headship the spate has become a flood; and, unfortunately, the increasing pressures on all teachers, not least on headteachers and their senior staff, have reduced the time available for improving the professional knowledge base.

It is becoming increasingly accepted that school management is merely a subset of general management practice and principles. Nevertheless, adaptation from one culture to another is no easy matter, and teachers are often put off by what appears to them to be an alien language. What this book does so well is to select in such a way as to point up the relevance of the management literature which the authors cite.

If the authors have any axe to grind it is that school management is not a concern reserved to the headteacher. Management is the responsibility of the staff as a whole: leadership, decision making and accountability must be thought of as corporate concerns. This book has a significant contribution to make to the way in which our schools will be managed in the next decade. It deserves a wide readership.

Cyril Poster

CONTENTS

CONTENTS

DIAGRAMS

INTRODUCTION

Over 100,000 teachers in UK schools hold posts with managerial responsibilities. It is to such headteachers, deputy heads, house and departmental heads, curriculum co-ordinators and so on that this book is mainly directed. However, the remaining 400,000 teachers and related staff form an equally important group because their work is influenced and sometimes directed by the managerial activities of others. Also, many of them aspire to gain promotion to posts with managerial responsibilities. In addition, the way schools are organised, and the nature of teaching mean that all teachers have considerable control over their own work patterns, and they can become involved in many ways in the management of their schools. Indeed, since members of both groups spend, or have spent, most of their time in the classroom, this differentiation of teachers into two types must be viewed with caution since it is more apparent than real. In addition, both have managerial responsibilities not directly associated with their teaching. Even newly-appointed staff have to assume general oversight of certain activities such as liaising with parents or carrying out playground duties. More significantly, their professional capabilities and knowledge make them potential contributors to management decisions affecting activities beyond their classrooms.

Interest in school management has increased since the mid-1970s with the work of more senior staff receiving greatest attention. Potentially these teachers have the most influence over school activites, while their managerial accomplishments and failures are highly visible both within the school and outside. Headteachers, for example, are seen by parents, pupils, governors and councillors as being ultimately accountable for everything that goes on in the schools, a perception which has been reinforced in law. Not surprisingly, as arrangements for school management training began, from 1983 onwards, to be developed on a formal and systematic basis, the DES chose to concentrate activities upon the needs of headteachers and senior staff (DES, 1983a). The fairly recent appearance of such training arrangements in the UK as compared with North America (Leithwood, 1986), parts of Western Europe (Hegarty, 1983) and Australia conceals the initiatives of LEAs, schools and individual teachers in this respect. Before 1983 most LEAs organised some form of induction course for newly-appointed headteachers, while many staff with managerial responsibilities made their own arrangements in an attempt to extend and

1

refine their skills. By contrast relatively few senior members of staff in the UK had the opportunity to attend COSMOS courses organised by the Committee on the Organisation, Staffing and Management of Schools (Poster 1976). However, the range and scope of such courses and activities have expanded even at a time of financial constraint, as both DES and LEAs have placed more emphasis on the centrality of management training for teachers in schools (Dennison, 1985b).

Undoubtedly the main cause of the continuing and rapid increase is related to the changing environment in which schools operate. Schmuck (1974) suggested six factors likely to produce such changes in secondary schools:

a growing demand for increased individualisation of learning;

a need to ensure that what is taught is relevant, particularly in relation to vocational requirements;

closer attention to evaluation and accountability;

increasing awareness of technological change;

re-organisation of the traditional fields of knowledge and a breakdown of conventional subject barriers;

greater emphasis on the socialising and humanising capacities of the school.

A set of very similar factors could easily be derived for primary schools. Since the 1970s the cumulative effects of these factors on attitudes and behaviour within schools have been compounded by problems of contraction both in pupil numbers and in financial support. In brief then, schools have been expected to achieve more in terms of identifying and satisfying pupil needs without the benefit of the resources to which staff had become accustomed in the mid-1970s.

In such circumstances the superficial attractions of increased emphasis on management techniques can be very appealing because they contain a hint of better value for money. Drucker (1974) for example, suggests that the management of any organisation has three main components. First, the purposes of the organisation have to be decided. Second, its work must be made productive in relation to these purposes. Third, the social responsibilities and impact of the work require attention. The real problem in schools and all other organisations is to staff them with individuals who possess skills and attributes to enable the requirements of these components to be fulfilled.

In schools this certainly does not mean that the headteacher or other senior members of staff define the objectives which dominate the design of working practices and control contacts with external agencies as do some industrial managers. It does involve utilising and extending the whole of staff knowledge, experience, contacts and expertise so that the identification and satisfaction of the changing needs of young people take place, irrespective of the conditions in the environment of a particular school.

This book therefore looks towards the management skills and attributes of school staff and the ways in which these can be developed. In particular it concentrates on the provision of a theoretical framework through attempting a comprehensive survey of management thinking as it can be applied to schools. Always the main emphasis is on problem solving. At the same time a prescriptive approach is avoided.

The book is based on four main premises:

skills and attributes associated with effective management can be learned;

the important element in the acquisition of these skills and attributes is the understanding of the learning methods used by adults;

the effectiveness of managers is influenced by insights about themselves and their work;

knowledge gained by learning about management can improve managerial performance, despite the differences in the two activities.

The last premise is of particular significance to teachers who have had the benefit of a long formal education often involving complex subject matter and ideas. Most teachers, therefore, have the confidence to analyse and criticise any guidance and information offered to them. If, as part of management training, they are asked to reflect upon their experience, they would acknowledge that any conclusions they appear to be able to draw should have at least some theoretical underpinning. In particular, specific advice - for example that individual feedback should be given on performance, or that teamwork rather than competition should be rewarded (Hollingsworth and Hoser, 1985) - will be more readily acceptable if the supporting evidence and theoretical background appear convincing. However, busy teachers, even including those fortunate enough to be released for a time to study management practice, do not wish to risk being overwhelmed by such evidence (particularly when much of it may appear contradictory) and have little desire or opportunity to devote their time exclusively to a study of the vast literature on management and related topics, particularly when that on school management is growing rapidly, as this Croom Helm series demonstrates.

Within all of this literature there is much of value to individual teachers who are trying to construct a base for the development of more effective management practice at all levels in the school. Under normal circumstances the immediate demands of a teacher's work are dominant, and difficulty is found in searching for what may be available. This book, after surveying the enormous literature which relates to school management, attempts the processes of selection, analysis, criticism and synthesis. Where appropriate, reference has been made to the management literature, not limited to that derived from school studies, in order to substantiate and reinforce the discussion, and also to indicate to the interested reader where futher information may be sought. Although there may be significant differences between the perspectives of teachers and those of members of other professions (Lowther and Stark, 1984), educational managers must not allow these differences to blind them to the applications of 'management theory' in schools. The intention of the present book is to strengthen the theoretical framework by placing schools within the broader context of studies about organisations with a view to exploring how the management of schools might be improved.

The dominant theme, then, is learning , not because the book concentrates on schools, but because the way in which improved performance of both teacher and organisation can best be achieved is through this process. Therefore, after a consideration of the changing environment of the school in Chapter 1, learning for managerial effectiveness receives attention in Chapter 2. Chapter 3 concentrates on the key issue of leadership in schools, while Chapter 4 looks at the problems of management expertise and credibility. Power and authority provide the core themes in Chapter 5, with particular reference to the participation of staff in decision-making. The response of management to changing demands and constraints is the focus of Chapter 6. This leads to consideration of the contribution of interpersonal skills to effective management in Chapter 7, and the fundamental importance of personal, group and organisational communication is studied in Chapter 8. The final chapter returns to the issue of learning by individuals, sub-units of the school and the school itself, through a review of appraisal, staff development and team -building, so that the role of the individual manager in contributing to the school's capacity to respond flexibly to both internal and external pressures can be fully appreciated and developed.

CHAPTER 1

DEMANDS, OPPORTUNITIES, CONSTRAINTS AND INFLUENCES

Changing demands

Managers in education, as elsewhere, are at the centre of conflicting demands. That is part of the job; it cannot be otherwise. Demands are made upon their time by children, other staff, parents and people outside the school who think that staff with managerial responsibilities ought to be concerned about, or intervene in, some particular matter. Competing demands for resources between departments and individuals have to be resolved. Demands to include new materials in the syllabus or adopt alternative teaching approaches will have to be answered: these will have come from parents or any one considering that they have a legitimate stake in the activities of the school. Increasing demands for greater accountability in relation to a school's or an individual's performance require some sort of response. Anyone who resists this notion of being the subject of numerous demands should not contemplate a post involving management duties in schools. Any school, even a small one, whose behaviour is to be shaped and modified as part of the management process, represents a complex organisation. Appointment to a senior post, as headteacher for example, does not permit a person to rise above that complexity. Indeed such a post heightens an individual's involvement with others, has an increased range and number of demands associated with it, and increases the complexity of the situation which the individual must confront.

To newly-appointed school leaders the debate about whether organisational life is primarily the product of the free will of its members or the result of determinism produced by environmental pressures may seem largely theoretical (Astley and Van der Ven, 1983). What such promoted teachers will soon discover, if they have not realised it already, is that both sets of factors, far from being mutually exclusive, contribute to a plethora of controls over action. Staff expect certain behaviour from school leaders who in turn feel obliged to respond to these expectations. To some extent, this provides some guarantee that the teachers will act in ways that they, as leaders, could approve. Externally, schools are fixed into a network of obligations and exchanges with other organisations including neighbouring and feeder schools, colleges, parents' organisations, employers and examination boards. These, as individuals and groups, or as members of groups, anticipate certain behaviour by schools; if their aspirations are not realised they strive to achieve their own perceptions of conformity. It is hardly surprising, in these circumstances, that schools, like most other organisations, are inherently conservative. Moreover, fixed into a pattern of relationships with other organisations and managers, they have to mediate between numerous competing demands which reflect the existing values, practices, structures and habits of staff, and to such people the achievement of changed behaviour presents immense problems (Pfeffer and Salancik, 1978).

In many situations there can be incentives for an education manager to raise the importance of these demands for continuity. Individuals have invested in a particular pattern of behaviour since it provides them with security and confidence. From the manager's point of view this avoids the new and additional demands that change might bring, without any certainty that these demands can be predicted or controlled. Some managers might argue that their free will is extremely limited; their freedom of action appears totally constrained by the social determinism of internal and external factors. That perception would be disputed by Stewart (1982). She, using a relatively narrow definition of demands (what anyone in a job has to do), goes on to establish empirically, through study of a large number of UK managers, that the choices available - those things that **can** be done as part of the job - are quite extensive.

Middle managers in school have the power to allocate their time and attention, either by concentrating their efforts on a small number of difficult pupils or by distributing their interest more widely to all their pupils; they can restrict their interest exclusively to their own field of activities or they can take an active part in issues affecting the whole school; they can involve their deputies in interviews with parents or assume this responsibility alone; they can see their duties as restricted to support for the teaching activities of the school or having a wider social function. Stylistically, in relation to their colleagues, parents, welfare agencies and children, they are free to adopt any position on the continuum from autocratic to laissez-faire (Tannenbaum and Schmidt, 1958).

Contrary to this view of their freedom of action many middle managers in school would claim that, in practice, most of such choices are illusory. Because of conventions, expectations, the nature of client- and workgroups and as a result of their own personalities, they visualise few alternative courses of action in any of these situations. A newly-appointed pastoral head would find it difficult to delegate interviews with parents, for example, if the previous holder of the post had established these as a personal responsibility. Indeed, a special problem for education in general in a no-growth situation is the potential dominance of demands for continuity. Less mobility means that staff-groups become well established, sometimes for long periods. In such a situation there is a tendency for staff to structure their work in such a way that predictability increases, and familiar and comfortable arrangements prevail, based upon routine or precedent. Some of the stresses of the work place may be reduced, but at a cost, as individuals occupying the same position for some time become increasingly less responsive to the challenging aspects of their jobs.

With greater continuity the temptation for managers is to respond only to certain demands, usually those evolving from the more immediate work-group. To personnel whose demands are seldom recognised, such as other staff on the margin of the work-group, parents and children in their role as consumers, the fact that their demands are only occasionally acceded to can be highly frustrating. Younger members of staff unable to gain promotion and others who think they have been passed over for the wrong reasons can make demands on the headteacher or departmental head for a change in syllabus, or an alternative teaching approach, but with little hope of satisfaction. Similarly, parents may demand more involvement in decision-making or a clear policy about homework but may not anticipate a positive outcome, particularly if similar requests have been turned down on previous occasions. Indeed, the most effective way of reducing demands is to demonstrate their ineffectiveness and the futility of making them.

Alternatively, if those making demands can establish a resource-dependency there is some certainty that other parties will pay attention to their demands. More directly, if A makes a demand upon B the response and its likelihood of satisfaction will relate to the extent to which B relies upon A for scarce resources (Aldrich, 1976). Under the 1980 Education Act all parents have a choice of schools. When, usually as a consequence of falling rolls, they are able to exercise that right of choice they are imposing a form of dependency in that their decision represents an allocation of resources in favour of one school but to the disadvantage of another. Their demands are thus less likely to be overlooked (Dennison, 1983).

The most significant change that has occurred in English education since the 1970s has been the growing tendency of the DES, followed more slowly by LEAs, to try to enforce particular views about the desirability of school activities. In this they have utilised the school's dependency upon locally provided, but increasingly centrally determined, resources. Because schools are almost wholly dependent upon public funds it is quite easy for ministerial or local advice about some aspect of the curriculum to be interpreted as an order; a request for information about whether a curriculum policy has been introduced may be regarded as an instruction to adopt the

7

new practices. In fact, of course, resource support levels from central government to local authorities and then from LEAs to schools are governed by criteria much more sophisticated than whether a particular policy or scheme has been implemented. However, in conditions of extreme resource scarcity there are few impediments to using a relationship of total dependence to create a climate of submissiveness. Individuals, groups and schools who do not wish to appear resistant to DES or LEA demands, risk a cut in resources, either in absolute or in relative terms.

It is no coincidence that the emergence of a more interventionist curricular position has taken place at the same time as the imposition of strict spending controls. To the increased dependency which retrenchment produces must be added the need to demonstrate value for money in an increasingly competitive environment for public expenditure. The DES obviously feels that this will more likely be achieved by greater central control of the curriculum, school practices and public examinations. Hence, there has been a steady production of discussion documents, policy guidelines, circulars and so on since the late 1970s (DES, 1985). LEAs and schools cannot ignore them, even when they doubt the quality of the content. With selectivity in funding the exploitation of dependency goes even further. Previously, LEAs and schools welcomed autonomy in resource matters: they were given block grants with ostensibly few specific instructions about spending patterns, but in fact this apparent autonomy was restricted because of high fixed commitments. Nevertheless, there was some freedom. When shortage of resources eliminated previously existing opportunities, the institutions found themselves increasingly reliant on specific grants, on funds from ESG (Education Support Grants) TVEI (Technical and Vocational Education Initiative), and TRIST (TVEI Related In-Service Training). In effect, the spending of centrally supplied money is being limited increasingly to the achievement of centrally determined objectives.

With TVEI the government has done little more than to respond to demands for a more technical and vocational bias in the upper years of secondary school. The pressure has arisen from employers, parents and government itself, concerned about high levels of youth unemployment and the inadequate wealth-creating potential of the country's commercial and industrial base. Possibly, such demands will be satisfied by a strategy to raise the technological literacy of pupils leaving secondary schools. Even without this initiative, however, schools find themselves at the focus of increasing demands from a constituency, based around parents and pupils, to concentrate on pre-vocational activities. This pressure has resulted from a tight labour market. Yet this demand is only one of many. It cannot be considered in isolation from all others, whether internally or externally generated; it should not be discussed other than within a framework of matching a need for continuity to the requirements for changed arrangements. The task of the manager is, first, to attempt to make an assessment of the totality of demand in any situation and the likelihood of change; next, to interpret the potential role of the school in the satisfaction of these demands; finally, to assist the sub-units in pursuit of this satisfaction.

Enhanced opportunities

Those involved in education management for more than ten years would undoubtedly claim that the demands upon them and others in their working group have risen, often dramatically. Caution, of course, is necessary in accepting such views. Everyone can recall when the demands seemed less than now, because the passage of time reduces perceptions of the stridency with which past demands were argued. In fact, any attempt to assess changes in the values of perceptions of individuals over time is beset with difficulties. Similar methodological issues arise when assessing changes in stress over time, if this factor is to be used as indicative of extra demands upon the individual. Certainly, interest in work-related stress has grown in recent years, in all occupations (Cooper, 1981a) and particularly for teachers (Dunham, 1984); but increasing interest cannot be adduced as incontrovertible evidence that jobs are increasingly stressful and, in this context, necessarily subject individuals to additional and rising demands.

Most teachers would argue that such caution is quite unnecessary. They would point to general demands, impossible to quantify but nevertheless important, demands for increased accountability of both school and individual teachers, for example. These may have only limited direct effects but teachers would still argue for their significance. Essentially however, the systematisation of school inspections by HMI, complemented by a more monitorial stance of some local advisory staff, the publication of the results of these inspections and the availability of secondary school examination results represent tangible outcomes of greater accountability. Quite probably a formal appraisal system for teachers' performance will be introduced (DES, 1983), but without this, given the numbers of HMI and frequency of inspections, individuals are not likely to be in an inspected school more than one or twice in their careers, and, even less probably, be the subjects of an easily indentifiable comment in a published report. The counter-argument of teachers might be that it is the intangibility of accountability that produces additional demands. They would maintain that there is a new climate, only recently developed, which permits, and even seems to invite, criticism from pupils, parents, employers and the media regarding the activities and achievements of schools. Undeniably a change has occurred. Non-teachers are more willing than before to question what goes on in school; parents are less likely to accept the word of the teacher as an expert. What teachers must not overlook is that these phenomena extend to many other public services besides education.

Increasing demands however, invariably mean less choice for the individual and it is this development which teachers would claim has been most marked since the mid-1970s, largely as a result of stringent expenditure controls and the problems posed by a small school population. In effect autonomy and authority have been eroded. Clearly there exists a paradox. Fewer pupils should mean more flexibility for the individual teacher in interpreting job-components and also additional freedom for the school in organising classes and the curriculum because the range and extent of demands upon staff might be expected to be related to the number of children. The main contributor to this paradox arises from the differing perceptions created by growth and contraction. It is the association of pupil-numbers with finance which dominates discussion of the issue. During the time of expansion to the mid-1970s rolls were growing, both as a result of demographic factors and because more pupils chose to remain at school beyond the minimum leaving age. The actual expenditure per child rose. The main resource input is manpower, which may be measured by the pupil to teacher ratio (PTR), which in 1962 was 24.7 and fell by 1974 to 21.2. However, the availability of additional funding, even though intended to support the needs of more children, was the most important factor in providing additional choice. New classes, schools, options and equipment, the purpose of which was to cope with the additional children, actually offered extended choices and opportunities to the teacher.

With contraction, expenditure per child has continued to rise (PTR in 1984 was 17.9) but because there are fewer pupils the total spending has, at best, risen slowly and on occasion has declined in real terms. Previous choices for the teacher, the school and the LEA have been eliminated. If a school wishes to continue to offer the same curriculum with fewer children and teachers (even though with a lower PTR than before) each teacher must be prepared to teach in wider curriculum areas. Simultaneously, the staff of the school as a whole has to balance moves for curriculum adaptation with the pressure towards continuity with past practices which follows from less movement of staff between schools. Not all such pressures are externally generated. What the lack of expansion has done, however, is to transfer outside attention towards what school and teachers actually do, and how well they perform their tasks, rather than to focus concern on the need for more resources. Without doubt this transference would have occurred even with rising school rolls, for it is a function of increasing control and scrutiny of public expenditure. The fact that there are fewer pupils has provided an additional rationale for more external interest and introduced a new perspective. So has the pace of technological change both through its impact on structural unemployment (with public expenditure implications) and also through long term effects on school processes. Micro-computers in the classroom can be seen as only the initial stage of a movement towards alternative learning arrangements resulting in great changes in the role of the teacher.

Yet despite these fluctuating parameters the choices available to the teacher in the immediate work-situation of the classroom remain largely undiminished. There may be fewer resources, less homogeneous groupings of pupils, new topics to teach and little chance of promotion, but teaching style, class arrangement and attitudes towards the children remain matters of professional autonomy. The example of the micro-computer illustrates this. The individual teachers will decide whether or not to be users; if users, when and how they will become trained; they will choose whether they will design their own programs or use packages; finally they will determine the extent to which they will modify their teaching methodology to encompass this new resource.

In the same way, such freedoms extend from the classroom to the broader area of school management. Headteachers and others with managerial responsibilities are able to interpret their jobs with a wide degree of latitude in terms of modes of performance and actual duties. In this they are no different from managers in most other occupations although the combination of the demographic, financial, social and technologically-induced pressures may be perceived by some post-holders to restrict these freedoms in schools. Alternatively, of course, the changes which result from these pressures can be viewed as opportunities which enhance the prospects of managerial activity in schools. If this view is accepted, it may be felt that schools have been the potential beneficiaries of effective management techniques for many years, but most of that potential has remained untapped until now, and for the first time circumstances are making teachers realise this. Probably there will never be a more opportune time to analyse the managerial needs of schools and their teachers.

Enhanced opportunities, however, have to be converted into actions and these in turn must satisfy the need which created the opportunities. In this case changing demands have to be assimilated into the school statement of objectives so that appropriate responses can be developed. To do this the individual teacher with any responsibility beyond the classroom needs to become more competent in relation to management tasks and responsibilities. What this involves provides an important component of this book. However, individual competence - even at a high level - is insufficient. A single teacher cannot function alone in a managerial context. This fact indicates the main difference between teaching and managing and also places co-operation among staff as an essential pre-requisite of effective management. Such a development is facilitated by the procedures and arrangements which the school can establish. Co-operation is much easier when the school offers a climate to facilitate intra-staff support. By far the most important outcome produced by such a climate is an appreciation by all staff of the intentions and strategies of the school. As a result school activities which reflect corporate thinking and changing internal demands are likely to be developed. Finally, managers in the school require heightened personal awareness of environmental demands, both as part of their own managerial competence and also so that they can alert others to the potential effects of external factors upon school activities. All such demands do not require a response; most can be used, however, to modify objectives and support arrangements chosen for their achievement.

Overcoming constraints

Many teachers might dispute that the time is ripe for the pursuit of more effective and visible forms of management in schools. On the other hand they might accept that some quite specific management approaches could be desirable, perhaps in the field of public relations to make what schools try to do more understandable and acceptable to a wider public, consisting of society in general rather than simply the parents of the pupils. Demands might then be based on a sounder knowledge of school activities and problems. There is also likely to be agreement on the need to manage resources more effectively through utilising political skills to achieve additional funds for the school and by developing financial skills to make sure that those acquired are not misused. However, even such limited managerial approaches would only be acceptable to critical teachers if they neither infringed upon the performance of their perceived professional duties, nor contradicted views they hold about the role of the school and the functions of education. Staff, while readily agreeing that the school needs a teacher responsible for public relations, will just as quickly repudiate the idea when told by the teacher appointed that they should alter their attitudes or teaching styles to improve the image of the school. Teachers vociferous in their demands for more resources may well resist the notion of private fund raising, for in their view this reduces the responsibility of the state or local authority. Similarly, an acceptance that misuse of resources must be avoided may only extend to the prevention of misappropriation of funds; one teacher's priority for more pre-vocational work during periods of high unemployment is to another the misuse of scarce resources.

The issue illustrated by these examples is that a predominant constraint in establishing a high profile for management approaches in schools is derived from a perception held by many staff that such a development runs counter to teacher professionality. A number of factors are consistent with this view. First, there is the matter of professional judgement. Because of specialist training and experience the teacher is best placed to decide about such things as teaching strategy and resource allocation. The involvement of managers must occasionally mean the overturning of professional decisions. Second, the notion of management implies the formalisation of the organisation and the existence of a hierarchy. One person must, as a result, be placed above another and invariably the professionalism of the former is felt to be transgressed. Third, the education and training of the professional focuses upon the individual, who studies, passes examinations and receives accreditation in a largely solitary capacity and in a competitive atmosphere. There is little experience of co-operative teamwork during training. In teaching, particularly, few opportunities are available for working with others in the early stages of professional life. The idea of the cellular teacher, working alone with a group of children, unobserved by other adults, remains powerfully entrenched. This is in contradiction to the management objective of individuals functioning as part of the staff-team. Fourth, management carries with it an impression of 'big business', with connotations of ruthlessness, lack of respect for the individual, manipulation and the pursuit of profit maximisation to the dismay and even revulsion of the teacher contemplating management in the school.

It is suggested by Handy (1984a) that the conflict between management and professionalism can be traced to the confusion between leadership and administration, and between policy and execution. In the business world the work of the manager covers both leadership and administrative functions. In education this is not the case since the taking of power from the professional is avoided, and therefore the pursuit of professionalism is safeguarded. Rightly, the view of the individual professional is prized; the training that is necessary, the skills which are developed and the commitment that results are all desirable attributes. The school as an organisation could not function without them. Leadership in this situation is provided by senior professionals; no other arrangement is possible as young professionals wishing for guidance or advice turn to more experienced staff. The headteacher and other senior staff are all experienced teachers, and most senior members of staff continue to have a teaching timetable. As a result they are well placed to give professional leadership. Confusion arises because simultaneously they must adopt an administrative role. Many tasks involved in the day-to-day running of the school are not, as for example in the legal profession, handed over to ancillaries, largely because schools are seriously under-provided with clerical staff.

Policy and executive functions present similar confusion. In a professional partnership policy-making is led by senior professionals but there are arrangements to allow all others to participate. The resultant policy represents a consensus. By contrast the executive function requires hierarchy and control mechanisms to facilitate the implementation of whatever policy is decided. However, professionals are much more likely to accept the existence of a hierarchy if they participate in the policy-making which establishes it and if they have some element of control over it. In schools these functions are totally intertwined; few schools, even those with only a handful of staff, have been able to establish policy-making procedures in which all teachers feel involved and able to participate. As a result a firm foundation for the executive function rarely exists. Professional staff can find themselves directed without having been involved in the decision-making which led to this direction. More disconcertingly, from their point of view, they find themselves asked to participate in decisions which only impinge upon executive functions, while being simultaneously excluded from decisions about policy. A teacher may have responsibility for ordering and checking the delivery of major equipment requisitions, yet be excluded from decisions on how the funds for resources should be allocated; or be charged with ensuring that complex examination procedures are adhered to, yet have no say in the selection of syllabuses appropriate to a preferred teaching style.

Changing demands upon the school can increase the difficulties arising from functional confusions. However because these demands require a response the school must produce policy decisions. The position and competence of senior staff involved in this process of arriving at such decisions is vital. If, because of the rapidity of change and the increasing complexity of issues, senior members of staff become more introspective and even unwittingly less able to involve other teachers, then both the leadership and policy-making functions are compromised. Possibly, the headteacher and a few other members of staff establish a policy-formulation team. Limitations of time, the difficulties of discussing issues with the rest of the staff and the need to maintain consensus among the policy-group can make this an attractive option in some schools. It can, however, lead to an abrogation of professional leadership. Other teachers cease to look towards members of the group for leadership, as they are unable to provide it if they perceive their roles in narrowly managerial terms. Conceivably, a situation could be reached in which professionals play no part in the policy function, which has been taken over by teachers who once were professionals but now act as managers. A more effective means of reducing the commitment and involvement of professional staff would be difficult to devise. As a result when a school moves close to this extreme situation the executive function is hampered. Teachers not associated with policy-making support it grudgingly, question its purposes and carry out delegated tasks with little enthusiasm. Often the policy-makers in the management group have no alternative but to perform many of the administrative chores, and therefore have even less time for policy-making.

The achievement of a policy consensus is time-consuming even in a small school. With changing demands there may seem to be insufficient time to establish and utilise procedures which sustain a wide measure of agreement. This problem and several others are easily related to the central theme that teacher professionality and school management are potentially at odds. That provides the main constraint in the development of management practice; others, such as the rewards structure of the Burnham salary scales, reinforce the concept of hierarchy and tend to take the good professional away from the classroom. The shortage of non-teaching staff to carry out administrative chores reinforces the centrality of this theme. If the enhanced opportunities for management are to be realised then this constraint has to be overcome. The professional attitudes of teaching staff must be safeguarded; they require nurturing because they provide the central element in assisting children's learning. To promote this learning however, schools must simultaneously respond to changing demands and attempt to maximise their own effectiveness. In this context the notion of the independent professional is outmoded. Schools cannot avoid the need for the formal designation of duties, the establishment of some form of hierarchy, the delineation of objectives and the adoption of common practices, since without them the school is no more than a collection of individuals as much working against each other as working together. In the current climate excessive individualism erodes the capacity to define and achieve group objectives. Nevertheless the opportunities for teachers to use their professionalism have to be strengthened at the same time as the organising competencies and skills of co-operation, which tend to be overlooked, are developed. Simultaneously, despite the reservations of teachers, organisational procedures may have to be strengthened. Given the way that the conventions of teacher professionalism have evolved, this will not be a balance easily achieved. Procedures have to be established, attitudes given time to develop and functions redesignated, so that individual and organisational behaviour appropriate to the management of a team of professionals is able to emerge.

Dominant influences

In one respect, schools are fortunate when they contemplate approaches to management. Senior staff, even when their professional leadership attributes are well hidden from other teachers, have, without exception, been professionals for some time. Invariably, they participate in the main function of the school, classroom teaching, for some part of the working week. Therefore, the first criterion in managing professionals has been satisfied. Professionals do not take kindly to the imposition of an outsider to manage them, irrespective of the alleged competency of the outsider. Yet the tradition of promoting classroom practitioners to managerial positions poses its own problems. Promotion relies less on potential to manage than on success as a teacher. There is some commonality in skills required, the refinement of oral communication techniques for example (Gronn, 1983), but there is no certainty that a successful teacher will prove effective in school management. Skills relating to the organisation of children's learning or classroom management are quite specific. It would be unreasonable to expect teachers who spend several years developing them to evolve simultaneously a range of more managerially useful competencies, particularly when there is no guarantee that they will have the opportunity to use them professionally.

Not only are there differences in the skills demanded by teaching and by management but these skills are exercised in different areas.

For most teachers the activity of teaching, as distinct from that of management, involves little interaction with other adults. Team-teaching, group-work and open-plan classrooms all exist, but the teaching cell remains the dominant organisational mode. Children, often excellent critics, tend to demonstrate disagreement or non-acceptance of teaching style by misbehaviour and absence. A teacher who moves into a school management postion becomes exposed to more articulate and sustained comment. For, by accepting managerial responsiblities teachers make their actions more visible and consequently the issue of individual competency is heightened. As a result they are potentially more vulnerable. Decisions, because they affect other adults, will be scrutinised and mistakes cannot so easily be disguised or hidden as in the classroom.

All of the training and professional life of teachers until they accept managerial responsibility bears the stamp of privacy and they are insulated from everything except 'closet' criticism. Now, as managers, they must become aware of the wider arena in which they function and the consequences for others. However, acknowledgement of this represents no more than the smallest step. In addition, they have to find ways of 'exploiting' the needs of their fellow professionals for co-operative working, when some are not even aware of the existence of those needs.

The capacity to work with other adults provides one of the main differences between teaching and managing activities especially in relation to objectives. Teachers have experience of establishing objectives for their own classes within a framework for the whole school or department. As managers, however, their task is to organise procedures for the review of objectives, so that the policy-formulation element functions. Moreover, this should occur in ways that allow staff to participate so that they feel committed to whatever is required by the ensuing executive aspect of management. The teaching-managing dichotomy also raises issues associated with job environment. The demands of the classroom physically and temporally restrict a teacher's capacity to appreciate the broader environmental factors which impinge upon the school. This limitation is detrimental to the individual's ability to contribute to school policy-making. The effects of government or local authority decisions, changes in financial provision, and demographic and socio-economic factors are all potential influences on decision-making. The teacher's lack of opportunity to be aware of, monitor and assess such environmental factors has to be compensated for by the staff with managerial responsibilities.

While differences between teaching and managing point towards certain requirements in the selection and training of senior staff (Morgan et al.,1983) they should not detract from the fact that the main influence on attitudes, no matter how senior the position, is firmly entrenched in the traditions of teaching. Research in the mid-1970s suggested that heads, even of large schools, still regarded themselves as teachers, not managers (Bernbaum, 1976). There is little to suggest that the significance of the perception has altered. Headteachers and other staff with management responsibilities wish to give, and to be perceived to be giving, academic leadership, but believe this to be made more difficult and, on occasion compromised by the requirements of having to manage the school (Hughes, 1977). The accelerated rate of change of demands will, of course, heighten this dichotomy, compound the difficulties and raise the likelihood of actions perceived as compromises. The answer is not create or import professional managers to help run the schools, although such is the nature of resource dependency that government or local authorities could introduce such a scheme. Professionals, even in formal organisations, perform best when managed by fellow-professionals, and the conversion of headteachers and deputies into professional managers is not desirable. The process would be too slow and, more importantly, it would exaggerate the gap between them and professional teachers. More generally this can be a contentious issue since in the US context senior management positions in schools are non-teaching posts for which the incumbents must hold a higher degree qualification.

There is no need for conflict between academic leadership and professional management provided that the staff concerned can develop the skills, behaviour and attitudes which focus upon the key issue of the management of professionals. Clearly, it is much easier to describe such a situation than achieve it in the practical context of schools. The opportunities for management may be enhanced, staff may be willing to be managed, but their assessment of what is offered will depend upon how it assists in the pursuit and interpretation of school objectives and how satisfying it makes the work situation. Professionals are well able to judge how they are being managed. Indeed, there is a circularity in that the more effective they assess the management to be, the more likely they are to support it and the greater this support the more effective the management. The main item in managing professionals then becomes an issue of learning (Handy, 1984a). The ability of the teacher to learn how to manage fellow professionals in the specific context of the individual school or department is crucial. Without question the learning has to concentrate upon the situation produced by the interaction between the people involved and the school as an organisation.

Bolman and Deal (1984) have identified four diverse approaches: structural, human resource, political and symbolic. These can be described as follows.

- In the **structural** approach the importance of formal roles and relationships is emphasised, because it is assumed that organisations exist to achieve established goals and a structure appropriate to the goals must be set up. As that structure will depend upon the environment of the school staff preferences will have little influence. Co-ordination of the specialised activities of staff is accomplished through impersonal rules. When problems arise in this approach the most likely reason is that the structure does not fit the situation, and therefore the structure has to be changed.

- In the **human resource** approach the importance of individuals working in the organisation and in particular their views, needs and prejudices dominate. Organisational members have the ability to learn and so involve themselves in new behaviour, and equally they have the facility to defend old attitudes and actions. However, the needs of teachers and schools are complementary; each requires the other. With a mismatch, both parties suffer. The teacher will not feel able to achieve and as a result the school will fail to meet its objectives. Alternatively, with a good fit the work is satisfying, and the school has its teachers performing in ways which suit its purposes. The salient feature of this approach is that the school provides conditions enabling staff to perform effectively.

- The **political** approach concerns itself with issues of power and influence. The allocation of resources among groups and individuals controls the organisation and its behaviour. Because of differing interpretations of needs and varying perspectives, different groups must necessarily be in competition for scarce resources. This results in bargaining, coercion and compromise. Such processes, therefore, represent essential components of organisational behaviour. As a consequence of these activities, decisions are taken and control is seen to revolve around positions of power, which are dependent upon authority, knowledge, coercion, control of rewards or personal attributes. The ability of the individual or group to utilise political skills provides the control theme in this approach.

- The **symbolic** approach abandons the assumptions about rational behaviour implied in the other three approaches. Instead, the assumption is made that common values and culture provide the framework which holds the school, as an organisation, together. Intentions and policies are much less important in this approach because of the assumptions made about the nature of human behaviour in organisations. Because events are frequently determined more by people's perceptions and interpretations of what has happened, rather than by what has actually occurred, uncertainty and ambiguity are inevitable, and rational consideration of policy-making is undermined. Consequently, members turn to symbols centred around the perceived values and culture of the organisation, in an attempt to resolve confusion and increase predictability.

Presented as frames - attempts to help individuals order their world before deciding about the appropriateness of actions - each of the four represents a main theme in the literature about organisations. However, it is not intended that managers should adopt a particular frame or allow one to dominate their thinking. More realistically the four frames highlight the diversity that pervades all aspects of organisational behaviour and, therefore, stress the range of perspectives needed if this behaviour is to be understood and, in part at least, managed. As a result, they also provide a structure within which teachers as managers can contemplate options available to them and the possible effects of particular actions in any situation. This process comprises an essential component of management learning on which the next chapter concentrates.

Management learning does not take place in isolation; like the organisational behaviour on which it focuses attention, it takes place within the constraints of, and makes use of opportunities provided by, the prevailing environment. This determines the dominant influences both upon management actions and the associated learning. In itself, a knowledge of frames, for example, is of little practical use. Indeed, too much concentration on the concept of frames and too great a reliance on one of them in helping to guide action may well produce unwelcome distortions in managerial activity. However, when the influences of the immediate situation become too dominant, the educational manager can be helped to maintain an awareness of longer-term issues and even begin to see how some of the constraints might be reduced. The frames, therefore, provide a context for analysing the influences which exert pressure on the teacher with managerial responsibilities, and the effects which such influences are likely to have on the educational processes they attempt to manage.

CHAPTER 2

LEARNING TO BE EFFECTIVE

Knowledgeable but skill-less

Management is a practical activity: learning about management and learning to be an effective manager are therefore very different issues, a fact not always appreciated by teachers and lecturers. In many school and college courses the dominant concern is knowledge transfer. The teacher will doubtless claim that a much broader range of intentions exists, but the fact remains that concentration upon content and processes provides for ease of syllabus design and objective assessment of individual pupil attainment. These factors become more important in secondary schools and further education, owing to curricular specialisation and increased inter-pupil competition for success in a declining labour market. Many educational staff, themselves relatively successful products of the system, view teaching-learning essentially in content terms, especially in the light of their current experience as teachers. Initially, then, teachers are not well placed to distinguish between knowledge related to the management tasks and the accomplishment of these tasks. Other factors add to their difficulty.

It is now accepted that for schools and colleges, as for all other organisations , there is no single theory which even attempts to consider the whole range of organisational and administrative behaviour. For educational organisations appreciation of this point has not always prevailed. Griffiths directed attention towards the natural sciences, using the example of Kepler's Laws of Planetary Motion, in the pursuit of a general model(Campbell and Gregg, eds., 1957) with the intention of creating a Pure Science of Educational Administration (Hughes, 1984). That line of approach has long since been discarded. Even the simplest cases, involving perhaps two members of staff discussing minimal alteration in teaching responsibilities, introduce a host of variables; the values, needs and perceptions of the two teachers, alongside the immediate context and broader environment in which the discussion occurs, all impinge upon the outcome and the actions which follow. With additional issues and the involvement of more staff, the range of potential results from any interaction, and the influence of interactions on each other, rise exponentially.

Most teachers know from their day-to-day experiences that organisations are incredibly complex. A significant contributor to this complexity is the limited knowledge about human behaviour and therefore the inability to predict it with any degree of accuracy. There is no certainty, nor even likelihood, that a certain action by a headteacher will lead to a particular outcome; no assurance can be given that an approach to staff development used successfully in one school will work in the circumstances of another school; no guarantee that tactics to persuade one teacher to adopt a new approach will be successful with any other teacher. Searches for simple answers to complex issues may be as attractive in educational management as elsewhere (Bolling, 1983) but they divert attention from the greater importance of facilitating the development of managerial skills in school leaders, and the capacity of those individuals to apply them in the contingencies of the different situations.

From the perspective of social psychology, Weick (1979) suggests that organising is the key word, with a fundamental building block of a double interaction; the first person acts, the second person responds and the first person readjusts on the basis of this reponse. A school leader may suggest a new teaching arrangement and then, depending upon the subsequent actions of teachers, may modify not only the programme but even the intentions which led to the original suggestion. Throughout this process the leader works in an environment of uncertainty, since reactions of individual teachers to any initiative cannot be taken for granted. It is relatively easy, for example, to over-estimate the extent to which teachers can be expected to act rationally, or for the leader to assume more power to direct teachers than actually pertains. In most situations the great majority of problems faced by school leaders will centre upon people - the teachers, pupils and others - who through their attitudes and behaviour can have an effect on the work in the particular area. Consequently, technical knowledge is insufficient for effective co-ordination or innovation. In the same way, there is no guarantee that knowledge of the behavioural sciences will lead to successful practical outcomes. The ability to convert knowledge into skills appropriate to the situation is a necessary adjunct to any knowledge. The senior member of staff may have learned a great deal about management but still be unable to manage. In certain situations a teacher with refined managerial skills may be better at implementing the new arrangements than someone with more knowledge about a particular curricular area.

The knowledge-base and skill-base

Even without formal preparation either before or after selection, anyone appointed to a managerial post in a school arrives with a certain knowledge-base about performing the tasks which constitute the job. A new headteacher, for example, has both observed others in action and received advice, and this alongside other experiences, in work and elsewhere, provides some sort of base or starting point. An initial concern, however, is to extend that base in relation to the school and then to the environment in which it functions. Therefore, the new postholder will want to know something about the background of the staff, the curricular objectives of the school, the links with other activities, the likelihood of resource availability and so on. To extend their knowledge-base along this dimension most new headteachers rely on other, more experienced headteachers (Dwyer, 1984). Significantly, they appear to be even more reliant on colleagues when it comes to widening their knowledge-base along the management behaviour dimension. When they want to know the best way of dealing with a certain situation they welcome advice from another headteacher who may have been confronted with a similar situation. Thus they seek to take advantage of a pool of expertise built up by their more experienced headteacher colleagues who collectively have dealt with most school situations.

For all with responsibilities in education the process of knowledge accretion about management behaviour is continuous, but, unfortunately, both random and lacking in co-ordination. Too few staff are able to categorise their knowledge in ways that will achieve the optimum in skill deployment; too few realise the full potential of their learning processes and learning needs. For individuals, the broadening of the management knowledge-base represents an essential component of Mintzberg's (1973) informational role as performed by managers. Here it was noted that much of the in-flow about organisational behaviour utilised small and unco-ordinated pieces of information. Much information-gathering relies upon chance conversations and the coincidences of meeting between events; many other activities are monitored in this general and unsytematic way. Nevertheless, without formally recording or categorising it, the manager processes a great deal of information, thus extending the knowledge-base about organisational behaviour and the methods by which it might be influenced or controlled.

While the uniqueness of each management situation demands the individualisation of objectives there is still need for categorisation of the items with which managers ought to be familiar and the areas in which they require skills. Such classifications have their value in that they can provide a framework which facilitates the organisation of learning experiences and activities. The potential danger of examples cited in the literature is that the tasks of management become perceived as separate entities; in practice the whole unified performance is the important matter.

Nevertheless, as a starting point, management can be viewed as consisting of two contrasting and, on occasion, conflicting strategies - political and technical (Bower, 1983). The manager must know how to deal with the political processes that permeate organisational behaviour, in particular those skills that relate to working with other people. In addition, there is a need for familiarity with the technical procedures of the school, curriculum design, the definition of educational objectives, teaching arrangements and so on. In practice, the acquisition of these political skills may be facilitated (Torrington and Weightman, 1982) as many of them are carried over from everyday life. Moreover, Katz, (1954) argues that, while the technical skills can be taught, political skills have to be learned experientally. This can be a long process particularly when in schools, and so many other organisations, staff are appointed to managerial positions after achieving competence in a different functional area. The salesman becomes a manager, the teacher is promoted to headteacher, and in both cases the knowledge-base of the new postholder is found to be inappropriate at the outset. A newly appointed primary headteacher is certain to know much more about classroom practice than about the managerial demands upon a headteacher. Indeed, Handy (1984b) argues that this imbalance may be particularly difficult for teachers to correct because of the compromises which the refinement of political skills demand. This contrasts sharply with some of the certainties that they have developed in relation to the material they teach.

For most analytical purposes, however, the political dimension is too broad. Even the highly influential classification of skills given by Katz over thirty years ago offered division into interpersonal skills (the ability to work with and through people) and conceptual skills (the capacity to see the organisation as a whole, and the direction in which it might develop), and a third element, a knowledge of the technical processes of the organisation. Many other divisions of the political domain are possible. In one of these, (Eilon, 1984), the ability to analyse situations, to define problems, to evaluate potential solutions, to infer from the particular to the general, is placed alongside experience - the facility to utilise lessons learned from earlier events to provide insights as to how to react in alternative situations - and the personal qualities which allow an individual to relate to the needs and values of other staff. Mintzberg (1973), after a study of managerial behaviour, identified eight skills:

peer skills: the ability to establish and maintain a network of contacts with others in the school and outside;

leadership skills: the ability to deal with other staff and the related issues of power and authority;

conflict resolution skills: the ability to contain and resolve conflict, including a capacity for working under stress;

24

information processing skills: the ability to extract, collect and disseminate information about the work-place and contingent factors;

unstructured decision-making skills: the ability to discover solutions when the conditions are ambiguous and sometimes others do not realise a problem exists;

resource allocation skills: the ability to decide about the allocation of scarce resources, including time;

entrepreneurial skills: the ability to see opportunities and implement innovations, sometimes through taking risks;

introspection skills: the ability to understand the position and behaviour of self, relative to that of the organisation.

Many other classifications can be constructed. Those evolving from managerial self-development exercises are particularly attractive as they try to identify the skills and knowledge which managers might concentrate upon to improve their own effectiveness. The list suggested by Pedler et al.(1978) for example, includes eleven items:

- a command of basic facts about the organisation, present functions, plans for the future and external factors which might influence its development;

- the skill of being able to up-date regularly professional knowledge relevant to the functioning of the organisation;

- a capacity to be sensitive to events and to changing conditions in the organisation, through perceptiveness, a feeling towards others and the ability to assess situations;

- an ability to solve problems, to be analytical and to make decisions and judgements, often in circumstances where there appears to be inadequate information;

- a range of social skills and abilities demanded by the numerous situations in which the needs, views and emotions of other staff must be considered and reacted to through effective communication mechanisms;

- an ability to develop the emotional resilience to cope with the stress and anxiety produced by the often ambiguous and uncertain conditions in which a manager must work;

- an inclination to respond purposefully to events, rather than allowing management behaviour to be controlled or manipulated by others, or becoming involved in the seemingly unavoidable pursuit of urgent but relatively unimportant activity;

- a capacity for creativity - that is, an ability to generate new ideas or novel ways of looking at problems which previously appeared insuperable, and a willingness to try out such ideas;

- a mental agility relating to both a skill in processing a large volume of sometimes contradictory information rapidly, and an ability to cope with several diverse tasks at the same time;
- a skill in developing balanced learning habits so as to be able to generate conclusions potentially utilisable in future situations from previous experiences, and the ability to relate these experiences to aspects of theories about organisations;
- a capacity for self-awareness, heightening knowledge about goals, values and feelings, in addition to the ability of self-analysis into the causes and effects of personal managerial behaviour.

Whatever the comprehensiveness intended in such a categorisation, further refinements or reclassifications are always possible. In this last example there is no mention of maintaining staff commitment as a managerial skill, nor does extending the power of a manager through an ability to influence others receive a specific mention. The process of refinement can continue almost indefinitely. Skills associated with communication, for example, are capable of being grouped in numerous ways. Therefore, while interviewing is integral to interpersonal communication, it represents only one aspect, because different types of interview have different skill components (Honey, 1976). At the same time all interviews involve the manager in listening, which itself requires certain skills. Indeed this exemplifies why a search for further refinement into separate skill-areas offers little reward; listening skills, rather than constituting an independent category, are best viewed as required components of other skill areas already mentioned.

The methodology for producing such listings relies on a mix of prescription (what managers ought to do to achieve more effectiveness or greater success) and observation (watching managers at work). As such they are open to considerable criticism because of both the methodological problems in such observations and the disadvantages of generalising from a small collection of results. It would be highly misleading to ignore the fact that management performance is unique to the person, the environment and the time. Even the most comprehensive catalogue of skills runs the risk of omission because of some contingency in the prevailing circumstances. In most situations the appropriate deployment of a collection of skills is much more important than the capacity to use one particular skill. What skill classifications provide in the context of management is a framework for the individual, so that needs can be identified and, as a result, the skill-base widened. To do this, though, the management knowledge-base has first to be broadened. The manager needs to know which skills to use and should have the confidence based upon some knowledge that they can be deployed effectively

The Methods of Learning

At first sight it would appear that there are three aspects of the way in which the knowledge of managers may be improved - what ought to be known, how it should be learnt, and how it can be applied. In practice, such a sharp three-fold division can easily disappear. The manager acquires knowledge through a variety of routes, each of which might contribute to the three elements. The commonest routes are probably:

receiving instruction: usually by attendance on a course;

working with a mentor: receiving assistance and advice from a more experienced individual;

reading: about management, the organisation and factors related to its technical competence and how to deal with people and organisations:

observing others: how they act and react in organisational situations;

group work: working with others and discovering that there can be alternative ways of viewing the same situation or problem;

direct experience: in the workplace;

alternative experiences: these help to develop alternative perspectives.

In the same way that the three foci of learning are often inseparable, so the potential learning routes overlap. In effect all are experiental. The manager undergoes a series of experiences and therefore learns, and whether that learning takes place as a result of formal instruction, work experience or group activities is much less important than ensuring that learning does occur and at an appropriate rate. Non-conventional arrangements have to be explored. Revans (1980) whose views are based on practice and research extending over many years, recommends action-learning in which small groups accelerate the development of individuals by examining and re-interpreting their learning experiences. It has long been acknowledged that experience matters in managing. Indeed, in this context, it has to be demonstrated, particularly in relation to schools, that there are more routes to learning than those which are available from 'on the job' experience, and that an intuitive experience-base can be usefully extended into a more broadly-based knowledge facility.

However, while employers (the LEAs and schools) accept that experience counts, they are often reluctant to accept the role of educators; most feel they would be more likely to perceive that this role should be handed over to course-providers, colleges, universities and management trainers. It is now generally agreed that there are many advantages in extending school-based learning as well as promoting other routes. However, the various components have to be mutually supportive, and complementarity among them is a necessary concomitant of effective learning.

For all managers in education, learning from work-place experience provides the foundation. It gives a framework around which other learning experiences can be assembled, and supplies a focus upon which learning activities can easily be concentrated. Invariably, though, there is a need for a better personal understanding of what has been learned from work-experience, and the relevance of such learning. In direct terms, then, the experience ought to be made to work harder for the individual. Often headteachers, for example, find it difficult to assess what has been learned; they are only vaguely aware of the skills that have been refined since they have taken up office. This is where the role of more formal instruction and monitoring achieves prominence.

In sequence, the manager participates in a range of experiences and then, most usually as part of course attendance or through discussion with a colleague, is persuaded to go through a period of organised reflection. The purpose of this is to help rationalise what has been learned from all routes about the performance of job-tasks, to identify what additional learning needs exist and, more generally, to relate experience to professional and personal development. Once such needs have been identified, further experiences which might lead to their satisfaction can then be considered (FEU, 1984). The individual, therefore, consolidates through a steady cycle of experiential learning consisting of four phases: concrete experience, reflective observation, abstract conceptualisation and active experimentation (Kolb, 1983). It is the combination of concrete experience and active experimentation (which are normally most closely related to specific problems that have to be solved as part of job-tasks) with abstract conceptualisation and reflective observation (processes more usually associated with conventional educational ideas about learning) that provides reinforcement. As a result, the individual participant has access to a learning methodology which is both holistic and adaptable to changing needs and situations.

The manager as adult learner

For education managers the association between learning and successful management both provides an opportunity and poses a problem. The opportunity arises because, unlike in other occupations, learning and its organisation is the school's business. The problem arises since so many of the conventions and practices that have become established in pursuit of learning in school run contrary to those which offer greatest promise in a managerial context. The need to maintain cohesive groups and classes, the differing requirements of the subjects which comprise the curriculum, the pressure on resources and the demands of examinations all combine to produce a particular learning strategy. Traditionally, this involves a group of children starting together and proceeding through similar pre-determined material at more or less the same pace, although some schools do work in other ways. In every respect this contrasts with criteria appropriate to management learning. In the first place it assumes that the teacher is best placed to determine both content and pace (and with younger children such an arrangement has powerful attractions) and, secondly, it has to take account of the fact that the teacher (or controls in the system) may construct artificial boundaries around the content.

It would be difficult to exaggerate the differences between suitable conditions for management learning for adults and the arrangements for school lessons for pupils. The teacher has to package, refine and simplify the material at the same time as making it both sufficiently interesting to motivate the pupils and so organised as to fit within the constraints of daily and annual timetables. Whether the resulting procedures may or may not be the most effective way to develop children's responsibilities for their own learning processes is not the issue. What is pertinent is whether, given this context teachers can adapt their own learning requirements to conditions so different from those that have prevailed in their professional work and training.

Teachers as learners have the same needs as all other adult students (Main, 1984). In this context Knowles (1984) actually identifies two distinct models of learning: pedagogy (traditional learning, based upon school practices) and andragogy (a model more appropriate to adult requirements). He suggests five fundamental differences:

the concept of the learner (and, therefore, the learner self-concept). Pedagogically the learner is regarded as a dependent person, with the teacher held responsible for the what, when and how of learning, as well as any assessment of whether the learning has occurred. The submissive learner can be contrasted with the andragogical model of the self-directed learner. Undoubtedly this latter model implies a psychological climate of mutual respect, trust, collaboration, supportiveness and openness rarely achieved in schools;

the role of the learner's experience. Children come to school with little in the way of experience which might be used as a learning resource. Accordingly the dominant learning mode is transmission from teacher to taught. Quite clearly, adults have a greater volume and variety of experience, part of which provides a learning resource, particularly when, as in educational management, many of the learning objectives relate to work-based experiences. In formal situations, therefore, group discussions and exercises will offer many opportunities because of the varied experiences of the participants;

readiness to learn. In pedagogical terms readiness to learn is largely related to age. Children are taught certain topics at particular ages and those unready, as demonstrated by slow progress, are deemed backward. Andragogically, readiness occurs when adults perceive a need to know. In terms of management learning, this may be when they, and those who work with them, decide that some part of job-performance requires improvement;

orientation to learning. The normal curricular arrangements of schools provide children with a subject-oriented view of learning. This remains particularly true for secondary schools. For adults, requirements tend to be more problem or task-centred; they take a conscious decision to learn because of a particular need and the more clearly the 'need to know' can be determined and the processes of learning made relevant to the satisfaction of that need, the more likely is the learning to be effective;

the motivation to learn. In the main, children are motivated by parents and teachers, as well as external factors such as examinations and competition with other pupils. According to the andragogical model the main motivation in work-related situations is derived from self-esteem, self-confidence, the ability to do a job more effectively and achieve greater recognition for it, alongside the capacity to have more influence in the work situation.

The strategy of andragogy is not without criticism. Mouton and Blake (1984) have extended it into the notion of synergogy which, while accepting the participative involvement of the learners, suggests that andragogy still tends to leave them too dependent on an instructor for social context and emotional growth. Instead, the authors concentrate upon membership of a team of learners as the most effective means of promoting learning. More important, the strategy of andragogy fails to come to terms with the particular characteristics of the individual learner. The significance of intellectual maturity - that is, the ability of the student to cope - has been noted (Lam, 1983) and in more general terms the different learning styles preferred by individuals (Honey and Mumford 1983) require consideration. There are activists, those who enjoy new experiences from which to learn; reflectors, those who like to reach their own decisions about their own learning; theorists, those who wish to be intellectually stretched; and pragmatists, those who prefer the link between subject-matter and job-problems to be made clear. The weakness of this classification, as with so many, is that individuals are typecast, when in reality preferences are time- and issue-dependent.

The context of learning

The best designed andragogic approach will still not work unless education managers are motivated to learn. They must perceive that potential benefit can accrue from learning more about the ways in which schools behave and about their part in influencing that behaviour in their own school. Moreover, effective learning will lead to new behaviours and new patterns of action on the part of the individual and therefore the replacement of previous activities which may have provided security and confidence. In addition, most school management has a high profile. Alternative approaches are visible; resultant mistakes may be scorned. Therefore, all senior members of staff concerned about improving managerial performance have to be sufficiently competent to realise what learning is desirable, and sufficiently confident to invest in alternative forms of activity. Either alone or in combination, these factors can prove formidable inhibitors to management learning. They may be effectively disguised. A headteacher, for example, may claim to possess adequate knowledge about school management; a promoted postholder may be quite satisfied to have achieved that appointment and become complacent, another teacher may be unconvinced that the investment in time and effort will pay any dividends.

Such perceived motivational disincentives are easily compounded in education. The lack of a general theory to explain organisational behaviour in a profession orientated towards knowledge-transmission provides one such example; a view that schools, as collections of professional staff, have no need for management suggests another. In addition, the absence of real pressure to achieve tangible results and the many problems associated with evaluating achievement have isolated schools from the pursuit of the type of effective management that has taken place in commerce, business, nationalised industries and the armed services. Compared to Europe, moreover, British education has been slow to develop overt interest in school management (Buckley, 1985). There are no formal training requirements before promotion to headship, no systematic development programmes in schools or LEAs to prepare younger staff for senior positions, no staff college, except in further education, to assist staff holding senior appointments and no educational equivalent to the business schools that service commercial and industrial needs. Indeed, it was not until 1983 that DES first made funds available to support the management training of senior school staff (DES 1983a). Inevitably, if a government agency is to achieve maximum impact of activity in a short time with limited resources, the dominant strategy has to be pedagogic. Funding courses and ensuring staff attendance may be an effective means of demonstrating action, but care is needed in course design and delivery to ensure that they lead to increased motivation or establish the best learning strategy.

Even without institutional intervention from the school, LEA or DES, some individuals will still utilise opportunities to organise their own management learning effectively. Given the prevailing orthodoxies and attitudes in education, though, such people are too few, and the relationship between what they can achieve and what is required from school management in the context of rapidly changing demands is too haphazard. In addition, an environment which encourages complete personal autonomy tends to concentrate too much on the needs of the individual and overlooks such items as the importance of team membership and the centrality of interpersonal skills in the organisation of a school.

The resolution of these potentially conflicting demands provides the framework for the response to these key questions: What is to be learned? At what stage in the careers of individual teachers? Who ought to learn? In what environment should this learning occur? (Handy, 1984a). The first of these questions provides the focus for much of the remainder of this book, where the assumption is made that for school management to be effective those who manage require a theoretical framework (Landers and Myers, 1980). The other questions arise less directly, but they impinge upon the issue of translating knowledge about educational management into managerial behaviour. Without doubt the efficacy of this translation largely determines the relative success of managers in education.

CHAPTER 3

LEADERSHIP UNLIMITED?

Leadership demands

Explanations of organisational success abound, as do controversies surrounding any explanation which receives much publicity. Both phenomena are understandable. There is a natural desire to discover why two neighbouring schools, or even two departments in the same school, seem markedly different in their ability to achieve similar objectives. Causal explanations are attractive to both observers and practitioners, particularly in the non-education world where the rewards of relative success can be high. Controversy invariably accompanies explanation because of the need to simplify the complexities involved both in assessing success and in identifying its causes. A UK study (Goldsmith and Clutterbuck, 1984) exemplifies the interest aroused and the disagreements which can result. In a similar study (Peters and Waterman, 1982) of some of the best-known organisations based in North America eight characteristics of success were identified. These ranged from a bias for action (do things now and then modify with experience, rather than spending too long in pre-action analysis) through to simultaneous centralization and decentralization (a few important shared values among organisational members providing a framework for individual autonomy). Although initially the US study was favourably received, criticisms of both methodology and conceptual framework have been trenchant (Carroll, 1983).

More difficult to dispute though, in such studies of the business world, are the criteria that might be used in measuring success; profit levels, return on stockholders' equity and the like. Such objective criteria are rarely available to education. Yet the absence of output measures has not prevented authorities from arbitrarily identifying the quality of the leadership as the chief reason for a school's success:

'...in all cases the head's leadership is of paramount importance' (DES, 1982)

'leadership of the headteacher determines the quality of the education throughout the school' (HMI, 1984).

This view, however, is not supported by Miskel's investigation (1984) in North America of the effects of principal succession on school functioning. He found that a change of principal (headteacher) had no effect, statistically, on perceived organisational effectiveness, teacher job-satisfaction and student attitudes. Nevertheless the word 'leadership',used in the DES and HMI statements above, appears more often than any other in descriptions of organisations and probably no word is given so many varied meanings (Katz & Kahn, 1978). Yet such statements offer no new insights into why some schools or departments are judged to be more successful than others, because they make no real attempt to specify whether the leadership represents a personal attribute of the head or can be related in some way to the office of headteacher. Furthermore, there is no mention of whether it is a constant or varies to suit the prevailing situation. Mant (1983), for example, in commenting on the rapidity of the progress made under a charismatic leader, has observed that such a leader seems able to harness the mass intelligence existing within the organisation and put right what everyone in the organisation has felt to be wrong.

Leadership is a quality which all effective managers must themselves possess and must encourage in others; nevertheless the temptation to elevate it to some all-encompassing notion, or see it as a panacea, sometimes appears irresistible. It needs to be resisted however, not least because of the accumulation of empirical evidence confirming the complexity of the issues involved. As a topic, leadership and associated concepts retain a high profile. Because of perceived links between individual and organisational success, people like to know how they can be led most effectively, how they themselves might lead, who ought to be designated leaders, how such individuals might be trained and how staff view leadership behaviour. Possibly, the concept of leadership that implies the power of one person over another is becoming out-moded (Handy, 1985). Conversely, as management will at times involve one person directing another, there is a need for that style of leadership which inculcates in others a willingness to follow. However, despite all such interest over half a century of research has produced little by way of consensus about the determinants, processes and consequences of leadership (Stodgill, 1974).

Initially, studies concentrated upon the qualities or traits of personnel in leadership positions. Although some prescriptive approaches existed (Barnard, 1938) the main thrust was to discover common traits possessed by leaders, both to assist in selection and for use as exemplars. Even by 1936 the difficulty of summarising desirable personality qualities was recognised (Allport and Odbert, 1936). Clearly, no individual could possess all the traits listed. This was confirmed by the reviews of Stodgill (1948) and Mann (1959) which considered over 100 studies linking personality attributes to leadership. In addition, hardly any traits were held in common by those in leadership positions. Although these traits included above average intelligence, ability to initiate, independence and inventiveness, self-confidence and reasonably high aspiration levels, they can only be viewed as factors in, but not conditions for, leadership. This early, **congenital** approach to leadership (Paisley, 1984) relied upon two assumptions: first, that the world divides into two categories of people, leaders and followers; second, that this occurs because leaders have certain innate qualities not possessed by followers. To those privileged by birth such an approach had attractions, particularly when a definition of required qualities remained elusive. In the UK, unlike the USA, interest in this approach persisted (Adair, 1980) both as a reflection of a more stratified society and, relatedly, because of a reluctance to view leadership as a characteristic of rather than a potential denial of democracy (Gray, 1982). Even in the UK, the inadequacy of the congenital approach together with attitudinal changes towards leadership altered the direction of interest.

Attention switched to the **situational** or **contingency** approach, with the social setting in which leadership occurs becoming a dominant theme, on the assumption that circumstances create opportunities for leadership. Stodgill (1948) posited that persons who are accepted leaders in one situation may find it difficult to be effective in another. According to this view, not only is the setting a factor requiring attention, so also are the group tasks to which the leadership is directed. After a sustained programme of research, with both experimental and field studies in many organisations, Fiedler (1967) broadened the variables investigated to cover three potential contingencies:

the structure of the task to be performed;

the power position of the leader in relation to others in the group;

the relationship between the leader and group member.

The last was introduced because earlier work (Fiedler, 1958) had indicated, initially, that a socially distant leader had often produced a more effective working group. Closer study seemed to reveal the need for leadership to be both socially-supportive and production-directed. Burnham (1968) adopted this notion when he recommended that the support leadership should be provided by the deputy headteacher in a school whose concern for the well-being of the staff derives from close day-to-day involvement with them, while the headteacher as a director and organiser should supply production (instrumental) leadership. This view is consistent with Mant's (1983) 'Merchant Marine' Model of leadership in which he advocates a combination of a 'builder' leader and 'raider' subordinate as an effective combination. A **builder** leader is seen as uncompromising but fair in pursuit of standards and valuing the institution (school) as worthy of existence in its own right and not simply a place where pupils are taught. As a result of the influence of this type of leadership, teachers are encouraged to

35

understand and influence their own working conditions, and are likely to be ready to enter into discussion with pupils about the function and purpose of their joint activities and teaching arrangements (Fig. 3.1.).

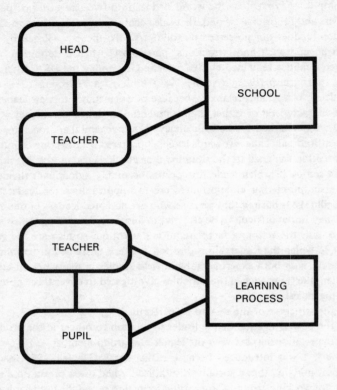

Fig 3. 1 Builder Triangles in Schools

The frame of mind in which **raiders** approach the problems and opportunities of leadership is quite different. They are more concerned with interpersonal domination and the power which can result. Their activities are characterised by conflict as opposed to consensus, win-lose confrontation as opposed to joint problem-solving, and they prefer to work in a survival (fight-flight) mode rather than seek to establish a working atmosphere in which there is mutual dependence between themselves and their colleagues. Again there may be consequences for teacher-pupil relationships resulting from the influence of such a headteacher (Fig 3.2).

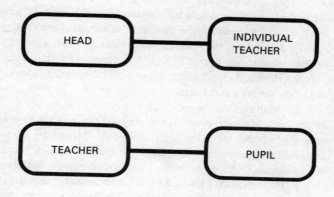

Fig 3.2 Raider Configuration in Schools

Mant's distinction between raider (binary) and builder (tertiary) modes of thought which determine the actions of leaders and responses to them is valuable, particularly as he maintains that it is virtually impossible for individuals to move readily between the two states. The suggestion that the roles, head and deputy, should be complementary if a healthy school climate is to be maintained, follows directly from this.

The two-dimensional approach to leadership represents an important strand traceable through much of the literature. Individual leaders, Fiedler suggested, appeared to favour one of two styles - either **structuring**, concerned with organising and directing the work, or **supportive**, looking towards the needs of group members. The structuring approach was most effective when the situation either favoured the leader or was very unfavourable. Favouring conditions arose when:

the leader was liked and trusted by the group;

the task for the group was clearly defined;

the leader had power over the group through rewards and punishment.

When the situation was only moderately favourable a supportive style appeared more successful. These conclusions are particularly significant in the context of interpersonal skills (Chapter 7). Interpreted as advice the Fiedler model and its derivatives include ambivalences. For headteachers as group leaders favourableness has to be sought: that is, the greater the extent to which they achieve power and influence over the group, the less is their dependence upon goodwill. Conversely, their performance as leaders relates as much to situational favourableness as it does to style. Therefore, work situation and style should be matched. If the tasks are routine and can be clearly defined and the headteacher is well respected, a directive approach which ensures task completion pay dividends. In situations involving ambiguity, however, headteachers and staff with senior management roles, with few rewards and sanctions to support their positional power, have little alternative but to be supportive rather than directive.

In schools the distinction between well- defined tasks and those displaying ambiguity is often far from straightforward. Moreover, many ambiguous situations include task completion conditions, usually because of time-limits imposed by LEAs or DES - a curriculum review, for example. According to Handy (1985) part of the confusion arises because the reality of leadership is more complex than Fiedler's contingency theory implies. This supports the view expressed by Argyris (1957) nearly 30 years ago that the choice of the correct way to act should be made by the leader only after an analysis of the reality of the situation. Handy continued to take leadership studies away from narrow-based trait and situational approaches into complex behavioural theories by introducing the following four groups of influencing factors which any leader must consider (described here for schools):

the professional style and personal
characteristics of the school leadership;

the style of leadership preferred by the staff,
and the dependence of this on circumstances;

the task: that is, the job, its objectives
and the associated technology;

the environment: that is, the organisational
situation of the head and the staff-group in
relation to the importance of the task.

From this is developed the 'best-fit' approach which argues that there is no 'right style' of leadership, but that the most effective leadership occurs when the requirements of the leader, group members and the task fit together. In any situation the three factors are placed on a continuum ranging from tight to flexible. For example, the combination of a headteacher who prefers tight structuring, a staff which expects autonomy and a loosely defined task, such as curricular re-organisation, does not represent a fit. The tasks and group members fit, the headteacher does not. If unresolved, the group will cease to function cohesively and the task is unlikely to be completed. A headteacher with a strong personality may seek for a better fit both by reducing the autonomy of teachers and structuring the task, but there is a risk of reduction in staff supportiveness as the project becomes more task-oriented.

Alternatively, the headteacher might adopt a new leadership style to improve the fit, risking reduced credibility. Whether this occurs depends upon the environment of the situation: for example, the norms of the school, the acknowledged expertise of the head in the curriculum area being discussed, or the availability of alternative strategies. Exact prediction is impossible because of the huge number of dependent and independent variables which can influence group and individual behaviour. Yet as demands for improved leadership in schools grow, because of its association with success, so do demands from headteachers and senior staff for advice and information. They would like guidance on how they might exert more influence in a range of situations, and how they might enhance followership within a constituency which, particularly in the case of some headteachers, can be large and varied. Because they perceive many limitations in their control over task and environmental factors they are attracted to the study of leadership style, believing that, if they learn how to adapt style to particular circumstances, they will be able to meet the demands of leadership.

Leadership styles and job satisfaction

The first use of multiple-leadership behaviour descriptions was by Lewin, Lippett and White (1939) who, following an experimental study, classified three styles, democratic, autocratic and laissez-faire. Nearly forty years later it was possible for Landers and Myers (1980) to report that more than forty style models had been developed, containing many different and sometimes conflicting features with styles per model varying from two to eight. The futility of searching for a single best style, even for one set of circumstances, was confirmed. For the headteacher there exists a range of behaviour which is acceptable to staff, rather than some single point on a behavioural continuum. However, each school leader will have a particular preference, depending upon the situation (Yukl, 1975). Confronted with the task of analysing such potential complexity, but at the same time providing simple guidance about style, many writers sought refuge in bipolar analogies. Democratic and autocratic, like participatory and authoritarian, can be viewed as two contrasting styles, but which is the more effective will be both situational and personality dependent. One style is not indisputably better than the other (Reddin, 1970).

LEADERSHIP UNLIMITED?

An alternative dichotomy as suggested by Fiedler (1958) was mentioned in the previous section, and appears in many other studies (Stodgill and Coons, 1957, for example) utilising **initiating structure** and **consideration**. The same notion appears under different labels: Etzioni (1964) with instrumental and expressive dimensions, Likert (1961) with production-centred and employee-oriented managers and Fiedler himself (1967) with task motivation and relationship motivation. Essentially there is considerable agreement about the separation of leader behaviour into two categories: one relating to the work or task, the other to people or relationships. The lack of a theoretical framework inhibits further consensus. The main impediment appears to be disagreement about whether the two categories represent independent variables, or are bipolar, that is, standing at different ends of the same continuum.

In support of the former view Stodgill and Coons (1957) reported that good leaders could score well on both dimensions, a finding which was developed by Blake and Mouton (1964) in their managerial grid. By representing concern for production as the X axis, with concern for people as the Y axis, and utilising scales of 1 to 9, they produced a matrix of potential management styles. The principle has been used extensively in management training in an attempt to persuade managers to aim for a 9,9 style, which shows maximum concern for production through maximum concern for people. In practice, of course, situational nuances have to be confronted. A headteacher coping with a member of staff under stress might advise the colleague to stop marking, contrary to school policy, until the personal problems have abated. The headteacher will be displaying a 1,9 style through seeming to be highly committed to the well-being of the individual to the apparent detriment of pursuing school objectives. Later in the same day, perhaps, faced with a LEA demand for information about the school the headteacher might seem to allow organisational objectives to dominate. A teacher will be ordered to make a return by a certain time; the headteacher in such circumstances will be perceived as production oriented.

The view that task and relationship interests represent opposite ends of a continuum has much support. Likert (1961) for example, analyzing managers of high and low productivity groups. found the former to be employee focused and the latter production centred. Representing these as contrasting spectral positions he produced four management systems.

System 1	-	Exploitive - Authoritarian
System 2	-	Paternalistic
System 3	-	Consultative
System 4	-	Participative

The last was considered the most desirable. Tannenbaum and Schmidt (1958) also posit four continuum positions;

tells   -   the manager (headteacher, say) makes a
                decision and tells the staff;

sells   -   the headteacher makes a decision but
                sells it to the staff;

consults   -   the headteacher listens to advice and
                does not make a decision until the staff
                have had opportunity to comment upon
                the issue;

joins   -   the headteacher delegates to the staff
                the right to make decisions and joins in
                that activity.

The similarities are obvious. Like Likert, they advocated a 'joining' style if the commitment of staff, both to the processes of decision-making and the outcomes, was to be maximised. A leader adopting such a pattern would more likely be successful.

Undeniably, the ends of the continuum are easier to identify than intermediate positions. McGregor (1960) made use of this advantage in summarising two polarised sets of assumptions held by managers about attitudes towards work. According to Theory X personnel dislike work, have little ambition, want security and require to be coerced, controlled or threatened with punishment. In contrast, Theory Y holds that staff will seek responsibility if the conditions are appropriate, exercise self-direction and control if they become committed to organisational objectives, and respond to rewards associated with goal-attainment. In practice, a Theory X headteacher would be task-centred; one adopting a Theory Y approach would exhibit System 4 or 'joining' features. Alternatively, by demonstrating maximum concern for school tasks through maximum concern for staff performing them, a Theory Y headteacher might be able to sustain a 9,9 leadership style.

Once again, though, the potential for practical application is flawed, because, despite a great deal of activity, no adequate theoretical framework has emerged. Even with the range of approaches adopted and the number of theories proposed causal relationships remain elusive. A plethora of terminology with much ambiguity surrounds leadership behaviour. The main thrust of Yukl, (1975) has been towards such a behavioural theory. Aware of the fact that so many of the empirical studies were situationally specific, while other 'theories' were largely discursive, he returned to initiating structures and consideration as dominant variables. However, he added a third, decision-centralisation; the extent to which the leader makes decisions. A high score on this variable is indicative of a 'tells' or 'sells' leader.

The issue of continuum however, still requires resolution. Possibly there are two continua - initiating structure and consideration (as before) alongside decision-centralization and consideration - for Gomberg (1966) reports that in the context of schools an autocratic headteacher may also be able to score highly on consideration. However, Yukl went on to develop a 'Multiple-linkage Model of Leader Effectiveness' which can be used to determine the performance of a group of teachers. In this model his three original variables interact with three intermediate variables (the motivation of teachers towards a task, their skills in that task area, and the technical quality of decisions relating to the task) and situational variables. Therefore, to improve performance the headteacher, in this context, must show an increase in one or more of the intermediate variables, while being aware of the various correlations and interactions that are possible among all the variables.

Nias (1980) utilised this model when studying the leadership patterns of primary school headteachers. She proposed three styles:

the passive   -   who gives more freedom than staff desire;

the bourbon   -   who maintains a social distance in an attempt to assert authority over staff;

the positive   -   who sets high professional standards, as well as consulting with staff.

To these styles she tried to relate the constructs of initiating structure, consideration and decision-centralization, according to young teachers' perceptions of their heads. For initiating structure, it was suggested that two aspects of commitment distinguished passive from positive headteachers. First, positive heads seemed able to demonstrate a high level of personal involvement in the work; second, they portrayed high professional standards. In the consideration category positive heads were both visible and accessible, passive heads were not only inaccessible but seemed unable or unwilling to support young teachers, while the apparently overbearing and authoritarian manner of bourbons aroused displeasure. Some preferred a head who took all decisions, that is, scored highly on decision-centralisation; the majority preferred discussion and a consults/joins style.

More specifically, a positive headteacher was high on consideration and initiation but low on decision-centralisation; a passive headteacher was fairly low on consideration, lower still on initiating and bottom on decision-centralisation; by contrast a bourbon was high on decision-centralisation and low on consideration. In some ways such an analysis runs the risk of over-simplification, particularly when translated from the general to the particular cases, but nevertheless it does highlight important issues. For example, it is significant that passive heads appear to cause more dissatisfaction than bourbons, despite the importance attached to professional autonomy by teachers.

Most important of all, however, the work of Nias alerts leaders in schools to the needs of staff and how these might be fulfilled or frustrated. Some sources of dissatisfaction have already been mentioned; others, such as inefficiency and disorganisation, or working in a school which seemed to lack purpose, proved equally powerful. When these prevailed, teachers' expectations of their heads were not being met, most usually by passive and less often by bourbon leadership styles. and only a positive stance seemed able to contribute effectively towards job-satisfaction. Such a stance was marked by clear, understood and accepted school policies, about which staff could negotiate within limits, high standards of professionalism, competence and personal commitment, together with a capacity for supporting and encouraging individuals. These factors can have a significant effect on the school climate (Halpin, 1966).

Such a conclusion replicates Herzberg's seminal study of job-satisfaction (1966) with 200 engineers and accountants in North America. Asked to remember times and events when they felt exceptionally good (or bad) about their jobs, they revealed in their replies that factors leading to job-satisfaction (achievement, recognition, attraction of the work itself, responsibility and the possibility of advancement) were markedly different from the factors producing dissatisfaction (company policy and administration, inappropriate supervision, low salary, poor interpersonal relations and working conditions). The elimination of these factors had little effect on positive job-attitudes; it served to prevent job-dissatisfaction. As a result they were entitled 'hygiene factors' because of their preventative and environmental roles.

By contrast, satisfaction arose from the individual's wish and ability to fulfil potential within the work situation. Yet another dual-continuum has produced its own controversies, not least the positioning of pay within the dissatisfaction segment. According to Herzberg, high salary may reduce dissatisfaction but it will not increase job-satisfaction. However, a sense of achievement from the work, a perception that what is done appears to be recognised by others in the community, the attractiveness of teaching as a career - all contributors to job-satisfaction - cannot be separated in the minds of many teachers from salary levels. If they feel underpaid they may believe that society is undervaluing their contribution. In the classroom they may still experience fulfilment; but outside of it society is implying that its recognition of what teachers do, and the importance of what can be achieved through teaching are not particularly valued. In an empirical study of the satisfaction which 410 Canadian school principals derived from their work, Fiesen, Holdaway and Rice (1983) found general agreement with Herzberg's work, but there were three significant differences:

interpersonal relationships were viewed as satisfiers;

advancement was not mentioned as a satisfier or dissatisfier;

overall constraints, pupil attitudes and performance, stress and attitudes of society did not appear on Herzberg's list.

For leaders in schools, unable to influence general salary levels and probably as concerned about them as other staff, the thrust must be towards organising the school and the managing of interpersonal relationships in such a way as to maximise the satisfiers and reduce the dissatisfiers. Indeed, years before Herzberg's work, Mayo (1933) showed that groups of workers who felt themselves valued by management improved output significantly compared with those who were resentful or suspicious of management. For teachers there can be little doubt that achievement and recognition are substantive contributors to job-satisfaction; and, compared with many other occupations, the opportunity for the individual teacher to attain a 'pleasurable emotional state' through appraising that the job is 'achieving or facilitating one's values' (Locke,1969) remains high.

Even with curricular and resource constraints individual teachers have considerable freedom to evolve a particular style of working and develop a characteristic set of competencies. In doing so, each tries to match a unique collection of needs to those that might be fulfilled by the job. Progress towards that match enhances job-satisfaction and should lead to more output. As a result the role of leaders in this context relates to awareness about the uniqueness of the needs of each individual with whom they work and the extent to which these are, and can be, fulfilled within the working environment. That represents the nub of leadership demands upon them; it therefore transfers attention to the issue of teacher motivation and the leader's role in its maximisation.

The leader as motivator

By implication, leadership involves influence: it means the process of influencing staff to strive to achieve group intentions (Koontz, O'Donnell and Weihtich, 1980). More specifically it represents:

'the influential increment over and above mechanical
compliance with the routine directives of the organisation'
(Katz and Kahn, 1978).

If members of staff of a school perceive the leadership is non-existent they may continue to do what is statutorily required of them, but the level at which they perform will be determined by the degree to which they are motivated. Self-motivation will only take staff so far. Leadership means that some organisational members are trying to influence the behaviour of others, despite Mant's view that 'good leaders don't do things to people; they release deep-seated urges and understandings' (1983). His concept of motivation as 'communicable enthusiasm' contrasts sharply with the type of management training which focuses on helping an individual exert influence over others, a feature which raises several ethical issues which have received little attention (Wright and Taylor, 1984), not least because this influence may be taking the organisation and the individual in directions which are questionable in the long-term. The securing of the commitment of members of the organisation to its values and objectives would seem a more defensible function of leadership than a perception of motivation which verges on exploitation and manipulation.

The study of motivation is, in effect, the study of human psychology, because almost all behaviour has some definable purpose. Work-place motivation does not differ markedly from other types of motivation (Vroom, 1964). It is suggested by Miskel (1982) that motivation represents ....'the complex forces, drives, needs, tension states or other mechanism, that start and maintain voluntary activity towards the achievement of personal goals'. He sees two types of motivational models - **content** and **process**. Content models attempt to identify the factors that exercise or initiate behaviour: needs, motives and expectancies as well as job-related items such as security and recognition. Process models, however, give a more emphasis to how behaviour is started, maintained and stopped, and concern themselves with issues of expectance and goal-setting.

Within the content model those theories that concentrate on needs fulfilment seem to offer most to organisational studies. Given that the energy and enthusiasm which individuals are prepared to bring to their work depend upon motivation, then the task for managers is the identification of situations in which individuals expend maximum energy to realise particular intentions. In this context the needs theory Maslow (1954) has probably attracted most attention. He suggests a Needs Hierarchy (a series of needs through which individuals progress) as the fundamental structure of human behaviour. The needs are:

physiological:	hunger, thirst, sleep;
safety:	structure, security, stability, order;
social:	acceptance, understanding, belongingness, friendship;
esteem:	attention, recognition, prestige, respect;
self-actualisation:	personal development, self-fulfilment.

When one need is satisfied by a person's behaviour, the higher order need becomes dominant. Within the theory there is no attempt to explain the intensity of needs, while the potential blurring of the edges between categories receives little attention. Even an issue as basic as the number of categories can be disputed, with, for example, Porter (1963) including the need for autonomy between esteem and self-actualisation. Nevertheless the theory does have credibility because individuals do look towards the satisfaction of pressing physical demands before progressing towards the needs which relate to a desire for a high evaluation of themselves. Teachers, like most other workers, act in ways which enhance and sustain their self-esteem and reputation in the eyes of those around them.

Of the highest needs, self-esteem satisfaction allows individuals to perceive themselves as useful and necessary, while self-actualisation refers to the desire for fulfilment, the need for a person to become actualised and to realise potential. Criticisms of the notion of self-actualisation (which Maslow claimed was only achieved by a relatively small number of people) abound, both because of its nebulousness and its inability to account for the very large range of situations and routes by which a person may realise individual potential.

Indeed, Locke (1976) contradicts Maslow over the limited achievement of the self-actualisation state by pointing to the danger of neuroticism as individuals in striving to achieve their full potential, and try to solve innumerable conflicts among the main choices open to them. Additionally, longitudinal studies, for example, (Hall and Nougaim, 1968) challenge the sequential patterning of the hierarchy and there seems little support (Miner and Dachler, 1973) for the suggestion that the five needs are inherent to human beings. A similar theory (Alderfer, 1972) based upon the needs of existence, relatedness and growth resembles the Maslow hierarchy, and therefore can be subjected to the same criticisms, but its credibility is enhanced by its greater flexibility and particularly by the notion that circumstances can produce variations in both the dominance and strength of needs and the probability that more than a single need will be present at any time. For leaders in schools these theories draw attention to the higher order needs of would-be followers. Existence, safety and physiological needs play little part (except, possibly, the threat of redundancy) but the capacity of the leader to offer conditions which enable the teacher to gain recognition through achievement and perceive self-development as a result of school experience should be an important motivating factor. However, teachers, even those working in similar situations, do not have the same collection of need strengths.

It was to this issue that McClelland (1961) and Atkinson and Feather (1966) turned with separate studies. The former identified three basic motivational needs in individuals, **power** (a concern for exercising influence and control), **affiliation** (a tendency to want to belong to social groupings and an unwillingness to be rejected by such groups) and **achievement** (a desire for success, through accepting challenging tasks and holding high aims -but a fear of failure is also involved). Need-achievement, and its significance for organisational issues, receives special consideration, based on the view that much behaviour is directed towards attaining high standards, and the assumption that it represents a basic personality trait (individuals can be labelled as having low or high need-achievement). Therefore, to staff a school with high achievement teachers should lead to success, in view of correlations with attributes such as perseverance, determination, receptivity and respect. With such personnel, organisation and leadership should present few problems, although Klinger and McNelly,(1969) conclude that the successful organisation in a competitive environment will produce staff exhibiting high need-achievement. More significantly, teachers with high need-achievement may strive in their own areas of work but may be indifferent, in the view of the leaders, to the needs of the school or the activities of other colleagues.

There are two main shortcomings in the usefulness to leadership practice of needs oriented theories. First, the implicit view that an individual's personality represents a stable phenomenon must be questionable. Indeed, modern theories about personality recognise that the unique features of the situation in which an activity or interaction occurs provide a significant variable in determining the personality mode. Numerous additional determinants can be isolated, of which two are particularly important:

constitutional: differences in the genetic structures of individuals which result in varying potentials for learning activity, energy and tolerance of frustration, each of which can influence needs and expectations;

group membership: differences resulting from the responses to beliefs, values and attitudes to which the individual has been, and is, exposed during up-bringing, social life, and in the work-place. Additionally, within each group the individual accepts or adopts a position involving behaviour expectations largely determined by other group-members.

All these factors make some contribution to the determination of personality. The second and related shortcoming of needs theories is that they tend to ignore the behaviourist perspective. More directly, the benefits which might accrue from precise identification of situational variables in any consideration of needs-related motivation far outweigh measures of changing personality, characteristics and dispositions, based upon some permanent classifications of needs. This is particularly so, when the empirical support for such classification is limited (McCormick and Ilgen, 1981).

Cognitive-rational theories of motivation, in contrast, emphasise an individual's expectancy of goal attainment and the extent to which a particular outcome is valued, alongside the strength of psychological needs, as the determinants of motivated behaviour (Taylor and Sluckin, 1982). Such theories place motivation quite clearly within the area of volitional and conscious decision-making. It is Vroom (1964) who adapted them to the work-situation, although they have a longer history (Tolman, 1932).

Essentially, individuals at work are viewed as rational decision-makers guided by three basic perceptions about any course of action:

expectancy - the expectation that effort will lead to desired performance;

instrumentality - the relation between performance level and the attainment of particular outcomes;

values - the value placed upon each of the outcomes.

Handy (1981) develops the subsuming concept of **motivation calculus** (E) as the mechanism by which individuals determine how much investment to put into any activity. This may require considerable private effort, possibly unrecognised and unappreciated by those with whom they work. His term 'E' represents the amount of Energy and Effort an individual is prepared to devote to satisfy his needs, along with the Excitement, Enthusiasm, Emotion, Expenditure of time and Expenditure of passion.

Criticisms of such approaches to motivation tend to focus upon the excessive reliance on calculation, which is little more than metaphor, when most personnel are more limited in their information-processing capacities than the theories demand. Less specifically, though, teachers gradually do acquaint themselves with the total environment in which they work, through perception and observation, and, as this occurs, they make judgements about which actions will meet needs and achieve personal satisfaction. In any situation several courses of action are available, and anticipations of further developments relating self to environment direct teachers towards activities which they think will maintain or enhance the satisfaction to be derived from work. However, since computation of expectancies and the assessment of values are introduced as directive parameters, rather than instigators of behaviour, cognitive-rational theories seem to offer some opportunities to leaders. If an individual's preference for certain outcomes is regarded as a motivator, then organisational tasks and attitudes require an appropriate design.

Because it includes the implicit assumption that individuals are able to distinguish between work-related variables the Herzberg (1966) study of job-satisfaction concentrates attention upon work-place organisation and the quality of relationships. As a result it is given a rational-cognitive classification although Handy prefers to consider this study as needs-oriented. Nevertheless by itemising factors leading to job-satisfaction -achievement, recognition, responsibility and advancement - and pointing out an individual's desire to fulfil potential within the work situation, a leader's attention is drawn to links between satisfiers and motivators which might enhance performance and effort.

Although all these theories offer insights, no single theory, from whatever perspective, has so far emerged to explain all the complexities associated with human motivation. Perhaps the greatest challenge to school leadership is the need to strive for incremental influence over not one, but many individuals, each with specific motivational characteristics. Each one has a unique collection of needs, which vary with time and are contingent upon situations; each has idiosyncratic aspirations, and as a result performs independent calculations about the likelihood and desirability of success relative to effort expenditure; and even when experiencing a similar concentration and intensity of needs as a colleague, each has developed a characteristic pattern of behaviour, which is a function of personality, in order to achieve satisfaction.

In addition, every teacher will react to frustrations when needs cannot be satisfied, or intentions appear beyond reach, by an individualistic collection of defence mechanisms consisting of some mix of rationalisation, repression, compensation, aggression or withdrawal. On top of all this, as the theories attempt to make clear, the interactions between the individual teacher and others in the work group may change any or all of these factors. At the same time leaders are not immune from interactions; they have their own needs and their own motivational requirements which are influenced by activities and outcomes within the group.

Any teacher looking for specific guidance from leadership theory to cope with particular situations cannot do other than rely on eclecticism. For schools, given the standard of education of the staff and the nature of the task, approaches directed towards servicing high order needs and raising the expectancy levels of teachers about achieving desired outcomes appear to offer most opportunity. With such strategies, motivational levels could be raised, with commitment and quality of work heightened. Practically, though, such strategies have to be devised and sustained within parameters imposed by the preferred styles and characteristics of both the leader and group members, while the framework imposed by the tasks of the school, department or any sub-unit, and the relevant organisational situations cannot be overlooked.

Leadership in practice

Throughout the majority of management studies, the issue of leadership skill has received relatively little attention. Most theories that relate to leadership are behavioural, with behaviour described at a relatively high level of abstraction. Similarly, the style approach is vague with little in the way of direct help to a leader in an actual situation (Wright and Taylor, 1984). A fruitful avenue for consideration lies in research on the work pattern of staff. As might be expected, such research on management activity has been restricted to the most senior staff. More surprisingly, little of it has occurred in the UK. A large-scale study of what teachers did was not focused on management tasks (Hilsum and Strong, 1978). Nevertheless, studies of the work-patterns of high school principals in North America can provide a useful framework for considering the improvement of leadership practice. In surveying the work of the school administrator, Bridges (1982) identified seven main foci. The first four of these, attitudes, behaviour, traits and impact, are person-related while the remainder, effectiveness, expectations and power, are more concerned with occupancy of the role. He further suggests that these concentrate on antecedents and outcomes. March and Cohen (1974) had already identified five analytical skills related to managerial areas which they regarded as basic:

analysis of expertise:	management of knowledge;
analysis of coalitions:	management of conflict;
analysis of ambiguity:	management of goals;
analysis of time:	management of attention;
analysis of information:	management of inference;

while Hodgkinson (1983) suggests the addition of a sixth:

    analysis of values: management of meaning,

maintaining that 'administration is philosophy in action' and leadership is 'the effecting of policy, values and philosophy through collective organisational action'. He asserts that issues of values are at least as important as decision-making, since 'the world of fact is given, the world of value made'. He argues that one function of the leader is to carry out values audits, pointing out that value conflicts need not be resolved, that the effective tension can be tolerated, provided that it is recognised.

Translating these skills into perceived activities is not easy, but the work of de Bono (1979) forms a good link with more analytical work. From his work on thinking processes he derived the following activities:

organising, compiling information, investigating, researching, generating ideas, synthesizing, reacting, explaining, communicating, selling, organising groups, using diplomacy, taking responsibility and making things happen.

These activities indicate the responsibilities of leadership which must be carried out in order that the organisation can continue to function, let alone achieve its goals. However, it is clear that all these activities of leadership cannot be performed even in a small school by one person - the designated leader. Moreover, distributed leadership has numerous advantages because of the possibilities it offers to service the higher order needs of other organisational members. The time actually given to the various tasks associated with designated leadership also demonstrates the futility of an individual trying to avoid a non-distributed leadership. For example, Martin and Willower (1981) observed the activities of a number of high school principals over a period, and recorded the time actually spent on thirteen different types of activity:

desk work, scheduled meetings, unscheduled meetings, exchanges, phone calls, personal, tours, monitoring, trips, announcing, observing, processing and teaching.

Records were kept of each principal's correspondence (input and output) and of the contacts made during the time of the study. A significant aspect of the research involved the ascertaining of the purpose of the activities, and indicated that 53.9% of tasks, involving 35.5% of time, were devoted to organisational maintenance itself. Only 7.6% of tasks were concerned with the academic programme, suggesting that considerable delegation took place in this area, consistent with the notion that relationships in the instructional sphere are more loosely coupled and autonomous than in the organisational area. Techniques outlined by Austin (1979) enable staff to perform their own studies. The Martin and Willower study also supports the sixfold characterisation of managerial work depicted by Mintzberg (1973):

> volume and pace; variety, brevity and fragmentation;
> verbal media preference; preference for live action;
> the contact network; blend of rights and duties.

A UK study on a selection of secondary school headteachers did not attempt to assess in such detail the activities of headteachers (Morgan et al., 1983). Relatedly, though, a classification of the skills demanded of headteachers was attempted. The team chose the three-fold generic grouping of Katz (Chapter 2) based upon technical, human and conceptual skills, but also added a fourth - those related to the management of external relationships. What is required, however, in developing leadership in practice, is more information on the day to day tasks performed by staff with managerial responsibilites and the priorities they give to them. With this information about what staff actually do, classifications of skills would provide a more useful framework for the design of learning programmes.

An appreciation of the skills required for effective leadership and the self-discipline demanded on the part of both the leader and the led, in refining these skills, can do much to improve the effectiveness of the organisation. Hodgkinson concludes his philosophy of leadership (1983) with four maxims in which he embodies the leader's requirements:

> know the task;
> know the situation;
> know the followership;
> know oneself.

How effectively a particular school leader is performing may be difficult to assess. On different occasions the evidence may be contradictory and convoluted, but, in broad terms, members of staff both demand and welcome what they perceive as good leadership within the context of effective management; at the same time the school's clients expect it to be provided. The business of those in positions of responsibility in schools must be to learn to satisfy this expectation, for, as Mant has observed, 'the problem ... is therefore to harness, as best one can, the manager's natural tendency to learn from his own messy experience' (1983).

Whichever component of leadership activity receives attention, however, task-performance cannot be separated from either the totality of the organisational environment in which it occurs or the acknowledgement that leadership provides only one element of management. The two chapters which follow will therefore examine the expertise and credibility of teachers as managers, and the power and authority they possess or are perceived to possess.

CHAPTER 4

EXPERTISE AND CREDIBILITY

Procedures, Rituals and Traditions

The reason why learning through experience is so often 'messy' is that it cannot be isolated from organisational existence: casual day-to-day events cannot be organised to maximise learning. A curriculum co-ordinator in a primary school may be confronted by an angry parent or find that some teaching material has gone missing. Such events have to be dealt with immediately. The experience may result in better handling of future situations but mistakes made during the original events can be difficult to rectify. Yet such 'messiness' cannot be avoided. Even when a headteacher attends a management course anything learned must be related to the job of organising the school if it is to facilitate improved performance. On this basis, though, learning can be too specific, relating to only one school situation. Indeed, there are examples where a headteacher or departmental head, apparently successful in one environment, is much less so on transfer to a similar post elsewhere. Adding the extra element of promotion, when a teacher moves into middle or senior management for the first time, compounds the problems which arise from over-specificity of learning because of the change of tasks for which the new post-holder is unprepared.

Notwithstanding these dichotomies in the learning process, normative arrangements for promotion to managerial responsibilities involve a steady progression through the middle and senior management on to deputy headship and headship. In most cases, candidates for a headship, for example, would already be deputy heads, A suitably qualified candidate who was already a head elsewhere, perhaps in a smaller school, would have a particularly strong claim. In contrast, even someone with a good educational background, but from outside school (a training officer in a firm perhaps) would be unlikely to receive much attention. The implicit assumption is that only those staff with a particular type and (probably) length of experience will have gained the necessary expertise. Undoubtedly, selectors intend that the post-holders they choose should strengthen their expertise, but during recruitment they look for a basic level, accruing from certain experiences. However, for senior positions in particular, the search for the most relevant expertise is elusive. Much of it relates to the nature of schools as organisations.

Schools, like all organisations, are inherently conservative (Wildavsky, 1972). They involve structures (houses, departments etc. in large schools) which have been established; they utilise the values of members to help them function; they encourage staff to adopt roles, and allow habits to evolve in the accomplishment of these roles. Alongside there are also on-going networks of obligations and exchanges, both between organisational members and with other organisations. A school interacts with its Parent-Teacher Association and Governing Body; it forms certain relationships with the LEA advisory service; it generates certain expectations among parents about what it can offer their children; pupils anticipate a particular education (Aldrich, 1979). Any of these parties, if disappointed or frustrated, will attempt to use the networks for amelioration. Even when satisfied they try to strengthen the level of obligations and the nature of ex-changes so that school activities fit more readily into a framework they would approve.

Newly appointed senior staff, therefore, should beware of overestimating the freedom available to them in discharging their respon-sibilites. They may have their own views and convictions as to how the job should be done. They may even have been given a free hand by the headteacher or the school governors, with the inducement of minimal in-tervention. What they soon realise, in practice, is that others, both within and beyond the school, have been able to shape practices and develop working procedures which they expect will continue without too much disturbance. Even when a school is new, staff move there with pre-determined intentions about the priority of tasks and their performance. Simultaneously, parents expect the school to provide an education not too dissimilar from that available elsewhere, while the LEA, governors and so on, wish the school to accord with practices already introduced.

An important effect of these constraints is that schools, through their organisational members, often seem to resist change. It is relatively easy for a headteacher or departmental head to utilise an already established network of relationships and exchanges with other staff to thwart the in-troduction of new arrangements, claiming, for example, that a proposed alteration in fourth year options would impose insuperable timetabling constraints. Similarly, a headteacher may oppose a new science scheme, even if recommended by DES (1985b), on the grounds of lack of resources. Indeed, in all such cases, there is a contradiction between the stability that organisational structure produces and the process of adaptation and development.

In many situations this contradiction is strengthened as procedures evolve into traditions and become, as a result, very difficult to change. The pace with which traditions become established is often remarkable. Sixth form colleges and middle schools were rare until the late 1960s; now both collectively and individually they include traditions which attract strong support as some LEAs have found when trying to convert sixth form colleges into tertiary colleges or to eliminate middle schools. In such circumstances the network of obligations linking parents, teachers, governors and local politicians is easily utilised to defend even the most recently established institutions. Within them traditions are even more rapidly introduced. An arrangement for examinations or an additional subject in the curriculum, even soon after introduction, can be portrayed as a part of some long-standing procedure, and any attempt to change as a threat to the stability or well-being of the institution. In particular, staff searching for continuity are attracted by the possibility of converting established arrangements into unchallengeable traditions.

As well as circumscribing new or alternative activities, traditions can also be used to legitimate (Pocock, 1973). An illustration of the way this has occurred, and in some situations continues, is relative to the authority of the headteacher. Musgrove (1971), for example, concluded that 'schools are underpowered in relation to the goals they try to attain'. More broadly he suggested that teachers' power fell so far short of their authority that 'most teachers live in a state of crisis and chronic apprehension'. Such a view, although exaggerated, does go some way towards explaining the attractiveness of traditions to some staff if they are perceived to enhance stability in relationships and allow a sense of purposeful discipline to permeate school activities. Historically, the authority of headteachers has been represented as unchallengeable and their powers limitless, particularly in the eyes of the pupils. Some teachers may choose to attempt a perpetuation of this myth because they think it assists in the exercise of pupil control.

However, like all myths it represents only part of reality (Lutz and Ramsey, 1973). Many other factors intervene in determining pupil behaviour: the competence of teaching staff, curriculum design, teaching style, the environment of the school, the attitude of parents. A teacher who relies on a perception of headteacher dominance to control pupil behaviour is likely to be disappointed. In other parts of school life the authority of the headteacher is reduced both by the traditions of the schools themselves and the personalities of the staff, factors of which teachers have been conscious for years. The steady decrease in the number of people in all walks of life who unquestioningly accept authority has further eroded the myth of headteacher autocracy. Yet, some elements of it can still be detected. Nias (1980) reported the willingness of some primary teachers to accept high-handed headteacher behaviour, and to prefer it to a non-interventionist approach. In the secondary sphere Berg (1968) illustrates a similar attitude from teachers when their school was experiencing problems, by reporting the statement 'We have a right to be led'.

Any study of educational management, or anyone trying to improve management performance, would be unwise to belittle the importance of rituals and traditions, both generally and in relation to a school, department or other unit. In many situations they provide a most significant element in institutional functioning and dominate aspects of individual behaviour. Without an understanding of their role attempts to re-orientate management processes will be defective and ineffectual. For many schools the most public statement of procedures appears in the 'school management scheme' or 'staff guidance notes', often supported by written school rules for pupils and a brochure for parents. While the purpose of such documents may be to inform, they can convey, perhaps quite deliberately, an element of the bureaucracy in the school.

In the context of its management the extent and form of this bureaucracy requires consideration. Hall (1963) suggests that the degree of bureaucratisation in a school can be measured by a six-dimensional organisational inventory:

Hierarchy of authority - the extent to which the loci of decision-making is prestructured by the organisation into departments and houses with the main areas of executive function remaining with departmental and house heads, who in turn are responsible, possibly through the deputy head, to the head teacher.

Pressure of rules - the extent to which the behaviour of organisational members is subject to organisational control. School rules, for example, circumscribe pupil behaviour and also make considerable demands upon staff freedom of action because it is they who must enforce them. Lists of duties, related to functional responsibilities place more direct controls upon members of staff.

Procedural specifications - the extent to which members must follow organisationally defined techniques and procedures in dealing with situations they encounter, as when a teacher wishes to have a formal meeting with a parent.

Impersonality - the extent to which members and outsiders are treated without regard to individual qualities.

Division of labour - the extent to which work tasks are sub-divided by functional specialisation: in secondary schools with the division into departments and faculties, because of the curriculum specialisation of staff, and with the evolution of pastoral structures between curricular and pastoral specialisations. In primary schools such divisions are less marked, but with the emergence of curriculum co-ordinators functional specialisation is growing.

Technical competence - the extent to which organisationally defined standards are utilised in the selection and promotional procedures.

More recently, Sousa and Hoy (1981) attempted a synthesis based upon both this six-dimensional categorisation and the Aston Studies on organisational structure (Pugh and Hickson, 1976). The latter used statistical analyses to investigate the relationship in a large number of industrial organisations between the primary dimensions of bureaucracy they devised and individual behaviour. As a result, Sousa and Hoy suggest four underlying dimensions which provide the underpinning of all school structures:

Organisation control: the hierarchy of authority rules and specified procedures as they exist in the school,

Rational specialisation: the specialist use made of the particular tecnical competencies of individual staff,

System centralisation: the extent to which centralisation of decision-making by headteachers and senior staff determines teacher autonomy,

Formalisation of routine: the degree to which routine arrangements are formalised in rules, regulations, job and task-specifications.

One needs nevertheless to bear in mind that the individual caught up in some part of the arrrangements may have a very different perspective. An aggrieved parent, told to see the year head instead of the headteacher, or a disillusioned teacher, expected to complete a cumbersome report form, may well view the school as bureaucratic and verging on the uncaring or possibly hostile. Paradoxically, of course, the same parent or teacher might well defend the stability that results from well-defined procedures, without realising the associations between these and the underlying bureaucratisation. The degree of bureaucratisation along various dimensions provides an important component of school management because of its influence on behaviour.

Locating management

Much of the discontent of aggrieved parents or disillusioned teachers occurs because it appears to them that they have been subjected to an adverse decision made within a bureaucracy, on which they have had little or no influence. In addition, it may be difficult for them to locate where decisions occur. The conventional approach to bureaucracy theories, as applied to schools, requires further extension. In this context, Mintzberg (1979) suggests five viable configurations: simple bureaucracy, machine bureaucracy, professional bureaucracy, divisionalised form and adhocacy.

Schools were categorised as professional bureaucracies. He further suggested that all organisations have five parts - not two as in the classical theory of line and staff (Fayol, 1949) - related in a characteristic way. The headteacher and his deputy, and in larger schools increasingly the senior management team, constitute the **strategic apex.** Secondary curricular and pastoral heads, or primary curriculum co-ordinators are the **middle line** providing the link with the **operating core,** the teaching force. The **techno-structure** consists of professional support, from HMI, LEA advisers and officers and other agencies. Finally, there is the **support staff** of cleaners, meal supervisors, technicians and so on.

Mintzberg then defined six distinct characteristics for professional bureaucracies:

the key part of the organisation is the operating core, in this case, the classroom teachers;

the members of the core, the teachers, are well trained and well qualified professionals who are given considerable autonomy over the control and design of their own work;

the main co-ordinating mechanism lies in the standardised and special skills of the teachers, and the acknowledgement of a pre-determined end-product, the educated child;

since these standards are isolated within the school, many teachers feel that they have more in common with their peers in other institutions than colleagues in their own;

there is emphasis on 'expert power';

techno-structure and middle-line management (of the type prevalent in industry) is not highly developed, since the need for planning direct supervision is limited.

Mintzberg thus suggests that the school is a decentralised structure in which the classroom teachers not only control their own work, but also seek to exert collective control over the administrative decisions which affect them. Co-ordination is therefore by mutual adjustment, a democratic process, with liaison devices in the middle line management rather than in the operating core. Because of their qualifications and professional ability, those in the lower regions of the hierarchy, the classroom, have a fair measure of autonomy. Significantly, most primary school teachers, for example, even from their first day of work, are assumed to be competent to meet the total educational needs of their pupils.

Because senior staff are unable to control their professional colleagues directly, Mintzberg sees power as developing from a series of roles that can be adopted. Thus, although solutions cannot be imposed on colleagues, the skill with which disturbances are handled and conflicts resolved between members of staff and between parallel hierarchies will give senior staff increased prestige and influence, even though technically their base of power is restricted. In occupying boundary positions, too, they are in a position to gain support from the 'other side', in winning resources, for example, and act in other ways which appear to legitimise authority. Power is thus acquired at the loci of uncertainty and senior staff can create a feeling of dependency in colleagues as an additional source of informal power. Fuller consideration is given to the role of power and authority in the next chapter.

If the school is large enough, combining the five parts of the professional bureaucracy with a conventional organisation 'family tree' presents few problems (Cooper, 1981b) for either a primary or a secondary school (fig. 4.1). The construction of such a chart may be comforting, particularly to senior staff who strive for formalisation on the four Sousa and Hoy dimensions, because:

it suggests a hierarchy which may help to legitimise their authority;

it purports to define those relationships which are encouraged and therefore may improve communication flows;

it appears to delineate responsibilities by enabling clear role-classification for individuals holding positions on the chart;

it gives the impression that the organisation is neat and tidy with a unity of purpose;

it imposes certain relationships which they would wish to see nurtured. Such notions may be attractive, not least because of their disarming simplicity, but they do not come to terms with the dynamics of school functioning. The overlay of Mintzberg, through its relationship to the notion of professional bureaucracy, concentrates attention upon the complexity of organisational life. In schools the activities of teachers are not conducive to well-differentiated managerial roles and a steep hierarchy. Additionally, a number of working relationships develop which are either obscured by the chart or receive no mention.

Packwood (1977) identifies several of these. For example, there are co-ordination relationships in which some staff organise the work of others without assuming responsibility for the actual oversight of the work. A Health Education co-ordinator in a secondary school may link the activities of several departments. Additionally, monitorial relationships exist in which some teachers have to review the work of more senior colleagues: a curriculum co-ordinator in a primary school will monitor the teaching of a

59

EXPERTISE AND CREDIBILITY

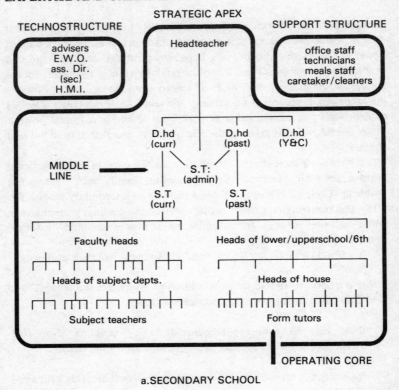

a. SECONDARY SCHOOL

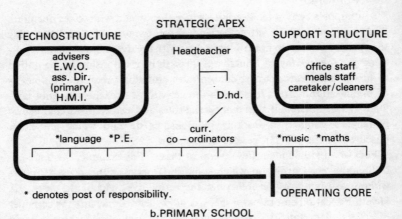

* denotes post of responsibility.

b. PRIMARY SCHOOL

Fig 4.1 Relation between Mintzberg's structural elements and typical tree diagrams for primary and secondary schools

deputy head; in some situations in a secondary school a curricular head may be a tutor under a pastoral head, who, in turn, is a junior member of someone else's department.

While such relationships undoubtedly influence behaviour in schools, they do so in ways which a more formalised view of them does not take into account. More significantly, they draw attention to an element of organised anarchy in school functioning. Cohen, March and Olsen (1972) suggest three factors in particular which induce the severe ambiguities that are characteristic of institutions displaying anarchic tendencies. First, there is no clear or consistent view about what they are trying to do. Because of limited agreement about their aims and objectives school staffs cannot define their preferences with accuracy. Some teachers place more emphasis on academic standards through examination results, others on extra-curricular activities, and so on. Second, even when an objective is agreed the staff are unsure of the processes by which it might be accomplished. The technology of teaching is unclear. Much of it is organised 'on the basis of simple trial and error procedures, the residue of learning from the accidents of past experience, and pragmatic inventions of necessity' (Cohen, March and Olsen). Third, participation in decision processes tends to be fluid. The interest of individual staff is activated to different extents dependent upon the issue, the timing, the pressure of other issues and such factors as whether the decision is made in a staff meeting, the headteacher's office or by a working party. A secondary teacher may be interested in the design of fourth year options but feels excluded through not being a member of the curriculum committee. Alternatively, a teacher who organises extra-curricular activities cannot attend lunchtime meetings, or a parent, unhappy with the non-availability at a parents' evening of a particular member of staff, might pursue that issue, but not feel inclined to stand for election to the school governors.

All organisations exhibit tendencies towards organised anarchy at some time. This applies particularly in schools and other educational institutions because of the potential impact of these three factors of aims, technology and choices on behaviour. Moreover, with the loss of public confidence in schools, and the reduction in resources at a time when major curricular changes are taking place, the possibility of anarchic tendencies is increased. There is more likelihood that the choice mechanisms display 'garbage-can' features: that is, the choices which some staff prefer, and the search for organisational problems to which they and other teachers have their own favoured solutions, produce a confusion of questions and unrelated answers. Such a situation runs contrary to the conventional view of decision-making in which, before a decision can be made, first one

61

considers the possiblity of choice, then the range of choices available and finally the likely effects of each choice. The apparent attractiveness of the garbage-can approach is the flexibility it could promote in school decision-making if it were not constrained by the strictures of conventional choice mechanisms: it appears to obviate the need for agreement over objectives, and this can be extremely appealing in a school confronted by conditions of extreme ambiguity. In practice, the attractions are often spurious.

The same benefits of more flexibility can also be put forward for the related notion of 'loose-coupling' (Weick, 1976). According to this the sub-systems of a school, of which only a few are visible in the organisation chart, are loosely linked. Consequently, the headteacher may be part of a sub-system with the science staff, or with a curriculum co-ordinator, as well as being a member of task-induced sub-systems. If the sub-systems have autonomy then the facility with which the whole school can respond flexibly to changing circumstances should be maintained. If, however, the coupling is excessively loose then the organisation as a whole ceases to exist (Padgett, 1980), certainly in the context of having a unified set of management procedures. Lutz (1982) takes this reasoning further by arguing that while garbage-can and loose-coupling models might accurately describe some educational institutions they tend to be used as an excuse for uncontrolled organisational behaviour or even organisational anarchy. Tighter coupling might well produce improved communication, more effective control mechanisms, additional participation for staff and enhanced opportunities both for choices and ultimately the education of pupils.

The Visibility of Management

If the parents or teachers who are unhappy with decisions which affect them are sufficiently persistent and perceptive they will realise that there still remains a missing dimension in their search for the location of decision-making. It would appear that in the professional bureaucracy of the school many staff make inputs into the choice processes; both formal and informal groups can have a powerful influence. In some parts of school activity, bureaucratic indices are high; in others there appears to be organised anarchy. Some sense can be made of these apparent contradictions by looking at the visibility of the decisions made by the school. This might provide the missing dimension, by concentrating upon varying degrees of visibility (Fig. 4.2.).

In the 'public' sector are those management tasks and decisions which have visible or tangible effects on teachers and pupils and which carry over beyond the boundary of the institution. There are two distinct levels of public activity. The first of these concerns the school's clientele - the parent body and the pupils themselves. The second is more concerned with

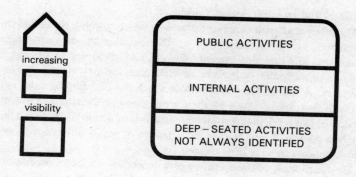

Fig 4.2 Visibility of Decision – making (Management)
Process in a School

the school's neighbourhood and community. The 'well-managed' school will seek to have its management problems visible to that wider community through, for example, work experience in the secondary school. The procedures and rituals resulting from decisions which directly involve arrangements for the education and well-being of the pupils are contained in this sector. However, if parents feel shut out from information about these activities, this indicates a need to re-appraise amd improve the communications across the school boundary. The governing body can often be regarded as providing the means by which the accountability of the school to the community it serves is maintained, and it might be thought of as being in the 'public' sector. However, the constraints of confidentiality over many issues lead it to operate through LEA officers and therefore internally. Accountability to the school techno-structure takes place at another level, but since this is within the operating core of school, such accountability is also internal.

To the outsider then, the structure usually appears stable and well suited to the production of the outputs demanded of the school. It appears at this level that the complex work of teaching, or attending to the welfare of pupils is well under the organisation's control; disciplinary procedures are clearly established. Most pupils complete their school careers without ever realising the time and effort devoted to the creation of the school as a system. The illusion created is that teachers just walk in and teach. Goffman (1971) has drawn attention to the 'behind the scenes' activities in other types of institutions which help to present this united front to outsiders and establish public confidence.

The **internal activities** are those processes which establish the united front developed by the organisation. The production of departmental syllabuses, and the deployment of staff and resources to achieve the school's or individual objectives, develop from the activities carried on at this level. Although the **framework** in which pastoral care operates in the school is developed at this level, there are so many personal and confidential aspects of this work that considerable freedom of action is granted to those teachers who work with individual or groups of pupils within any 'system' which appears to have been created.

The functioning of the operating core depends upon fellow professionals who use skills which may be difficult for individuals to acquire, and the well defined procedures developed in most schools rely upon the assumption that it will always be possible to recruit teachers with the appropriate training and skills. This may not always be possible under conditions of falling rolls and the solution may lie in the provision of school-focused in-service training (Chapter 9). The purpose of the internal activities is to create an environment complex enough to require the use of the sophisticated and caring techniques of the teachers, but stable enough to enable these skills to become standardised or even institutionalised. Weick (1976) maintained that schools are in the business of building and maintaining categories ('pigeon-holing') of pupil needs, in terms of set procedures, and then applying the appropriate procedures. In order to respond to needs in this way, managerial decisions must be made by individual staff or, if the school is large enough, centres of management operating at this level, usually acting autonomously.

Even so, the professional bureaucracies which attract the loyalty of staff serve to control and standardise the procedures developed, since they are, in general, conservative bodies. They are hesitant to change well-tested and proven ways of working both because they represent security to many teachers and as they have only been achieved through the investment of considerable time. At this level of internal activities senior staff in particular require enhanced skills in decision-making and negotiation if changes are to be introduced. Innovation and problem-solving require inductive reasoning to appreciate new concepts, and divergent thinking which can break away from established strategies and standards, rather than concentrating on the refinement of existing ones. Often the introduction of 'new blood' to help work at this level may be effective, through the recruitment of different staff. This is an option which, with reduced staff mobility, may be restricted. At all levels of visibility, these management activities concentrate attention upon the interactions between middle line

teachers both among individuals and within groups. The former is discussed further in Chapter 7; the latter in Chapter 9. However, an additional
level of managerial tasks and decisions still demands attention.

At the deepest and least visible level managerial activities are concerned
with major decisions and policies affecting the whole school organisation,
usually in response to pressure for change and development. For this purpose the school can be compared to a living organism, able to respond to
both internal and external disturbances, either by adapting to the new conditions or assimilating parts of the innovation. Often there is little evidence
within the school as to the source of the influences which have an effect at
this level. However, the cumulative impact of many decisions taken by
several teachers can produce evolutionary change in the organisation, or,by
compensation, lead to adjustments attempting to restore the status quo.
This homeostatic view of school organisation can be developed to show
how autonomous decisions made by teachers, sometimes working in apparent isolation, may be incorporated into the working life of the school.
There are, however, three main influences on this process of assimilation,
working at all levels from the 'public' to the 'possibly unrecognised'.

More significantly, school planning and development may well be dependent on the intrinsic aspirations of influential teachers who seek to establish
what is meaningful and satisfying to them in their own centres of management. Insignificant changes may take place in this way, but these are
cumulative. From the interaction of these patterns of behaviour, experiences and attitudes, and in the context of external pressures or constraints, the status quo may be called into question at all levels in the
school, and changes may become assimilated into established practice.
Thus the process which actually takes place is quite the opposite of the anticipated rational planning process during which aims and objectives are
publicly stated and methods devised to achieve them. The deep-seated interactions are to varying extents masked by the degree to which procedures
have become routine as the school has evolved. This gradual evolution has
taken place as a result of the accumulation of decisions arrived at by processes taking place independently and separately, and having become diffused throughout the school. The task of senior management is to monitor
these developments and also to ensure that the school organisation remains
capable of responding to internal and external pressures - that is, the
maintenance of an adaptive environment within the school.

Balancing formality and freedom

For educational managers the issue is not only how to achieve the tightest
possible coupling or the fewest garbage-can characteristics in the school
decision-making. In practice, thrusts designed solely to meet these ends

would be counter-productive. For while even the smallest schools display elements of formal organisations - a hierarchy encompassing a decision-making structure, rules and regulations, a division of labour - they also have ambiguous goals, unclear technologies and variable participation rates in choice mechanisms. Therefore, a headteacher, for example, who tried to constrain all decision-making within the formal structure would not only produce a stultifying atmosphere in the school but would also exacerbate the worst aspects of inter-personal relationships among the staff. There would be little chance for staff to feel committed to choices, while motivation could easily be reduced. What the headteacher ignores, of course, are the elements in school functioning which point towards organised anarchy. No matter how well organised the debate there must always be some disagreement among staff about objectives. In schools the scope for that disagreement intensifies because of the intangibility of goals and no action by a headteacher can alter this situation. A broad statement of aims may be accepted by all staff, but within that framework groups of individuals assess their own subgoals. In contrast, a specific set of behavioural objectives may be designed for a course but debate, discussion and possible dissension about their appropriateness are always present (Raven 1977).

A headteacher can have even less influence on technological clarity. The learning processes of children as individuals, or as part of a group, are not well understood. When these potential uncertainties are added to factors related to social background, classroom dynamics and so on, a teacher can have no guarantee that a certain technique or a specific input will produce a predictable outcome in terms of pupil performance. All teachers must therefore come to terms with an unclear technology, and also the near inevitability of variable involvement, both in terms of those included and their level of interest, in most decisions, a dominant feature in allowing the school to drift towards organised anarchy. If, however, the school reaches a state in which anarchy in the organisation predominates, perhaps because it is thought that such a condition promotes academic freedom or maximises the adptability of the school to confront changing circumstances, then this is an abrogation of management. As such, the school is not being managed, except as a set of separate sub-systems. However, such an extreme rarely arises because of the balance of routine and stable decision-making which continues with little change over a number of years.

Indeed, there is always the chance that such routines can become over-dominant, inducing rigidities and militating against the introduction of new working practices. Teachers and pupils alike may welcome the apparent stability the routinisation of school procedures can produce, even if this means conforming within a bureaucratic framework. Possibly such an arrangement increases their sense of power in the classroom, thereby allowing them to be adaptable in a discrete area, while working within an apparently stable environment (Moeller and Charters, 1966). If such attitudes are reinforced by structures within the school then ossification follows. In secondary schools this represents a particular problem with the potential rigidities that a departmental or faculty configuration can introduce. Originally sub-dividing the school into subject departments that reflected the curriculum made sense, but only so long as the curriculum could be kept stable, with additional subjects coinciding with extra staff. As contraction has occurred at the same time as demands for more inter-disciplinary activities, such as multi-cultural education, pre-vocational courses and health education programmes, the deficiencies of the existing structures have been exposed. Possibly, new inter-disciplinary departments could be established but with fewer resources this would prove difficult. More significantly, this solution would exaggerate the problem, because such departments would be permanent, while the specific curriculum problems they remedy may well be transitory. The more fundamental error was to allow the ossification of a structure based upon departments, because of the assumption that was reinforced that a particular collection of departments would always be able to satisfy all needs.

In such a situation the school cannot, with existing arrangements, adequately confront the variables of fewer resources and changing consumer demands. The need is for a more flexible arrangement of sub-systems than that provided by the departmental structure, even if supported by competent pastoral arrangements (Dennison, 1985). In any new arrangement the key issue is the tightness of the coupling. The role of staff subject co-ordinators, programme organisers and so on, who co-ordinate the sub-sytems and those who provide linkages between them is vital. They have to confront the uncertainty inherent in any situation because of the inability of any one individual to be aware of all the relevant information. Yet within this constraint they must try to relate the interactions of environmental factors, parental attitudes, fewer resources, which influence the school, with internal issues, competence of individual staff, relationships with other sub-sytems, relative to the situation they manage (Fig. 4.3).

In broad terms, therefore, changing arrangements and attitudes, together with more demands for development, direct schools towards a more organic, as opposed to mechanistic, form of organisation (Burns and Stalker, 1961). Consequently, as for all managers, teachers have little alternative but to work out their own version of contingency theory, regarding

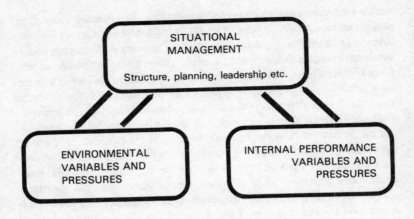

Fig 4.3 Contingency theory applied to a school

the school as an open system subject to environmental influences, and consisting internally of a matrix of interacting sub-systems all faced with uncertainty. The task of the manager is to devise a structure, a planning strategy and norms of managerial behaviour in order to maintain tolerable levels of certainty and stability, while maximising the capacity to respond to change (Lawrence and Lorsch, 1969). For schools the level of differentiation between the activities of sub-systems, and the tightness of coupling clearly represent key elements (Hanson and Brown, 1977). If the coupling is too tight then the school risks inflexibility; if too loose, management has little part to play.

The task of the managers in schools, therefore, is the maintenance of balance in a range of overlapping contexts: structurally, so that the organisation is not too rigid to produce an adaptive environment; attitudinally, so that the requirements of staff for predictability and continuity match the changing requirements of their pupils; and behaviourally, so that responses to short-term issues do not over-reflect expediency to the detriment of strategic planning. In addition, the decision-making processes require that a balance is maintained between garbage-can characteristics and a clear identification of the real problem (Drucker 1974). It is the latter which is often the most neglected area of school management.

Invariably, the expertise required to sustain such balance remains intangible, certainly to a teacher who can only be aware in part of the activities of a senior manager. To the teacher, that expertise is important only in so far as the headteacher appears to be an effective manager. Success in previous posts, qualifications and other experiences may convince a selection committee that the headteacher has the necessary expertise. They will need also to assure themselves that such qualities can be transferred from senior to top management. The teacher, viewing the headteacher in post, will be more interested in credibility. The capacity of the headteacher to convert expertise into acceptable management procedures is much more significant.

CHAPTER 5

POWER AND AUTHORITY

Making things happen

The most effective means by which any educational manager maintains credibility is to be judged as being able to make things happen. If the routine procedures of the school, such as the administrative chores of checking registers, completing requisitions etc. can be improved then the standing of the staff member responsible for the improvement rises. Similarly, if the school's reputation seems to grow so does that of the school staff, and particularly the more senior members. Such developments, though, rarely happen by chance. Even a school in a favourable catchment area has to formulate and implement a policy designed to attract more pupils. Except in the very smallest schools of course, it is not the job of the headteachers to be the sole formulators and implementers of policy. Their responsibility, however, to ensure that the processes for making choices are well-designed, responsive to changing circumstances and continue to function efficiently cannot be denied. The more senior the personnel (headteacher, senior management, middle mangement) the greater is the range of school activites which others perceive to be within the areas of responsibility of such staff; but whatever degree of responsibility is exercised, the capacity of the individual to establish, expedite and complete arrangements represents a most significant component of management.

The problems of an exaggerated thrust towards getting things done are only too obvious. The temptation always exists for individuals, particularly when recently promoted, to concentrate upon job redefinition and finding new ways of completing the tasks associated with their new post. By this means they seek to prove themselves to be good managers. In doing so, however, they tend to overlook the complexity of the factors associated with working alongside other staff. To be high on initiating structure (Fiedler, 1967) or viewed as a 1,9 manager (Blake and Mouton, 1964) may expose deficiencies in other areas of management activity. In the case of someone with pastoral responsiblities there is no alternative but to work through, and with, other staff so that things do happen, with the intention that an improved pastoral system for example, does actually evolve. Issues related to the commitment and involvement of the other staff are central to task completion. Such a middle manager may not make all the decisions, but does ensure that the establishment and refinement of the system takes place so that the most appropriate choices are made and implemented.

Once again, as in the previous chapter, the key issue of balance emerges. In practice there must be an awareness that the factors associated with achieving a suitable balance in each situation and the subtleties that each factor introduces are complex. The pastoral head, in the example given, needs to balance a perceived requirement for new procedures, perhaps gained as a result of experience elsewhere, with the apparent need felt by some staff for the security that continuity provides. Perhaps an unwillingness to change, or even to think of new arrangements, on the part of other teachers arises not from insecurity but lack of time to consider the defects in current procedures. Someone fully stretched in working on an existing scheme is not well placed to realise the potential for improvement. That in its turn indicates the need for another balance: the amount of attention given to the continuation of existing arrangements (a reactive mode) must be assessed against the time required to modify these or change to new arrangements (a proactive mode). In this context the pastoral head may well be more proactive than other staff (Pedler et al, 1978) through greater opportunity for awareness of pupil needs, but too much proaction may result in the neglect of routine procedures, while too much reaction tends to ignore the requirements of adaptation.

In addition, the views of personnel outside the immediate span of control of the middle manager cannot be ignored. It is here that they would be helped by an appreciation of the attitude of the headteacher and a knowledge of the position of other sections of the school. The former may well want new procedures to be developed but insist on reliable continuity of existing arrangements as changes take place. Headteachers do not willingly defend chaotic procedures, even if they are only temporary phases. Generally, the concern at this level of management will be for a balance between continuity and change in this case, but over a wider range of potentially inter-active situations. If, for example, curricular changes in a department take place at the same time as changes in pastoral procedures, this can affect the work of members of staff quite dramatically and the individual needs for security, stability and predictability are reinforced in at least some parts of their work. The headteacher and other more senior staff should be better placed than class teachers to take an overview because of the breadth of vision their position allows, the range of information sources available to them and greater attention they can give to appreciating the many balances being sought at any moment, the interactions among them and the time scales involved.

In the search for such balances, however difficult and frustrating, one

71

issue emerges clearly - the need to maintain an adaptive environment in the classroom, school and sub-unit. Without this as a main intention of school management, the problems of identifying and satisfying the needs of the children cannot be solved. In most schools, contraction and the related issue of reduced staff mobility add a further dimension which exacerbates the management problem of maintaining balances. As groups of individuals come together and work with each other for increasing periods of time a number of important factors can emerge (Katz, 1982). First, the tendency to structure work activities so that levels of certainty are enhanced. The members of staff of a primary school, for example, organise themselves so that the demands made upon them by the LEA for a curricular statement can be anticipated and easily met. Second, group members, through spending time together, gradually evolve standard work-patterns that are familar and comfortable, often in ways in which routine and precedent play significant roles (Weick, 1979). The teacher of eight-year-olds works out norms of behaviour and achievement with the teacher of the preceding class, and examples like this occur throughout the school, as stable relationships become established and each party enjoys a measure of confidence and security. Third, and largely as result of this stability, it is relatively easy to become isolated from sources of information and new ideas. Often, notions which challenge current practices may be ignored, as a consequence of the complacency induced by membership of a group confident in its assumptions. Fourth, as group members know each other well, the likelihood increases that they will communicate with group members whose interests and views coincide with their own (Rodgers and Shoemaker, 1971). For most staff the communicative search is for agreement and support, rather than for dissent and criticism. The main impact of these factors is that if group members remain in the same posts for some time they can become over-reliant upon the traditional ways of doing things. The incentive for pro-action will be lost and the motivation which drives them to search for and respond to changes in pupil needs will be diminished. Clearly, there is a danger of a downward spiral of receptiveness in such circumstances in relation to members who do not appear to conform to group norms (and whose alternative views are therefore likely to be ignored), and also to new recruits who can either conform or risk ostracism. The latter group, at least, if they are aware of the circumstances, have the option of not joining in, rather than having to opt out, but both situations increase the risk of complacent acceptance and continuation of current practices.

Perhaps an even more significant reinforcement of the status quo occurs when senior members of staff with managerial responsibilities also have long-term group membership. Some, frustrated in their career ambitions, find a complacent laissez-faire attitude attractive. As they are able to form stable relationships with their colleagues they establish predictability for themselves and acknowledge few demands upon them. They choose not to disturb a comfortable balance which has resulted in allowing the activities for which they are responsible to continue with as few changes as possible. In such situations they have accepted that the relationships which have become established over time, and of which they are part, have diminished their power to make things happen; this, to them, is more important than the maintenance of an adaptive environment.

The Sources of Power

With occasional exceptions (e.g. Musgrove 1971), in the study of schools as organisations the issue of power has received little attention, yet it would be difficult to deny its significance in the context of individual and group behaviour. Most directly, power represents the ability of **A** to get **B** to do what would not otherwise have been done (Pfeffer, 1981). As such it is a function of resources - cognitive, monetary, and sometimes even coercion. One member of staff, or a group of teachers, can undoubtedly exert power over others in many ways: **A** possesses knowledge (in the form of ideas, information, expertise, a form of behaviour, a type of analysis, etc.) which **B** would wish for, or perceives a benefit in sharing: **A** has some control over resources (such as time, personnel, access to money, use of facilities) which the other party would like to use.

Numerous examples can be quoted of knowledge-based power. Curriculum co-ordinators or subject heads possess power in their teaching areas so long as other staff acknowledge their superior's expertise gathered through experience, course attendance, additional reading and so on. The power deriving from such expert knowledge can extend to both subject-content and pedagogy and through these to curriculum and syllabus design, but its continuation depends upon acknowledgement. So long as junior members of staff accept that the views, ideas and knowledge of their senior colleagues are relevant and therefore can influence their behaviour, power is retained. Similarly, power derives from the possession of information and is supported by a capacity to discover and utilise other potential sources of information. The example of headteachers is apposite. For a number of reasons - more access to school-wide activites, greater opportunity to attend LEA and other outside meetings, as the first recipient of information inflows from outside sources - headteachers are extremely well-placed to know a great deal more about contingencies affecting the school than any one else. That knowledge represents a potential source of power, as when, for example, a headteacher, alert to LEA curricular guidelines, can persuade a group of teachers to introduce a new teaching pattern or an alternative syllabus.

Often this form of power is reinforced by that which relies upon control of resources. The headteacher, in the previous example, can offer the teachers more equipment or whatever is needed to help organise the innovation. In broader terms, because the teachers depend upon the headteacher for resources, the extent of that dependence equates with the headteacher's power over them. (Emmerson, 1962). Indeed, if knowledge is considered a resource, then power is little more than the control of scarce resources, and the power of individuals or a group within the school centres upon the skill with which the members can use their control over resources, and the extent to which they can strengthen this control (Pettigrew, 1972).

In many situations the reward and coercive routes to dependence may prove equally attractive. More overt dependency derives from the capacity of a head or deputy head to award for example, teacher time to departments, classes to teachers, space to activities and school finance to intended innovations. This exists alongside the more covert dependencies that accrue, for example, from the capacity of senior staff to help colleagues gain promotion in the school or elsewhere. Indeed, an individual teacher's need for praise, both for intrinsic satisfaction and as a possible indicator of more tangible rewards, leads to dependency. Moreover, to a person skilled in the utilisation of power, all such reward dependencies have an inverse potential since withdrawal or non-introduction of a reward can provide an effective coercion mechanism. Therefore, a department can be granted less teacher-time as a 'punishment' for not introducing new teaching arrangements, while a teacher may be given a poor reference when applying for posts as a sanction for non-compliance with some aspect of school policy.

In all cases, then, power (the ability of **A** to make **B** perform in ways which **A** requires and **B** may even partially resent) relies upon the strength of the dependence. Clearly, if a teacher ceases applying for other positions, adverse references are no longer a sanction. Similarly, some teachers, for reasons of lack of confidence or insecurity, are more likely to be influenced by hidden rewards than others. Often in such circumstances, the potential rewarders, through lack of awareness of the motivational requirements of others, do not realise the power they can exert. It is more difficult still for them to assess the extent of their referent power - which relies upon the attempts of other staff to model some aspects of their behaviour (French and Raven, 1960). Of course, there is also the possibility of an inverse effect when staff choose to avoid replicating some facet of displayed behaviour. The possibility of power accruing from these sources invariably relates to seniority in the school. The headteacher has more visibility in many ways than the deputy who has more than the other members of the senior management team; therefore, the likelihood that others will identify with a postholder and model behaviour, or refrain from doing so, increases with responsibility. The potential for determining resource utilisation and assimilating knowledge includes a similar relationship.

At all levels, however, power in the school centres largely upon the individual. A subordinate teacher, because of personal attributes or even as a union representative or through membership of the governing body, may be thought by many staff to be more powerful than the headteacher. However, while the potential for exercising power relates to seniority, the attributes and the aspirations of individuals prevent automatic alignment. Organisationally, therefore, power represents a form of illegitimacy. The notion of authority attempts to provide legitimation. Indeed, according to Weber (1947) the concept of legitimate authority provides the basis of any organisation. To a greater or lesser extent the authority of a headteacher, or any office-holder in the school and beyond, relies on agreement that certain powers should reside with that office. Therefore, while the designation itself as 'curriculum coordinator' provides a source of power, its usefulness to the post-holder depends upon the extent to which others agree that the holder of such a post demonstrates the right to exercise certain powers.

Undoubtedly, a school is disadvantaged if its authority structure bears minimal resemblance to the power structure. A perfect match, however, is quite unattainable. Individual teachers in a school will strive for power for a whole range of reasons, and in pursuit of a number of personal and organisational objectives. The strength of that pursuit will vary over time and be issue-dependent. To achieve their ends, individuals form groups, not necessarily reflecting the organisational structure of the school; The composition of these groups will also change over time and with issues. In this context, therefore, the school is best viewed as involving changing coalitions of participants since resulting choices are the outcomes of bargaining among individuals and groups (Hawley and Nichols, 1982). As a consequence conflict and negotiation emerge as central issues in studying the influence of power on behaviour in schools. Both will be considered later in this chapter.

In all schools efforts to change the power patterns are both inevitable and continuous. They are played out during day-to-day interactions involving staff as individuals and in groups. Most changes that result are small and barely perceptible. If it suits their purposes participants will utilise more formal choice mechanisms; if not they will try to introduce elements of garbage-can decision-making. Similarly, they might try to loosen or tighten the coupling between the sub-systems (coalitions) in ways which reflect their intentions. Unfortunately, despite efforts to modify the power structure there can be no guarantee that the outcomes will improve the adaptive properties of the school. Yet each school finds itself locked into an increasingly competitive situation for scarce resources and the only mechanism for reducing that tension is by demonstrating an ability to satisfy the changing demands of parents, pupils and the local authority, so that they have no alternative but to support the school.

Strategies of Change

Efforts by management to achieve compliance by subordinates are frequently met with resentment in schools and elsewhere; similarly, the wish and the ability of some personnel to pursue their own ends, while simultaneously damaging colleagues and organisational well-being, should never be underestimated. Rarely, if ever, will those personnel recognise the effects of their actions and accept responsibility for the consequences. In their perceptions, they feel compelled to extend their personal power, in their view solely in pursuit of desirable objectives. More normally, though, in the professional bureaucracy of the school, teachers do many things they would not have done if left to themselves. That is part of the process of exchange between themselves and the school, but provided that what they are asked or believe they are compelled to do is balanced by inducements, in the form of intrinsic and extrinsic rewards, they will continue to contribute much to the organisation (March and Simon, 1958). This includes an acceptance, within certain zones of tolerance, that controls, either from individuals utilising sources of power or resulting from sub-system membership, represent essential components of school life. However, individual and group achievements in making things happen do not, of themselves, produce an adaptive school climate. Additionally the needs of the children have to be identified and the most effective methods of satisfying them have to be sought and implemented. A single change from one set of arrangements to another represents too simple a perspective; instead a continuous process of adaptation in line with varying needs and contingencies must be the intention. To achieve this within the complex interaction resulting from variable coalitions of participants, as the political dimension of school life evolves, requires some sort of strategy. Bennis, Benne and Chin (1971) propose three possibilities:

Rational - Empirical:
This assumes that changed practices will be accepted if thought to be beneficial to children, staff or both. Staff awareness of potential benefits can be heightened by in-service activities and effective communication both within the school (to assist in diffusing ideas) and outside (so that experiences can be shared with other schools);

Normal - Re-educative:

This seeks to improve the problem-solving capability of the school through fostering the development of the staff. The focus is even more clearly on in-service work to support the training of staff in acquiring new skills and attitudes, while at the same time enhancing their confidence to work in changing circumstances;

Power-Coercive:

This strategy relies upon the principle that change occurs most readily through the application of power from the senior staff downwards. All sources of power may be utilised, not excluding the inculcation of guilt and shame among teachers for failing to appreciate the need to commit themselves to change, and maintain an adaptive environment.

Bennis and his co-workers suggest that no single approach should dominate, while the most appropriate overall strategy will depend upon circumstances and the changes sought. In assessing appropriateness, however, senior staff, in particular, are faced by a paradox. In the view of other staff and outsiders, they have a special responsibility for encouraging the adaptability of the school, but to do so they must remain heavily reliant upon the co-operation of their fellow-professionals. Especially within the classroom, the considerable autonomy individual teachers possess provides ample opportunity to frustrate the intentions not only of the headteacher or deputy head but also the intentions that fellow members of formal groups think have been agreed. In such circumstances even the most effective combination of power and authority cannot force every teacher to be compliant. All that can be done is to provide a context in which staff can feel confident to adapt and refine their approaches and in which mechanisms can be developed for group and individual support.

An additional element in the paradox occurs because willingness to consider change relates directly to a view that current practices are inappropriate. If it is clear that needs are being neither identified nor satisfied the case for a review of present arrangements can be overwhelming. Yet senior staff, except when newly appointed, have a particular responsibility for the current state of affairs, certainly in the eyes of other teachers. Within this framework the necessity of establishing an environment in which attitudes can become attuned to adaptation as a continuing process, rather than a series of discrete and possibly unrelated changes, becomes even more clear. Schmuck (1974) places this process within the context of organisational development, and introduces the idea of school 'self-renewal'. As argued in Chapter 9 however, such an approach cannot be distinguished, in practice, from developmental activities concentrated upon individuals and groups of teachers.

Providing facilities and support to assist teacher development requires resources. Simultaneously, the equipment and materials for alternative curricular approaches have to be funded. Such resource requirements add a further element to the paradox because of the association between reduced funding and the demands for adaptation. In brief, if schools suffer financial retrenchment the only means directly available to them to accommodate to such difficulties is by demonstrating their ability to confront such adverse conditions. That ability demands flexibility in staff attitudes and practices, which in turn requires resources. Under various conditions, as with TVEI or Micro-Electronics Project the offer of additional resources can be an effective mechanism for initiating change in a school. However, if such a strategy is to continue to produce change and the maintenance of an adaptive environment, not only must there be a steady flow of extra funds, but staff-related issues within the school still require attention. Creighton (1983) specifies a number of tactical issues relevant to the achievement of a single change:

- Is the change consistent with the expectations of the staff?
- What are the perceived advantages?
- What is known of possible consequences and associated risks?
- Has the change any precedent - in the school and elsewhere?
- What are the sources of opposition - in the school and elsewhere?

In addition, she suggests that the internal features of any change (complexity and compatibility with existing procedures, for example) are key issues. Alongside these institutional factors a number of personal items are also raised.

- Has the change been designed and propagated by people within or outside the school?
- Have significant people (in the eyes of the teacher) been involved in the development?
- Has it the active support of prestigious and influential parents?
- Is it congruent with existing beliefs, values and practices?

Lewin (1947) has devised a single diagrammatic representation so that all such features impinging upon a situation where change is sought can be considered. The intention of this force-field analysis is to identify all supporting (pushing) forces pressing for change, and all hindering (restraining) forces; and then to devise strategies whereby the former might be increased and the latter reduced. An example used in a school curriculum development project forms Fig.5.1. Here, as elsewhere, there may be practical advantages in lowering the restraining forces rather than adding to the pushing forces, since the latter can produce counter-reactions not present in the original situation.

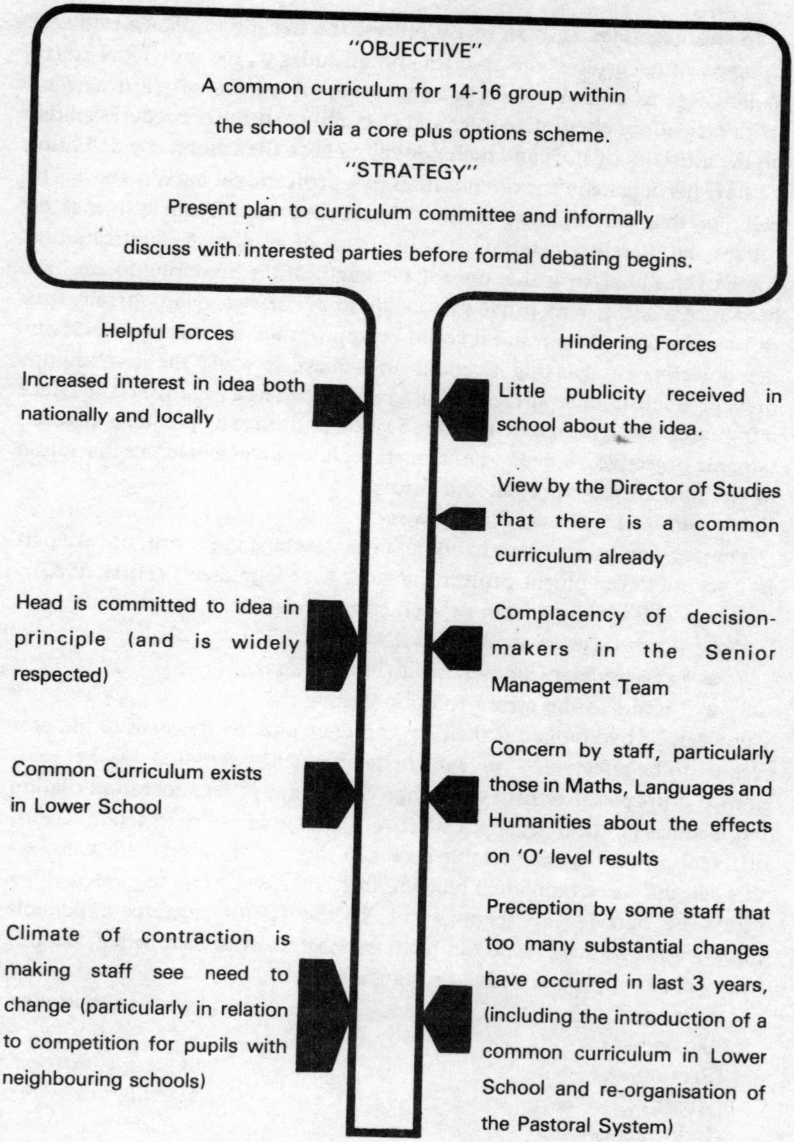

"OBJECTIVE"

A common curriculum for 14-16 group within
the school via a core plus options scheme.

"STRATEGY"

Present plan to curriculum committee and informally
discuss with interested parties before formal debating begins.

Helpful Forces

Increased interest in idea both
nationally and locally

Head is committed to idea in
principle (and is widely
respected)

Common Curriculum exists
in Lower School

Climate of contraction is
making staff see need to
change (particularly in relation
to competition for pupils with
neighbouring schools)

Hindering Forces

Little publicity received in
school about the idea.

View by the Director of Studies
that there is a common
curriculum already

Complacency of decision-
makers in the Senior
Management Team

Concern by staff, particularly
those in Maths, Languages and
Humanities about the effects
on 'O' level results

Preception by some staff that
too many substantial changes
have occurred in last 3 years,
(including the introduction of a
common curriculum in Lower
School and re-organisation of
the Pastoral System)

* The width of an arrow relates to the strength of each force

Fig. 5.1. Force-field analysis for Curriculum Innovation - after Craig (1978)

In this example, as in so many others, the likelihood of achieving the change centres around the abilities and attitudes of the individual staff. Willingness to consider the changing needs of pupils, to learn new activities, to adopt alternative roles and to modify existing procedures all rely on the attitudes of staff and their commitment to the school. By definition all staff participate in the organisation of a professional bureaucracy. The place of that participation requires consideration as it can influence attitudes and therefore determine the use made of ability. A significant outcome of this analysis is that once the strength of the hindering forces have been recognised it may prove impossible to devise strategies whereby they can be reduced. As a result it could be appropriate to consider modifying the objective or delaying attempts to achieve it while these conditions prevail. Such an outcome should not be regarded as a negative result, since it indicates that it would be unwise to risk loss of face by pursuing an unattainable objective. Indeed, the 'hinders' column gives a valuable indication of the state of play, present and future.

Participation, Involvement and Power

The decision by a teacher to adopt a new teaching approach, or take part in a school development project, includes four ingredients (Hirst, 1982):

- willingness to learn new practices (Vouloir);
- knowledge of what to do (Savoir);
- knowledge of how to do it (Savoir-faire);
- access to the means to do it (Pouvoir).

None can be overlooked if the new approach and involvement in the project are to be effective. It must be remembered however that teacher reaction to a proposed reform or change occurs not in technocratic isolation but includes political negotiation between individuals of divergent interests, different attributes and variable access to sources of power. All such factors can influence individual reaction to change when it is suggested either within or outside the school, and Reddin (1970) suggests a possible classification of these responses by those most likely to be affected, ranging from active support to active resistance:

Sabotage_____(Active Resistance)
Slowdowns
Protests
Apathy
Indifference
Acceptance
Support
Co-operation
Commitment_____(Active Support)

In any innovation which affects the whole school the active support of all staff through co-operation and commitment has to be sought. This is particularly true if the scheme requires a co-ordinated approach, and the capacity of individual teachers through their classroom autonomy to slow down and possibly even sabotage the new initiatives is always available. The starting point for change may well be the headteacher's perception that a new scheme is desirable for a number of reasons, such as dissatisfaction with the current practices, the example of other schools, pressure from local authority advisers or the availability of funding from the parent teacher association. Initially, then, it is the headteacher who 'owns' the problem; this is in direct contrast to the most desirable end-point when the headteacher and every member of staff have a share in the 'ownership': that is, there is agreement about the need for a new scheme together with the framework, if not the detail, of how it could be introduced in each classroom.

A number of issues require emphasis. The notion of joint-ownership of problems includes all the staff and the headteacher. It is not a matter of the headteacher handing over the problem to the staff. Indeed, if this were attempted, the likelihood of the latter accepting ownership would be minimal. More significantly, joint ownership commits the headteacher to ensuring that, as far as possible, the necessary ingredients for positive acceptance of the new scheme are available to all staff. In practice this can prove very difficult. There will be those teachers who, through lack of confidence or because they do not believe that the chosen approach is the most appropriate, resist any element of ownership. For some staff the resultant attitude will be determined by this single issue; for others it might extend to an unwillingness to accept part-ownership of any situation outside their own classroom. Yet, the headteacher often has little alternative but to proceed with the innovations in the face of active resistance from some staff. Even in a small school, if the introduction of alternative arrangements has to await the positive affirmation of all staff the probability of maintaining an adaptive environment within the school will be remote.

For the introduction of a new language scheme for example the political skills of the headteacher are clearly of primary importance since they relate to the perceptions, willingness, attributes and confidence of each member of staff. The changing coalitions among teachers about the issue, the utilisation of power and the interactions between this proposed innovation and others also need to be taken into account. Differences in time-scales may well prove a significant but unanticipated difficulty. The headteacher, protected from the more immediate demands of implementing the new scheme, should be better placed to maintain an overview of long-term benefits. Conveying such an overview to busy members of staff who may be struggling with the day-to-day demands of the new scheme may well prove difficult. A similar type of problem arises with information control. The headteacher may know from the LEA that a new language scheme is essential, but believes that some staff need protection from knowledge about the intrusions of the LEA into curricular matters within schools. A decision to withhold information may be well-intentioned but endangers the notion of sharing. It is particularly difficult to maintain a stance of joint ownership if some staff think the headteacher knows more about the change and its potential ramifications (in particular, what some individual could gain from it) than they do. This illustrates one of the worst dilemmas in participation: how can true participation take place when there is a difference in the power of the individual teachers concerned?

A politically inept headteacher may easily achieve the worst possible outcome, total personal ownership of the problem of implementing the new language scheme. In such circumstances the launch will be unsuccessful. The other sources of power available to the headteacher will be insufficient because the requirements of effective leadership have not been fulfilled (Chapter 3). The focus of Adair's work (1973) on the three elements which the headteacher must simultaneously consider is particularly apposite in this context (Fig. 5.2).

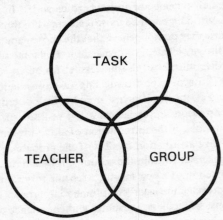

Fig. 5.2. The Interactions of Teacher, Task and Group (from Adair)

One element concentrates upon the individual teacher, with a unique collection of needs, values, aspirations and abilities, both in relation to the proposed change and more generally; the second relates to the interactions between those characteristics of the individual teachers and the group situation in which they work; the third considers the common task (in this case the introduction of the new language scheme). Diagrammatically, the three representative circles overlap, indicative of potential tension in them. The headteacher has to be aware of what is happening in all circles and the relationships between them, and must ensure that none of the interests portrayed is able to dominate. Simultaneously, the headteacher's influence ought to be both separate from the circles while yet remaining part of them: a personal commitment to the task and group's needs is required along with an independent view of group requirements. The relationship between independence and membership represents another key balance that has to be sought. To the headteacher group membership is central to the concept of professional bureaucracy - most clearly demonstrated by the retention of a teaching commitment by many headteachers - and also heightened ownership about school activities; but if the headteacher is regarded as no more than another group member the other teachers have a legitimate complaint about the additional salary and status the job confers.

From the headteacher's perpective, the achievement of balance centres around issues of staff involvement in decision-making. Conway (1984), distinguishing between delegation - the assignment of specific responsibilities by a headteacher or senior member of staff to other colleagues -and participation, has identified four aspects of the latter. First, there is the actual format of the processes by which attempts are made to involve staff in school decision-making. Three continua are suggested:

Mandatory _____ Voluntary
Formal _____ Informal
Direct_____ Indirect.

From a management perspective too great a skew along any of these continua has disadvantages. If all staff must be involved before a choice occurs, not only can this slow the decision-making system, but it ignores the differing abilities and interests of teachers. In particular it ignores the extent to which teachers' interests are issue-dependent. One teacher may be interested in the choices involved in placing pupils in classes, the other more concerned about syllabus design; but within weeks these respective areas of interest may be exchanged. Similarly, over-formalisation of participation mechanisms risks the failure to consider the particular and changing needs of individual teachers. Too little formalisation places less senior staff and those new in post at a disadvantage: they are not well placed to understand the nuances and subtleties that informality can produce.

The issue of perception also dominates Conway's second aspect - the degree of participation. He used a similar classification to that of Likert (see Chapter 3):

System 1	Exploitive - Authoritarian
System 2	Paternalistic
System 3	Consultative
System 4	Participative.

As Likert (1961) himself warned, opinions about the system which actually operates in an organisation vary with seniority of membership.

Headteachers and senior staff find it very difficult to see things in the same way as a classroom teacher, even though they are members of the same professional bureaucracy. Such differences appear particularly marked in relation to participation. In studying arrangements in UK secondary schools, Smith (1982) found considerable discrepancies between accounts of staff participation given by headteachers as compared with those of other members of staff. On many issues these differences related to the degree of participation: headteachers thought other staff were more involved in participation than the staff considered themselves to be. There were also differing perceptions among the staff concerning the remaining two or Conway's four aspects.

In the third, attention is focused on the content of decisions. In broad terms he classified choices as linked to system maintenance, personal or professional issues, with the willingness of individual teachers to become involved varying both across and within these categories. Indeed in earlier work on the extent of the participation which teachers felt desirable, Conway (1978) found that it was involvement in decision-making which was rated most highly. For example, in matters such as textbook selection or managing pupil problems, present and desired participation levels appeared to match, with both rated as high. Conversely, in areas such as dealing with staff grievances or problems in the community there was little agreement in the perceptions of head and assistant teachers. More directly, teachers were little involved in these items of school management and had no wish to be, regarding them as the responsibility of the headteacher and more senior staff. Most likely any efforts to increase staff involvement in these areas would produce 'decisional saturation' (Alutto and Belasco, 1972) as opposed to the more desirable situation of 'decisional equilibrium'. In fact Conway (1978) did not report any saturation in the schools surveyed; the inverse 'decisional deprivation', however, was apparent, most strongly in relation to choices about the appointment of new staff and plans for building changes, and less strongly in decisions about spending schedules and teaching timetables.

Smith (1982) contradicts some of these conclusions. Not only does he report decisional deprivation - although 9% of his teacher sample, most commonly senior staff regarded themselves as 'saturated' - he also suggests that, according to headteachers, decisions relating to new staff appointments and finance provide a greater degree of staff participation. It is in the areas of school organisation and the curriculum that teachers seek to make most of the decisions themselves, because they perceive it is here that they can generate the most effective power sources. Some of this apparent contradiction is resolved by Conway's fourth aspect of participation, the scope of the process. He suggests that teachers wish to be involved at the formative stage of the problem-solving, but think that on many occasions they are only invited to choose among a number of solutions after preliminary work by other more senior staff has restricted the availability of the choices. Often a headteacher and senior staff may sincerely believe that genuine and full participation has occurred, yet colleagues do not think they have participated in the decision-making process. Perhaps such teachers simply are not aware of how and where decisions are made, and as a result they cannot participate in an exploitive-authoritarian system.

In seeking to clarify the issue of participation Hoy and Sousa (1984) make a distinction between the sharing of decision-making authority in terms of delegating, and sharing in terms of joint decision-making. In their study of 55 secondary schools in New Jersey they found that a number of school principals allowed participation in discussion but reserved the final decision-making to themselves; it appeared that these principals were prepared to delegate the work but not the outcome if it resulted in the taking of decisions. Any teachers involved in this situation clearly placed little value on such a consultation process unless they perceived they had a real influence on the outcome. As Hoy and Sousa stated, 'delegation of decision-making maximises participation; consultation minimises participation.' They found, however, three main benefits which can result from the willingness of a principal to delegate:

- the teachers' perceptions of a weaker authority structure increase the likelihood of identification with the school's aims and objectives;
- a greater sense of job-satisfaction develops and this improves teacher attitudes towards their work and also towards colleagues;
- teachers show greater trust in, and loyalty to, their principals.

On the evidence available, any intention of maximising the participatory opportunities of all staff in every school situation represents wasted effort. Headteachers have different perceptions of what participation means to them, and individual teachers vary in their appreciation of what is happening in their own schools. Individuals also have different needs for participation and even for the same teacher these are issue-dependent. The design of satisfactory arrangements which enable teachers to maintain desirable perceptions of involvement presents substantial problems for senior staff. To attempt to solve them by so circumventing or limiting choice that none really exists, or restricting influence to situations which are thought to be unimportant, usually proves counter-productive. Whether introduced deliberately or through lack of perception of the real needs of other staff, such tactics make it much more difficult for junior staff to participate in other more significant decision areas. If participation is lacking then senior staff retain the ownership of all school-based problems, and an adaptive climate, in which teachers are willing to contemplate changes, may be impossible to maintain. Moreover, without conditions that staff feel to be appropriate for their involvement in decisions affecting their school, their job-satisfaction, and their desire for recognition, personal autonomy and a sense of achievement are unlikely to be realised.

However, perhaps the most potent factor which should encourage senior staff to establish effective participatory mechanisms, mainly through relating colleagues' perceptions about arrangements that exist to produce desired outcomes, derives from the potential for increasing their influence. Participatory systems can extend the power sources available, and further legitimise the authority of headteachers in particular. Over thirty years ago Gouldner (1954) argued that, by enabling other staff to participate, senior colleagues gain influence, and therefore control, over the actions of those staff. Not only is their commitment encouraged, particularly towards choices in which they have played some part but at the same time the headteacher and senior members of staff gain a greater awareness of the issues involved in each decision. Senior staff may feel that they are influencing rather than directing events but, in identifying this as a potential disadvantage of participation, they overlook the ineffectiveness of much intended direction in schools because of the relatively high level of autonomy possessed by teachers in the classroom. Therefore both senior staff and their junior colleagues stand to gain from an effective participatory system, first because it can apply across the broader range of their responsibilities, second in relation to the classroom and its contingencies. It would be naive, however, to suggest that such a system can be established and maintained without difficulty. Consequently issues of conflict and negotiation must be considered.

Managing Conflict

However well organised a school and whatever its success in sustaining an adaptive environment, conflict - disagreement about the outcome of behaviour in a relationship (Muth, 1984) - is quite unavoidable. Two members of staff will disagree about the appropriateness of teaching methods, one department will be in dispute with another over the availability of resources, parents will criticise aspects of school procedures, the headteacher will argue with various members of staff about their responsibilities. The job of management is not to view such occurrences as indicative of failure, and therefore events to be overlooked, or even avoided. Instead, concentration should focus on two main issues - the control of conflict and its resolution. Conflict control seeks to prevent the negative consequences getting out of hand and attempts to restore equilibrium. This should not be approached by way of denial, avoidance, capitulation or domination, measures which only preserve the unease which produced the original conflict. In contrast, conflict resolution considers the positive aspects of why individuals and groups get into opposing positions, by accepting that genuine differences in values, needs and goals provide an essential component of school life. As a first step to resolving non-realistic sources of dispute - such as those stemming from error, ignorance, prejudice, tradition, poor organisation, displaced hostility and tension release - the real causes need to be recognised and dealt with by improved communication and individual counselling.

It can be argued (Deutsch 1972) that, if managed appropriately, conflict avoids stagnation while stimulating interest, and therefore provides a medium through which problems can be raised and solutions sought. Indeed the provision of any facility by which teachers can assess their own views and judgements against those of others, so that they can appreciate the potential for conflict, may help promote motivation and self-esteem, and contribute a significant element to staff development programmes. In practice, though, the need for such a facility and the extent to which it might be used to maximise the positive features of conflict vary enormously among schools. Often it is the conflict control element which seems to dominate, and not always effectively. Litwak and Hylton (1962) claim that the potential for conflict tends to be greater in schools with more formal bureaucratic arrangements than when there is less attempt at central control. Just as significant are teacher perceptions of the effectiveness of the participatory mechanisms in the school, both in relation to the quality of interpersonal relationships they sustain (Chapter 7) and the details of the arrangements. In a different context Gouldner (1958) has described the ways in which management style can affect interpersonal tensions among a group of workers. The paradox is that the potential for conflict heightens in organisations which lack individuals able both to devise procedures and to exercise the appropriate interpersonal skills to contain and resolve the conflicts that emerge.

If the organisational climate is one in which win-lose confrontations predominate, the unevenness of need satisfaction among teachers will result in the kind of frustration which can fuel conflict - the Relative Deprivation Theory (Merton, 1957). However, such conflict between groups of teachers can improve the level of co-operation within such groups. For example, members of a department will 'close ranks' when threatened with a change they would not choose for themselves. Much depends upon the nature of change, the methods by which it is to be introduced and the perceived nature of the threat. On occasion, feeling within the group can be affected by the attitude and behaviour of a single individual. Reich (1970) has described situations in which people behave in destructive ways to those who apparently pose no threat to them, while Dollard (1939) has developed a 'frustration-aggression' model to illustrate this basic source of conflict. For example, frustrated leadership aspirations in one person may well provide a focus for other teachers who have developed resentments against specific features of the school organisation. At certain times, apparent over-reactions to minor crises indicate the ways in which tensions are lying below the surface of an apparently smooth-running school. The 'withdrawal of good will' by teacher associations as a move in national wage negotiations has different effects in different schools, due in part to ways in which resentments built up over time are discharged under these 'strike' conditions.

Boulding (1963) suggests that mechanisms to settle disputes should be built into the organisation. On an individual basis, conflict itself may not be too uncomfortable, but the frustration and anxiety associated with it can lead to stress if not dealt with. However, it must be remembered that having a consultative procedure does not necessarily result in effective consultation. Human relations cannot be separated from working conditions, especially in schools, and conflicts may well persist unrecognised and therefore potentially destructive. Pondy (1967) considers that organisational conflict takes place in a series of 'conflict episodes' and an understanding of the stages in such episodes could make a significant contribution to conflict management. Pondy's ideas may be summarised as follows:

Stage 1. **Latent Conflict** arises from the competition for scarce resources, drives for autonomy, and divergence of both individual and sub-system goals. Role conflict is regarded as an example of this situation.

Stage 2. **Perceived Conflict** may be due to misunderstandings of other points of view, and may well be suppressed or alternatively made the focus of attention so that it can be resolved at this stage.

Stage 3. **Felt Conflict** occurs when the conflict becomes personalised with attendant anxieties and tensions.

Stage 4. **Manifest Conflict** is best illustrated when teachers engage in such conflict-causing behaviour producing frustrations in others by blocking their goal achievement. Explosion pressure is the name given by Boulding (1963) to the condition which turns potential into actual conflict.

Stage 5. **Conflict Aftermath** results in inadequate resolution of conflict situations. If suppressed, the latent conditions for conflict still remain to flare up again at a later date.

Examples of these stages can readily be seen in school situations involving teachers, pupils and outsiders. Clearly the management of such conflict episodes must take account of the need for all involved to experience some degree of satisfaction from the outcome. In practice, the first stage in any resolution attempt is to achieve a situation in which those involved are prepared to accept the need to confront the issues in dispute. This demands active participation by those involved since conflicts cannot be dealt with by proxy. Ideally, all involved should attempt to put into words perceptions about the causes of the frustration, as well as anger and hostility relative to the situation as a whole. The role of the 'peacemaker' at this stage is to search for possibilities of common ground between the points of view. Unlike the processes of negotiation described in the next section, the resolution of conflict involves emotive issues on a personal basis with additional emphasis on win/lose confrontation and greater likelihood of personal suffering. In these circumstances participants have to be prepared to indicate their personal feelings on these issues if any discussions are to progress and if the conflict is to be contained and resolved.

Power through negotiation

The school organisation has already been described as one of shifting coalitions of teachers concerned about, and able to have a considerable influence upon, the outcomes of the bargaining processes which take place at all levels. The issue of the changing memberships of such coalitions is raised by March and Simon (1958) but, in general, teachers tend to join forces to exert pressure to gain control over the school's goals and procedures in order to reconcile differences in interests, objectives and perceived power. It is those differences which provide the potential for conflict. A manager skilled in resolving the conflicts which actually develop resorts on many occasions to negotiation, between individuals and groups within the school and outside. Most commonly a school leader is one party in such negotiations, and an important component in the skill of resolution revolves around the ability to use negotiation to extend power and influence.

Morley (1981) identifies five models of the negotiation processes which may develop in a school or any other organisational environment:

- **a game of strategy** in which the participants make guesses about the other's responses and plan their campaigns accordingly. The appropriateness of the moves determines the outcome;

- **a struggle,** or win/lose confrontation, where the participants pursue their own interests to the limit. The outcome represents a compromise when each side can claim an 'honourable settlement';

- **a collaborative venture** in which the inequalities in the balance of power between the participants are not exploited. Satisfactory solutions are favoured, rather than forcing concessions from participants;

- **a 'two track' or 'boundary role'** model in which discussion takes place between representatives of groups or organisations. The participants bring into the discussion pre-determined points of view directed by prior consultation with those whom they represent;

- **interpersonal and interparty exchange** in which the outcome is affected by the relationships which develop between the participants. Such negotiations are effectively 'co-operative' rather than 'individual' or competitive.

In all cases of negotiation power results from the negotiator's ability to choose appropriate tactics. In common with all assertive individuals, effective negotiators tend to advance a single point of view persistently, rather than providing reasoned argument in support. However, such tactics may well produce stress especially when both parties virtually ignore the other's point of view. Janis and Mann (1977) describe a condition of 'defensive avoidance' which enables individuals to 'escape from worrying about the decision by not exposing themselves to cues that evoke awareness of anticipated losses.'

In general terms, then, bargaining in negotiation allows mutual influence to determine whether the final outcome is closer to one or other of the original positions taken by the negotiators. In much of the bargaining which takes place within a particular school, individual and group prestige is at stake. The more public the negotiations the more self-esteem there is involved, resulting in progressive disenchantment with the proceedings if the decision goes against one of the participants. To be the unsuccessful participant in a 'win - lose' form of public negotiation, results in damage to the self-perception of the group represented and can produce recriminations.

Douglas (1957) has identified three stages in all negotiation processes ranging from national negotiations to industrial transactions:

- **establish the bargaining range**

  Attempts to reach premature agreement are avoided, despite the fact that such agreements may seem to reduce conflict. This stage is really one of 'cards of the table' in which information is exchanged between the participants with no attempts being made to reconcile the two differing positions;

- **reconnoitre the bargaining range**

  Social interaction takes place between the participants, positional weaknesses are not exploited, and both give sympathetic consideration to the other's point of view. Attention is paid to giving and seeking opinions and feelings on possible solutions. This 'sounding out' stage often develops into the creation of ambiguous conditions in which participants are invited to respond in ways which indicate willingness to proceed further along possible lines, without giving offence by formal rejection if the approach is considered unacceptable. As a result of such interaction none of the participants can be held directly responsible for initiating formal proposals;

- **precipitate the decision-making crisis**

  after the informal discussions have been completed, the participants look for some event to force them to return to the issues; then, if the range of options has been adequately explored, definite proposals may be put forward with some confidence that there is a basis for acceptance.

These three basic stages of orientation, evaluation and control are no less applicable to schools. They represent vital ingredients in successful negotiation: these small and insignificant compromises underpin the apparent smooth-running of all organisations.

Strauss and his colleagues (1963) in their analysis of the negotiated order found in hospitals have developed a view of organisational order which has ready application to schools. Issues leading to 'negotiated order' in schools would include: rules selectively invoked; disagreement and tension over placement of pupils into classes/sets to maximise learning opportunities; methods of dealing with disruptive pupils; timetable compromises; competition for scarce resources; response to pressures from internal and external sources.

The fluid and temporal nature of the negotiated order is stressed, as agreements, alliances and coalitions made in one context are not readily carried over into others. New ones are re-negotiated and replace them, often without the conscious activity of the participants. Preferably, the headteacher and other senior staff monitor corporately such changes because of the constraints they may impose on the adaptability the school can generate in confronting changing demands and circumstances. More positively senior members of staff can utilise the negotiated order as an effective means for widening their power-base and further legitimising their authority. In this way their capacity to make things happen is extended.

CHAPTER 6

CHANGE AND RESPONSE

Pressures for change

The organisational structure of a school is established in order to discharge the expectations and duties imposed on it by the society it serves, as well as to realise the goals of the teachers involved. Although there may be some goal dissensus (a term used by Prebble, 1978), a loosely-coupled system can accommodate some variation in goals as members are relatively free to negotiate their individuality without placing undue strain on the organisational structure. The appropriate operational and functional roles and relationships in a school are usually formulated rather than formalised, and in such a way that the abilities and inclinations of staff are able to be used to best advantage: for example, rigid and limiting job-descriptions are usually avoided although areas of responsibility may be mapped out. The word 'best' indicates that value judgements and perceptions lie at the heart of the organisational structure. The work of the school is thus arranged into units - classes, departments, houses - linked by management positions which help to define the relationships between them. Those holding managerial positions are invested with authority to communicate instructions and information to others within the conditions of a professional bureaucracy.

A school, however, is an organisation primarily concerned with the interactions between its members - teachers, pupils, office staff, technicians and so on - and these interactions produce a social climate peculiar to each school (Halpin and Croft, 1963). The school climate is the name given to the atmosphere which develops from the ways in which the headteacher and staff work among themselves and with the pupils, and can be assessed in several ways (Finlayson, 1973) depending on the priority given to the factors which influence it. These factors include:

- the spirit of co-operation and teamwork with which tasks are undertaken;
- the effectiveness of the communication system;
- the degree of commitment and loyalty of its members - teachers and pupils;
- the effectiveness of conflict resolution;
- the extent to which participation in decision-making takes place;
- the degree of mutual confidence - between head and staff, and between staff and pupils.

Halpin (1966) has stressed the importance of the headteacher's role and suggests six school profiles which can develop as a result of social and organisational behaviour. In an **open** climate the headteacher is constructive and flexible, a feeling of achievement pervades the working atmosphere, and good personal relationships develop. Where the headteacher remains aloof, impersonal and arbitrary, and firm leadership is lacking, the climate is described as **closed** and teachers gain little job-satisfaction or personal fulfilment from their work. In an **autonomous** climate teachers are given a fairly free hand in their work and this increases the sense of job-satisfaction, but social needs receive little consideration. An authoritarian headteacher may exert considerable control over the staff, and many teachers appreciate this as it creates a more **controlled** atmosphere. A **familiar** climate, however, is produced when the headteacher appears more concerned about social relationships than in giving firm leadership with the result that morale suffers because low achievement may become the acceptable norm. The 'seductive oversolicitousness' (Halpin) of the head in a **formal** climate is distrusted and there is little incentive for effective task completion among staff.

In seeking to explain how different school environments create their own characteristics, Handy (1984b) has developed the concept of 'organisational culture' or 'ideology' and applied it to the school to show how issues of staff attitudes, relationships and innovations may be affected. He suggests that there are four identifiable cultures in schools which he labels as the **club**, the **role**, the **task**, and the **person** cultures. The cultures vary considerably in the environment they create and the opportunities which exist for the exercise of power, selection of key personnel and capacity to initiate and respond to change. A knowledge of the type of culture which has evolved in a particular institution will clearly be of value to those who are contemplating the impact of innovations within that institution. Handy's approach also goes some way towards an explanation as to why so many attempts at change prove abortive. The ideology of the institution may be such that any proposed developments or strategies for producing them may be inappropriate.

In considering the appropriateness of strategies, if not the suitability of the changes themselves, it must be remembered that the school is interdependent with its environment, and that the school environment is turbulent and unpredictable. Thus the school must be regarded as an open system, in contrast with a closed system which requires either that the system is insulated from the environment, or that the outside forces which influence it are predictable. As an open system then, 'the behaviour of the organisation is contingent upon the social field of forces in which it occurs, and must be understood in terms of the organisation's interaction with that environmental field' (Katz and Kahn, 1978). It is the capacity for internal adjustments within the organisation which helps to maintain an adaptive environment. The demands for these adjustments may arise in response to changes in either external or internal situations.

Any educational institution is accountable in a number of ways - to parents, to children, to ratepayers and taxpayers, to governors, to the education committee, and to the community at large. Often the demand for change arises in response to the recognition of accountability. However, when this does happen the existing organisation and curriculum must be maintained at a satisfactory level at the same time as plans for response to anticipated future developments are being considered, developed and finally implemented. So when schools plan their responses to local and national curriculum initiatives as with the decision to introduce the General Certificate of Secondary Education (GCSE) they have to continue most existing activities while generating time and facilities to sustain any new arrangements. Frequently, such changes have to be introduced within the context of declining resources. Recently, there have been exceptions as government agencies have offered additional resources to achieve specific curricular change, as with MSC and TVEI in UK schools.

Such examples highlight the increased accountability of a school if a resource provider demands certain actions. The more dependent the school on extra resources and the more specific the requests of a sponsor, the closer the match between external intentions and school actions. In effect the sponsor pressurises for particular curricular changes, provides resources, and monitors the school's response. More generally, as resources have become less available both central and local authorities are better placed to influence curricular matters, through schools perceiving themselves as having to be more responsive. Increased competition for resources proves an effective mechanism for raising accountability.

Higher levels, though, are not restricted to schools' relationships with public agencies, especially in conditions of retrenchment. In a tight labour market secondary schools, in particular, become more accountable to employers. To a large extent this is transferred through the parents, concerned that schools are preparing children mainly through examination performance to compete for the few jobs available. Parents and employers have to be assured that school standards are being maintained to such a degree that public confidence does not erode. If they feel there is a decline some, at least, will try to correct matters. Sometimes they can express their views forcibly through membership of the governing body. Less frequently, they may have sufficient misgivings so as to want to utilise the media.

Increased visibility of school activities does not necessarily lead to more responsiveness to the views of employers or parents. Better educated parents, however (as a result of improved schooling), have the knowledge and the confidence to exercise their roles as consumers. Additionally, they are not likely to accept unquestioningly the advice of the teacher as expert. More probably they regard themselves as customers, and their views about what the school can do for their children as dominant. For example, parents who, instead of taking advantage of youth training schemes, decide to support their children at school with the intention that the qualifications and experience will enhance job prospects or enable them to meet FE and HE entry requirements, perceive themselves as direct recipients of the school's products.

Not all parents have such a vested interest in the quality of work done at school. Nevertheless it is significant that as public confidence in schooling has eroded during the 1970's and 1980's little attention has been paid to potential mismatch between school and consumer priorities. It is now some time since a Schools Council survey, (1968), indicated that the goals of pupils and their parents were in some ways quite different from those of the teachers. Parents gave examination results a higher rating than did teachers for example, while staff were more concerned about goals relating to the personal development of pupils. Since then, even with the criticisms of schools that have emerged, there have been few, if any, systematic attempts to see if such misalignment still occurs. Yet studies of successful commercial organisations both in North America (Peters and Waterman, 1982) and UK (Goldsmith and Clutterbuck, 1984) emphasise the importance of awareness about customer needs.

Using such a direct comparison with commerce to criticise schools may be deemed unfair, but schools are marketing a process, the care and education of children, and a product, the young person better qualified to cope with adult life. If consumers do not like what is on offer they may have little alternative but to accept, but they will do so unwillingly. Pupils become disaffected, parents show little interest, employers use perceptions about poor standards as an excuse to stop giving school-leavers jobs, governors criticise rather than support, and politicians stop lobbying for extra resources. Sometimes when the many 'stakeholders' in a school adopt such attitudes senior management is unaware of them. They have failed to inform themselves, but even if they did know they might claim that external attitudes are irrelevant to their problems in managing the school. According to this view professional staff are qualified by experience and expertise to be the sole determinants of school activities.

Practice demonstrates that such a policy of exclusion is futile. The work of schools is highly visible. Almost everyone, if asked, has an opinion about what they should be doing. At any time over 25% of the population is immediately involved as pupil, parent, teacher or governor. Teachers do not have the advantage of other professions of being able to erect barriers based upon confidentiality or complexity. Often there are fundamental differences, even among the staff of the same school, about what they are trying to achieve. More generally, goals are numerous and ambiguous in all educational institutions. In a survey of the goal structure of teachers in comprehensive schools Finlayson (1973) found that the teachers' top priorities were output goals which related to the balanced development of pupils' potentials, interests and skills. Of relatively low priority were output goals which reflected a concern for the maintenance of the authority structure and economic system of the wider society. Significantly, adaptation to the needs of the community had low priority according to the teacher.

Undoubtedly, such general statements disguise the great variations in priorities that do exist among the individual members of any school staff. Many polarisations are possible - between 'instrumental' task-based teachers and their more socially conscious 'expressive' colleagues, for example. Such divergence in views, combined with limited knowledge about the technology of teaching and learning, go some way in explaining why teachers want to be introspective. Introducing the opinions of outsiders into discussion will only further complicate matters, as they introduce their own views about educational goals and practices. Yet such opinions cannot be ignored, even if they are opposed to those of the teachers. The pressures that stakeholders can exert for adaptation and responsiveness is too great, if they have any control over resources, for schools to function in isolation.

Any tendency of schools towards introspection is heightened by the particular demands of a teaching job. Comparatively few teachers have the opportunity to visit other schools during the working day. Fewer still are able to spend time in a factory or office. Views about what schools ought to be doing, and their relative level of success, are therefore formulated very largely in schools by teachers with limited outside experience. For example, there is little opportunity for any market research, however informal. Schools and LEAs do not attempt to market their activities, although exceptions are now emerging in further and higher education institutions. The active marketing of a product does not mean pandering to the whim of the consumer: it does however involve gaining a knowledge of consumer requirements and the extent to which these are being satisfied. It does include efforts to educate the consumer about the benefits of the product (Willsmer, 1984).

The teacher as entrepreneur

Perhaps the best way for schools to improve their image, through increased responsiveness to group and individual consumer requirements, is by employing more teachers with entrepreneurial inclinations. To many teachers such a policy may seem abhorrent. To them entrepreneurs convey an impression of unprincipled profiteers, possibly with a role in industry or commerce, but certainly not in schools. In this context, though, entrepreneurship refers to teachers who are inventive and proactive and likely to achieve objectives far beyond those of their peers. In effect a school needs both teachers who are entrepreneurial, able to promote the image and well-being of the school in an external environment, and some who are intrapreneurial, possessing the capacity to work within the school and contribute substantially to its effectiveness. Undoubtedly, an outstanding departmental head can be simultaneously both an entrepreneur and an intrapreneur, managing a department with a high and growing reputation among parents and governors, while acknowledged as providing curriculum leadership within the school.

The concept of the school as a loosely-coupled organisation provides opportunites for intrapreneurial activity. The freedom available to teachers is considerable, and this can be used to foster 'centres of excellence' - classes, courses, departments or any separable entities - within the school. In contrast to teacher autonomy there are other factors which tend to stifle intrapreneurialship. Intrapreneurs, for success, need to be able to generate additional resources, most usually in terms of the energy and interest of other staff. Often these teachers will be suspicious about the motives of intrapreneurs. They wonder whether the ultimate beneficiaries of the extra work asked of them will be the pupils. Intrapreneurs are often perceived, correctly as it turns out, to be more interested in their own career progress. Even if the motives of an intrapreneur are sound there is also the difficulty of communicating both enthusiasm and ideas to other staff within the time constraints of the working day and the traditional 'cellular' arrangement of the school. It may not be that the majority of teachers are reticent about their classroom work, simply that the opportunities for communication are so limited that the school intrapreneur has difficulty in emerging.

Handy (1984b) suggests three ways of encouraging them within the culture framework of the work-place. These consist of trusting people by sacrificing some central control, rewarding success rather than punishing failure, and expecting good results and high standards with the anticipation that such prophesies will become self-fulfilling. According to this view senior staff of a school, and the headteacher in particular, have a responsibility for establishing a supportive climate for intrapreneurialship.

Simultaneously, though, they are best placed to adopt the role of entrepreneur. In its pursuit they have to cultivate the support of their own staff, parents, pupils, LEA officers and the wider community. In a few well publicised examples the headteacher has found that the demands of such a mixed clientele cannot be satisfied when trying to sustain radical change. Both McKenzie (1973) in striving for progressive teaching methods, and Fletcher (1985) in aiming for greater local democratic involvement in the school, would be regarded as examples of entrepreneurs, yet they met insuperable opposition.

What such examples should not detract from is the less publicised success of both intrapreneurs and entrepreneurs in the management of effective schools. Such people do create difficulties. A school staffed solely with teachers exhibiting entrepreneurial talents would probably be unmanageable. Problems arise because the values of such people can conflict with those of other staff. Also, an intrapreneurial departmental head can cause jealousy among other departmental heads by attracting a large share of resources; similarly a headteacher can create frustrations among staff and parents in a neighbouring school through entrepreneurial activities. There is always the temptation for LEA officers and headteachers to use the difficulties caused by entrepreneurialship as an excuse for stifling its effects. Yet staff with such skills are amongst the most able, and certainly the most likely to assist schools in adopting and responding to changed needs. In dealing with entrepreneurialship the leadership which emerges may become transactional or transforming.

Transforming leadership occurs when one or more persons engage with others in such a way that leaders and followers raise one another to higher levels of motivation and morality (Burns 1978). **Transactional leadership** may be thought of as consisting of the various processes of negotiation which take place within the school organisation. For the headteacher, one of the main problems posed by intrapreneurs in the school is that of judging the effect of such teachers on colleagues. These effects tend to polarize the views of co-workers into two camps. Some teachers disparage the entrepreneur's efforts and retreat into an entrenched position; others are stimulated into re-considering their own goals and work patterns, possibly from increasing awareness. There are also those who resent enthusiasm and are jealous of the attention entrepreneurial teachers may be getting.

Unlike in the industrial situation there are few external incentives for the teachers with entrepreneurial skills. They are not likely to increase sales, gain bonuses, acquire a greater share of the school budget, win recognition or immediate promotion, or even necessarily gain the respect and admiration of their colleagues. In fact, the reverse applies in many cases. Their motives are likely to be misunderstood, their activities misinterpreted, and they are likely to be taken to task when their efforts impinge on the activities of their more complacent and conservative colleagues. Although they may well be supported by sympathetic senior colleagues and advisory staff, it is frequently their own faith in the value of the work they are doing which sustains them, especially in the initial stages. The effect on the rest of the staff when one of their colleagues appears on television, or has work reported in the press can be quite alarming and divisive. Sympathetic leadership is essential in these circumstances in which conflict must not be disguised but resolved to the satisfaction of all participants if permanent damage to the organisational relationships is to be avoided.

A final problem posed by both intrapreneurial and entrepreneurial teachers is that if they are successful in gaining promotion (often as a result of their initiative) it is virtually impossible to replace them adequately. The nature of entrepreneurialship is that the goals are idiosyncratic, and the developments which result depend entirely on the personalities, interests and the contacts of the responsible individuals. Unless they have been able to influence their colleagues sufficiently to ensure that the innovations have been incorporated into normal school policy and practice, it is likely that, within months of their departure, the impetus for developments will have been lost. Many Mode 3 CSE schemes in secondary schools, or projects in primary schools, have been formulated by the enthusiasms of individual teachers, and the schools have found it impossible to sustain these activities when the particular teachers have left.

Shaping Attitudes, Behaviour and Work Patterns

The strategies for producing innovations in organisations described by Bennis, Benne and Chin (1961) have been discussed earlier (Chapter 5) and these can be viewed alongside some of the categories of tactics for shaping behaviour suggested by Olmosk (1972):

> **Fellowship.**These strategies stress good interpersonal relationships on the basis that, if the relationships between people are good, all other problems can readily be resolved as between friends. The initiatives for innovation may result in changes in such relationships causing a need for re-negotiation. Problems of maintaining the impetus for development will remain for a considerable time during the establishment of the new procedure.
>
> **Political.**If enough influential members of staff can be convinced that a particular change will be beneficial, it will be difficult to resist the legitimate authority of those who wish to establish the innovation. However, the difficulty of maintaining credibility and avoiding back-

lash may remain long after the innovation has become established.

Economic. The introduction of new measures into the school, or the redistribution of school resources can remove one source of opposition to the implementation of change. The problems of recurrent expenditure after the initial injection of capital must be discussed in advance of the acceptance of the change. Issues of job satisfaction may arise later as the implications of the change become apparent.

Academic. Job satisfaction and motivation have emotional overtones, and the would-be innovator needs to identify the initial causes for discontent in order to win sympathy for the new ideas. If not, the proposals will simply not command the attention of colleagues.

Engineering. If the environment is changed it is sometimes possible to bring about changes in the behaviour of certain teachers. Since this method is often used by the staff on pupils they resent it when the technique is being practised on them. The problem is that those affected are not taken into the confidence of those wishing to produce change, and so the process becomes time-consuming and difficult to control; there is also an element of deception which the members of a professional bureaucracy may find intolerable.

Confrontation. Provided that sufficient anger and frustration can be generated over the prevalent conditions, teachers will be prepared to expend energy to change them. The problem may be that a range of alternatives exists, or conversely, that there is no alternative to the existing situation, and so the innovator must seek to develop plans to be put into operation after the initial impetus for change has been created. Again, there is the danger of backlash from the more conservative members of staff who find the status quo quite comfortable.

In discussing the nature of responses to initiatives for change March (1981) states that 'what we call organisational change is an ecology of concurrent responses in various parts of an organisation to various interconnected parts of the environment'. Thus, different parts of the organisation are required to make - or actually do make - different responses to innovatory pressures, and some of these responses may be quite unanticipated. March lists six such consequences resulting from elementary adaptive responses functioning under special conditions. For example, organisations which are facing difficult times may well follow more risky strategies for change. The six consequences are as follows:

Learning from the response of clients

The assessment of the needs of consumers-pupils, parents, employers -in relation to the work of the school is always important, but March suggests that particular attention has to be paid to the accurate monitoring of consumer reaction in the aftermath of any major change in school activity.

Rewarding friends and co-opting enemies

March warns against the recruitment of change agents on the basis of their stated opposition to the current school policies, since it is impossible to forecast the results of such staff transfers. The incentive to continue to 'be difficult' in the 'new' school may well cause problems, since such 'difficult' teachers have apparently been rewarded for their awkwardness and retain perceptions of their 'independence'.

Competency multipliers

The practice of involving interested staff in decision-making is not without its dangers, in that such participation increases their competence and hence their desire for even more involvement. This can result in significant alterations to the processes which took place in the original group, especially when the decisions made were good ones, since the 'new' members have had little experience of failure.

Satisficing

Organisations 'satisfice', that is they seek alternatives that will satisfy a target goal, rather than look for the alternative with the highest possible expected value, in order to maximise the probability of achieving their target. Individual teachers often adopt this approach in setting targets for their pupils in the classroom, since they recognise that realistic goals for pupils are likely to be better motivators than goals which can only be achieved by a few. This compromise between 'satisfaction' and 'sacrifice' is found at many levels in the school organisation.

Performance criteria

The achievement of change—a new working practice, or an alternative syllabus—should never be considered to be an end in itself in schools. Therefore, an assessment of both the change itself and its effects on other activities must be an important element in appraisal of the teachers and sub-groups within the school.

Superstitious learning

Because of the need to confront continuously changing demands, which often introduce new factors, experience may not always be a good guide. Teachers must therefore always be cautious when applying successful former solutions to new problems. One reason for this is that both innovations and the goals of people within the school tend to be altered as a result of the processes of adaptation. The school is thus continuously evolving as the result of the goal-oriented behaviour of individuals relative to their own perceptions about school intentions. The aim should be that they learn, and contribute to the learning of the school, about the most effective means of achieving objectives (Chapter 9).

These factors illustrate some of the issues concerned with producing change and they have to be related in individual cases to the school climate in which negotiated changes take place. They are more likely to result in increased teacher satisfaction in those schools where the level of bureaucracy has been reduced, permitting greater opportunities for participation through the application of the principles of corporate management (Poster, 1976). The involvement of members of staff in senior management teams, academic boards and pastoral committees, for example, tends to reduce the formalisation and centralisation of the management processes in the school and lowers the degrees of anxiety and stress existing among the teachers. It is no coincidence that a high degree of teacher-participation is linked to the development of teaching styles which focus on pupils' needs. For example, the introduction of Developmental Group Work (Button, 1976) into form periods is extremely difficult in bureaucratic schools, whereas schools with a weaker hierarchy of authority seem to create a climate in which such developments are more readily accepted. The more centralised and formalised schools tend to produce teachers with less loyalty both to their senior colleagues and to the institution as a whole. Such 'depersonalisation', in the bureaucratic sense, can place the school climate at the exploitive/authoritarian end of the continuum (Likert, 1967) in which, under threat or pressure, interpersonal relationships are characterised by mistrust, lack of confidence and supportive behaviour, leading eventually to hostility. By contrast, participation systems tend to create warmer atmospheres in which supportive senior staff and well-motivated teachers share the responsibility for development and a high goal achievement. Some formalisation must, however, be present so that teachers' attitudes remain focused on the task-based aspects of the school.

It is perhaps appropriate at this point to ask with Greenfield (1975): does the organisation actually exist, or is it the product of the interaction of personalities? Can it accommodate new key personalities or will it change as a consequence of their introduction? In discussing educational planning, Larson (1982) refers to the 'mythology of organisational goals', pointing out that such goals are attractive to administrators, give the impression of parent and consumer participation, and suggest that the teachers' work is unified by a common purpose. However, goal-conscious development may well clash with the norm of behaviour in the school, in that attempts to establish school objectives as a basis for change are usually seen by the teachers as an interesting but fruitless exercise, quite unrelated to classroom practice. Once the school's aims and objectives have been worked out, the issue of how to plan in order to turn them into action remains a problem. Likewise a statement of the existing curriculum in terms of the school's goals is extremely difficult to formulate in behavioural terms. In individual subjects, the national criteria formulated for the General Certificate of Secondary Education have gone some way towards realising this, but over school policy, teachers prefer to discuss 'here and now' situations, not abstractions which are often felt to be for the consumption of outsiders.

Such abstractions are seldom felt to be the basis for action, but rather the provision of a rationale with which those occupying boundary positions have to be concerned. Wieck's (1976) loose-coupling concept suggests that a reason for this is that the school's sub-systems (classrooms) have their logical separations, and there is little to be gained in efficiency and co-ordination from trying to develop a subsuming policy which will not restrict the flexibility of the teachers. March (1981) further believes that 'behaviour is loosely coupled to intentions: actions in one part of the organisation are loosely coupled to actions in another part: decisions today are loosely coupled to decisions tomorrow'. The function of organisational goals, then, may well be to provide a kind of myth in which hopes and purposes may be built into symbolic representation of the future. During the process of goal-setting, the directed thinking of the staff may well result in change strategies being developed and in the revitalisation of communications. This is analagous to the way in which the Hawthorne Effect (Mayo 1933) produced change while purporting to observe what was going on. However, when a list of school or departmental objectives is finally produced, it seldom provides the basis for development. As Larson (1982) has said: 'The requisite conditions for institution-wide goal planning are seldom found in educational organisations'; and he asks: 'what planning processes will work within the context of organised anarchies and garbage-can organisations?'

In this context 'goals' are seen as creating an illusory sense of order and direction in an attempt to avoid uncertainty. The question is not one of identifying goals to pursue, but which of them can be supported from the resources available. In reality, the 'interactive planning' described by Mc-Caskey (1974) is based on individual goal-setting, on what the individual teacher finds satisfying or meaningful in the context of the classroom, laboratory or tutor room. The sequence of events, according to Shiman and Lieberman (1974) is that 'teachers talk, they move into activities, they examine the whole school programme, they raise philosophical questions and then they struggle with goals'. Thus, rather than looking to organisationally established goals, it is more profitable, as McCaskey suggests to examine the impact of innovation on individual teachers. Tracking exercises (DES 1983b) indicate ways of examining the relationship between what is intended and what is actually happening in the curriculum sphere.

Innovation is usually regarded as an opportunity by those who advocate it and a threat by others. It challenges complacency and established practice, and frequently new faces are to be seen among the school's key personnel, either because of new appointments, or, more threateningly, because new significant roles have been taken by existing members of staff. There is likely to be a vague feeling of discomfort in that something or someone must have been wrong, otherwise the status quo would not have been disturbed. The work of Bernstein (1971) may be cited as an example of one way in which the influence of a curriculum change may spread into the organisation, forcing changes there, and finally affect the feelings of individual teachers apparently unconnected with the changes.

The curriculum change he considers is a move from separate subject disciplines into a more integrated curriculum. The characteristic of the former 'collection curriculum' is oligarchic control with strong relationships among senior members of staff. Individual departments have strong hierarchies within them, and the work of junior staff is contained within the departments. The pupils are relatively isolated from one another. Movement towards integration results in less control and the development of increased horizontal relationships between staff in different departments, reminiscent of 'gangplank theory' (Fayol, 1949), or the role of 'linking pins' (Likert, 1967). Boundaries between staff and pupils, too, are likely to become weakened. 'The move from collection to integrated codes may well bring about a disturbance in the structure and distribution of power, in property relationships and in existing educational identities. This change of educational code involves a fundamental change in the nature and strength of boundaries.... It is no wonder that deep-felt resistances are called out by the issue of change in educational codes' (Bernstein, 1971).

In the redistribution of resources which inevitably occurs in support of planned changes, some teachers gain and others suffer. Reorganisation of teacher-time, non-contact periods (often seen as a status symbol by teachers, but although they relate to status, they are not symbols, since they are required for non-teaching tasks required by the organisation), rooms and facilities, or even of the time allowed for certain subjects may all take place. Since the relative provision of resources is also seen as indicating relative esteem for either teacher or subject, many emotive issues are raised. Thus teachers may be involved with change in size, either of the school or of individual departments (often seen as 'empires') together with a decrease in non-teaching time which may in turn result in decreased time for re-learning and renegotiation, both of which are vital during periods of significant change.

The changes may well mean greater opportunities for some teachers but fewer opportunities for others. Resentment at the creation of 'winners' and 'losers' may not be restricted to those members of staff actually af-fected; some disquiet and apprehension may well be felt by the 'spectators' since changes in the administrative or technological structure could affect them eventually. Further, it may be assumed that 'senior management' does not really understand the demands which are being made on in-dividual teachers, and that faulty assumptions have been made about the motives of teachers who have either supported or opposed the changes. What is vital is that the teachers must have the support of the school management team at this time, when they are having to work harder with very little recognition. The danger of taking the goodwill of staff for granted at this time may have repercussions later on.

In the initial stages of innovation, teachers are often 'de-skilled', especially when it comes to new teaching methods, and the lack of ex-perienced practitioners in the school could prove an insuperable handicap to development. The need for appropriate in-service training to ensure that teachers are properly equipped to teach new courses, take part in counsel-ling, organise work experience etc. has been stressed (OECD, 1982). As a result of these processes occurring throughout the school the organisation is continually evolving, but in ways which cannot arbitrarily be controlled. The changes depend upon a few stable processes and often reflect simple responses to demographic, economic, social and political forces apart from the educational advances themselves. The responses within the school are sometimes unexpected, and adaptation may result from a mixture of ra-tionality and 'foolishness'. 'Organisational foolishness' is not maintained as a conscious strategy, but is embedded in such familiar organisational anomalies as slack, managerial incentives, symbolic action, ambiguity and loose coupling' (March, 1981). 'Slack', he maintains, gives protection from normal organisational controls to individuals and groups involved in innovation. The freedom of action which follows may also be associated with high status and professionalism.

During the course of the establishment of a particular innovation within the school, several other possible reactions may occur amongst the members of staff. One of the most important of these is **cognitive dissonance** (Festinger, 1964) which concerns the state of discomfort within an individual when a conflict exists between two ideas both of which are accepted as true, but are contradictory. The teacher is then motivated to behave in ways which reduce the dissonance, and so escape from the feelings of unease. One method is to attempt to manipulate the information received so as to change one or more of the contradictory facts. Alternatively, some teachers seek to gather more information to support or disprove one or more of the cognitive elements. A third alternative course of action would be to attempt to decrease the relative importance of both of the elements, so that the whole issue can justifiably be forgotten.

Such an attempt, however, usually fails to reduce the stress produced at this time. Stress in this context is taken to mean the state of non-productive anxiety which develops, and is discussed in more detail later in the chapter. The teacher usually manifests, in an effort to escape the feelings of discomfort, symptoms of withdrawal, hostility and aggression. Each of these maladaptive responses, especially if adopted by considerable numbers of the staff, can exert conservative effects on the organisation's capacity to assimilate the proposed change.

At the same time it may be argued by teachers under stress that during times of scarcity and insecurity, the organisation should devote its energy to improving what it is doing, rather than working to produce radical changes. If there is sufficient support for this point of view, the traditional institutional values begin to dominate, the innovation becomes the scapegoat and the first casualty of financial cutbacks. Finally, the fact that teachers tend to attribute success to internal factors such as ability and effort, and failure to external factors such as luck and the difficulties of the task, makes true evaluation much more difficult. Thus, attribution theory tends to relate success to 'good internal management' and failure to 'those others outside', and reduces the need to evaluate critically institutional practices and beliefs. This attitude reduces the impact of external opinions and therefore the amount of conflict produced in the internal situation.

Teachers and stress

Unresolved conflict and pressure for change are only two of the contributory factors to the stress experienced by many teachers in today's schools. Other significant sources of anxiety are role conflict and role overload. Most of these result from pressures placed on teachers and arise from increased work load associated with the organisational and curricular changes described. The expectations of a society with uncertain values, in which young people are developing attitudes and behaviour quite different from those which were formerly apparent in schools and in society in general, represent additional sources of pressure. Lack of promotion prospects, deteriorating working conditions and uncertainty about the future all serve to aggravate the situation for teachers. Maslach and Jackson

(1981) have used the term 'teacher burnout' to summarize the feelings of stress and anxiety which are being indentified in teachers subjected to such pressures. Although the authors acknowledge that the term itself may appear 'trendy' and sensational, the feelings which they report give cause for concern. Three independent aspects are recognised:

- Feelings of emotional exhaustion and fatigue result in the depletion of emotional resources and consequently of energy for the job;
- Feelings of de-humanisation and de-personalisation result in negative and cynical attitudes;
- Feelings of negative self-evaluation produce a distinct lack of personal accomplishment.

The significance of these feelings in relation to the motivational issues discussed earlier, is for those responsible for maintaining school morale and climate, considerable. Even more important are the defence mechanisms which teachers can resort to in order to reduce these states of stress. Understandably, they seek to avoid painful anxiety and its disruptive effects and, as a result, do not have to admit to feelings of inferiority. Vernon (1969) has catalogued seven such defence mechanisms which can readily be seen in the staff of schools under conditions of stress, and particularly under extreme conditions, as when schools are to be reorganised or closed.

Rationalisation: teachers may seek to find a moral and rational explanation of their behaviour which they feel will be acceptable.

Compartmentalisation: teachers often show different types of motivational behaviour in different parts of their lives.

Projection: teachers may attribute undesirable motives to others, whom they can then blame for the situation.

Reaction Formation: the teachers may behave in a manner directly opposite from the way they feel in order to mask unacceptable motivation.

Denial: the perception of people and events likely to arouse considerable motivational tendencies in the teacher is distorted or even completely suppressed.

Repression: painful thoughts are repressed more or less completely into the unconscious mind so that they can be 'lived with' and not interfere with the teacher's day-to-day work.

Regression: during periods of excessive frustration the teacher may retreat into an earlier and happier state of mind until the immediate threat or anxiety is over.

In addition to these individual responses to situations which are experienced as painful and threatening, Bion (1961) has identified three forms of group defence mechanisms which may be developed.

Fight Defences: teachers are ready to attack those responsible for their discomfort by querulous interrogation, competition and expressions of cynicism.

Flight Defences: groups of teachers seek to 'retreat' from the situation by endless and futile intellectualisation, attribution, interminable attempts at re-interpretation and finally emotional or even physical withdrawal.

Group manipulation: teachers divide into pairs or groups of allies and derive satisfaction from mutual solicitude or by showing extreme sympathy for those colleagues who are visibly distressed.

More recently Dewe (1985) has referred to a number of ways in which teachers' actual behaviour betrays the stress which they feel, as they seek to find constructive, rational responses to the situation in which they find themselves:

indentifying the source and its possible consequences;

developing self-awareness, personal goals, expectations and feelings; maintaining a balanced approach to work which includes diet, exercise, relaxation and recreation;

the development of good supportive relationships through colleagues, family, friends and leisure.

He groups the specific elements of behaviour observed into six main strategies:

attempting to ride the situation; developing rational task-oriented behaviour; adopting a conservative approach to teaching; utilising colleague support; putting things into perspective; becoming less involved.

The sombre picture of the ways in which demoralised teachers behave has considerable lessons for the senior members of staff who have to sustain morale over difficult periods. Schwab and Iwanicki (1982) have drawn up strategies for developing school-based interventions to reduce role ambiguity and conflict and the associated emotional exhaustion. These strategies could well be built into the school organisation in advance of threatened change or development so that a framework would have already been established to help the staff overcome the problems which could develop. However, since the effects of changes cannot be worked out in detail prior to their implementation, all consequences cannot be visualised in advance. The value of Schwab and Iwanicki's suggestion is that the impact of such change may be absorbed by the organisation, rather than by the individuals in it. Their proposals are as follows:

- establish clean lines of authority within the school organisation;
- develop clear teacher job descriptions;
- involve teachers in the development of realistic system-wide as well as individual school goals and objectives;
- involve staff in the teacher selection and evaluation process;
- train teachers and administrators in conflict resolution skills;
- organise effective teacher support groups.

If this approach is used the task of the headteacher as leader of the school organisation is to establish feelings of mutual trust and agreement in relation to the strategies and operational procedures as they affect those involved in them. Steps have to be taken to reduce isolation and distance between colleagues so that the concerns of teachers who are caught up in situations of change and uncertainty can be promptly alleviated. Faulty communication is one of the major contributors to such uncertainty and is the result of the failure of those in authority to involve their colleagues in discussions about how the implementation of new policies will be likely to affect them.

Deprivation and distortion of information may produce a lack of identification with the purpose of the changes and can result in the excessive preoccupation of those involved with the effects of such changes upon themselves. The effects fall into three groups:

- personal consequences such as future promotion prospects and changes in formal and informal status and authority within the school;
- working conditions such as the interest and importance of the work contributed, work pressures and skill requirements, and the amount of work to be done in relation to time available;
- changes in relationships with superiors, colleagues, subordinates.

It is sometimes said that a teacher's life is one of thwarted expectation and this may be aggravated under conditions of change, with the result that the degree of frustration and aggression increases. Some teachers may leave the school or even the profession, but those who remain can respond by withdrawal of involvement in school activities; or they may show signs of depression through having to endure too much change in too short a time - Toffler's 'future shock' (1973). The teachers involved may also show a 'stress syndrome' (made up of negative emotions of anger, fear, helplessness and failure) and report difficulties in relaxing from work during their spare time. This represents a different dimension of the teacher stress problem, since relaxation difficulties relate negatively to job satisfaction (Mykletun, 1985).

Etzioni (1966) found a strong negative correlation between the level of ambition and the degree of success, and proposed a more gradual approach to the introduction of substantial change by altering a few components at a time. Advantages claimed for this approach are:

- lower levels of uncertainty and fewer unintended outcomes;
- major changes can be phased in over a longer time;
- monitoring of the effects takes place more gradually and information required for decision-making can be exchanged over a longer period;
- the impact of increased demands for resources can be lessened and tailored to possibilities of success as the changes proceed.

From the point of view of both the school and the individual teacher this approach reinforces involvement in the new activities, increases information flow and self-esteem and paves the way for the maintenance of an adaptive environment. The recognition that innovation frequently spawns sub-units in the school is an important factor in the maintenance of good communications. From the point of view of those not directly involved in the development there is the fear of being excluded from what is seen to be going on, with the attendant anxieties, while for those implementing the changes there is the perceived distrust of colleagues and all the emotions of the initiator described above. In both cases the 'effective teacher support groups' advocated by Schwab asnd Iwanicki could well prove effective in combating the problems. Such groups' ability to exert influence on others and provide mutual support for their own members capitalises on the needs of teachers to seek allies and express their viewpoint when things appear to be passing out of their immediate control. The dominant resources available to such groups include the size of membership, the cohesiveness of the group and the ability of the group to speak on behalf of the members. The support of, and the interaction with, other such groups, and the perceived correspondence of the group's goals with the basic values of the society served, are also contributory factors to the value of the group's effectiveness in dispelling the anxiety of its members. The contribution of the leadership, both within the group and as a point of reference for other groups, can ensure that the views and problems discussed are brought to the attention of the school management team or headteacher.

Since training is seldom provided in advance for those individuals who are to be involved in change, individual teachers have to find their own ways of dealing with the situation and resolving their anxieties. The acknowledgement of senior staff that such support groups can be invaluable for the health of the school organisation is vital and should not be left to chance. In looking at the stress which can be attributed to the organisation itself, Coldicott (1985) emphasises the need for in-service programmes to include the recognition and alleviation of stress by individuals and by groups of organisational members. More contentiously however, French (1985) suggests that teachers should clear up their stresses **before** 'becoming embroiled in organisational activities rather than after.'

CHAPTER 7

INTERPERSONAL PERSPECTIVES ON SCHOOL MANAGEMENT

Within the school organisation good interpersonal relationships among members of staff are essential if continuous re-negotiation is to be maintained and destructive conflict is to be avoided. The opportunities for such conflict are almost infinite when attempts are made to shape the attitudes, behaviour and work patterns of individuals and weld them into a school community able to adapt to change. Thus, in addition to the 'task' requirement in school management, there is an equally important interpersonal dimension, and also a need to apply management styles appropriate to different circumstances. All teachers need to respond to, as well as seek to create or modify, the organisational climate (Halpin, 1966) in ways which are suited to the parts they have to play in the functioning of the organisation as a whole. In order to achieve managerial success at the levels in which they operate, all teachers must therefore develop a proper balance of task orientation, personal relationships and effectiveness (Everard, 1984).

The Centrality of Interpersonal Skills and Managerial Self-Awareness.

Woodcock and Francis (1982) have suggested the following eleven skills and abilities which are required by managers in general:

- ability to manage oneself
- sound personal values
- clear personal objectives
- emphasis on continued personal growth
- effective problem-solving skills
- capacity to be creative and innovative
- high capacity to influence others
- insight into management style
- supervisory competence
- ability to train and develop others
- capacity to form and develop effective teams.

The suggestion is made that although each management task makes unique demands, any manager weak in one or more of these attributes will experience difficulties, or as they term it, 'a blockage'. The first step, then, to managerial effectiveness is that personnel with managerial responsibilities should set out to identify, and then establish a self-development programme to remove any 'blockages' they may find.

However, the traditional view of educational management in school is that the 'good professional teachers' will gain promotion and make the transition in such a way that they gain management expertise through experience, and that the 'jargon' of management theorists and the approaches of management trainers are not appropriate to the school situation. Indeed, many teachers holding higher level posts can be reluctant to see themselves as managers at all. This reluctance is based on the impression that much of the management training available to them unfortunately seems to be built on industrial models which have not been tailored to the school situation. The self-perceptions of teachers constitute another important factor, in that all teachers develop different views of their many skills and competence, and these views determine their response to training programmes (Dubin, 1962). The potential success of training programmes in relation to self-perceptions and competence is shown in Fig, 7.1.

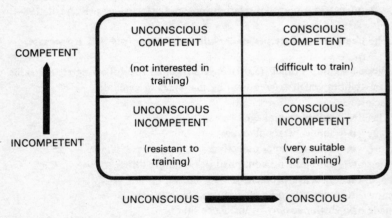

Fig. 7.1. Teachers' Self – Concepts and Training Potential. after Dubin 1962.

Nixon (1974), also writing of the importance of interactive behaviour as a skill to be learnt, states that it involves:

> perceptual sensitivity and accurate perceptions of others; warmth, rapport, affiliation and rapid response to others; a repertoire of techniques; flexibility; energy and initiation (since active people are more effective); smooth response patterns.

This cluster of attributes is not significantly different from the eleven skills and abilities listed by Woodcock and Francis. Both are applicable to the centres of management diffused throughout the school. In fact, as the power differential between teachers close together in the school hierarchy is less than that between, say, the head and a classroom teacher, it could be argued that the need for interpersonal skills becomes correspondingly greater at the lower levels, precisely because ideas must be 'sold' rather than 'told' to colleagues over whom no legitimate authority or power can be exercised. However, in practice, educational managers have less legitimate power than their peers in industry, because teachers are all part of the professional bureaucracy. They therefore are no more effective in the 'tells' mode than any other member of staff. Likewise, interaction between a teacher with pastoral responsibility and a teacher with curricular responsibility may be considerably improved if both have had training in management skills based on the development of self-awareness and sensitivity to others.

It is in this connection that the Johari window is valuable in illuminating an area of personal relationships which may have gone unnoticed in the hurly-burly of the staffroom and in the multitude of time-demanding tasks undertaken by teachers. In task-oriented situations, it is frequently the interpersonal dimension which has to be sacrificed; the instrumental needs dominate and the opportunity for improving relationships is hard to come by. Figure 7.2 shows how a modfied Johari window can be used to initiate self-awareness, so that teachers can gain a greater understanding of themselves and their effect on others, on the basis of feedback and disclosure.

Feedback takes place when the teachers indicate that they are willing to make constructive use of information which colleagues are prepared to share with them about themselves and their influence on the organisation. Their ability to accept feedback must be developed to the extent that colleagues feel safe in taking the risk of passing on unpalatable truths, in the knowledge that their candour will be respected and constructive use will be made of the information - it will not be rationalised away. A possible problem in the managerial situation is that teachers may well find it difficult to accept feedback from several individuals with the resulting accusations of having 'favourites' by giving only certain privileged people access to their time. The advantage of such disclosure is that the senior members of staff increasingly and consistently take people into their confidence as regards their personal and managerial perceptions, by letting people get close to them. The crucial feature is again one of trust, but as before, the reactions of colleagues who are not party to confidences may be a possible source of problems.

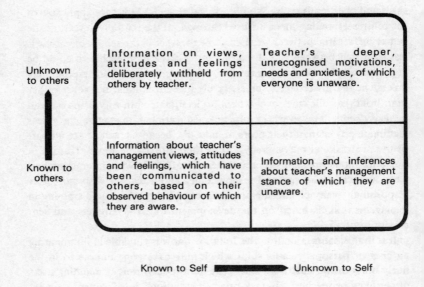

Fig. 7.2. Modifed Johari Window for the Teacher-manager - based on Luft (1970)

The appropriate school environment for such conditions of feedback and disclosure is in fairly close working groups with obvious specific membership boundaries, such as the school management team, or a group of probationary teachers who are being helped through their probationary year by an experienced member of staff. Under such conditions, disclosure and feedback can be of mutual benefit and support, both of which would result from the improved personal relationships within the group. This approach is consistent with the view expressed in Chapter 9 that the development of management **teams** within the institution is just as important as developing the management skills of the individual (Belbin, 1981) and would go a long way towards obviating the dangers of loose coupling and garbage-can developments described in Chapter 4.

The Personal Qualities of the Good Teacher-Manager

Probably the most important personal quality of senior management staff in a school is that of demonstrable loyalty to the institution and their colleagues. Where this is felt to be lacking, there quickly develops a feeling of anomie in the institution, and the credibility of the leadership may be sacrificed. This is apparent when, for example, a teacher fails to sustain the 'united front' to outsiders and criticises colleagues in public. Linked to this sense of loyalty and pride in the institution is the need to show respect for colleagues, their abilities, their rights and their privacy. When a professional leads other highly-qualified and trained professionals there are many occasions when contact counselling (Sperry and Hess, 1974) is required, and transgressions from the code of trust and invasions of privacy can quickly be seized on by demoralised colleagues who will feel that they have been betrayed.

Most professional associations have a formal Code of Conduct to which members are expected to conform. Teachers have only an informal code, entered into voluntarily by negotiation; but breaking this can have disastrous consequences for staff relationships. Thus it is important for senior members of staff to listen carefully to what is said to them in such a way that they detect what is implied as well as what is explicitly stated -Rogerian 'active listening' (Carkhuff, 1969). It is rare for junior members of staff to criticise their senior colleagues face to face without emotion, unless they are confident that their colleagues are genuinely trying to empathise with them and understand their terms of reference. There is a great danger that experienced teachers will respond with their own interpretation of a situation which to a junior member of staff appears quite different. This is especially so when there is little time for senior teachers to key into the situation and appreciate the worries and problems of their less experienced colleagues. In this connection, discussion papers like Young Teachers under Stress (HMA, 1976) are invaluable for reminding senior staff of the difficulties which they may have faced, but have now 'forgotten'.

The problems of the assimilation of newcomers into the school organisation should also be recognised. They need help in adjusting to the newness of the situation. Their difficulties may be due to confused perceptions of the extent of the personal adaptation required when adopting a new role or acquiring a different status. Schein (1971) has identified functional, hierarchical and inclusion dimensions for individuals seeking to establish themselves in the instrumental and social network of an organisation. The effect of 'surprise' resulting from the difference between an individual's anticipations and subsequent experiences in the new situation may be positive or negative and can have repercussions for task completion, the school organisation or the individual. Expectations might not be fulfilled, or self-concepts may have to be revised by individuals who discover that they find additional responsibility uncomfortable, or that there are aspects of the new job that they had not expected and which arc difficult to reconcile with their previous experience or attitude.

Coupled with this appreciation of colleagues' difficulties and problems it is important that the senior members of staff are able to communicate their understanding of these difficulties, and are also prepared to make known their own true feelings, albeit with discretion. In addition, they should endeavour to be aware of their own feelings and prejudices about the situation or persons involved, so that they can recognise their influence on decisions or on the advice they judge to be appropriate. Perceptive and intelligent colleagues can quickly recognise gameplaying and manipulation by senior members of staff and permanent resentments can be built up quickly. The situation may even develop into one in which ulterior motives are ascribed by uncertain colleagues to most management activities.

Of the more task-orientated qualities desirable in senior members of staff, the most important is preparedness to accept the inevitability of change, and acknowledge that such change and innovation, if properly managed, can lead to healthy developments. However, change, in common with many other aspects of effective management, involves risk. In dynamic situations (Burns and Stalker, 1968) it is vital that senior management in a school is able to delegate effectively, so that decisions can be made at the lowest level at which they are operative in the organisation. Once again, however, the theme of trust emerges, since all teachers holding managerial positions must have the confidence to give their colleagues genuine responsibilities without constantly looking over their shoulders.

Teachers possess considerable classroom autonomy and expect to be given a degree of managerial autonomy. However, the ability of senior members of staff to be specific and assertive is essential in this connection. There is considerable danger in the giving of vague and non-responsive answers to questions, coupled with a hint of ambiguity in policy-making, especially when a firm negative reply is called for. The ability to say 'No' without giving offence is a great asset. Non-specific delegation and woolly definitions of participation and consultation can only lead to frustration and dysfunctional conflict in the operating core of the organisation. Thus the main visible quality of senior members of staff is that they are able to meet their objectives and get results as a direct consequence of their efforts.

The final personal quality essential in teachers in senior positions follows directly from this. This is a willingness to devote time and energy to their colleagues' personal and professional development. Most teachers who hold positions of responsibility have demonstrated their adeptness at training pupils, but few of these teachers appear to have the will and self-confidence to undertake the development of their junior colleagues. It is perhaps worth noting that there are two aspects of this managerial inservice work with more experienced colleagues: manager training and management training.

'**Manager development** has as its focus the individual who has the potential to succeed to positions of significant responsibility for the resources of the organisation......**Management development** has as its focus the team of managers and others with managerial aspects to their professional jobs, who jointly run the organisation' (Everard 1984). Implicit in the latter statement is the belief of the teachers with managerial responsibilities in the value of team development and a vision of the cohesion and congruence of the centres of management diffused throughout the school.

Respect for a person's achievements in fields other than those of the work place is to be encouraged. Special knowledge, skills and background derived from activities in society outside education are valued even though the experience and expertise may be unrelated to the school's needs. The achievements of, for example, a physics teacher who is in the county rugby team bring 'reflected glory' to the institution. Healthy outside interests help to get the job into perspective and provide necessary relaxation. Religion or a unified life philosophy gives an ethical and moral dimension to the teacher's viewpoint. Hobbies such as reading can contribute to knowledge and perspective, and athletic activities may have beneficial effects. Membership of professional associations (e.g. ASE, BEMAS) enables all teachers to keep abreast of new ideas and methods, some of which may be applicable to their own situations. Many members of the teaching profession become involved in civic and church activities which help them to be aware of local community needs and of moral and political implications of their work.

Developing self-assertiveness

It has been suggested earlier that senior staff must develop interpersonal skills such as empathy, genuineness and spontaneity if they are to make effective contributions to their own self-development as well as to that of their colleagues. However, there are two warnings which must be heeded. The first is that 'task needs' of the organisation have to be balanced against 'people concerns' - an issue discussed in Chapter 3. The second danger is that this area of human relations is often regarded as 'soft' management. For it has to be acknowledged that, in addition to sensitivity to colleagues, there must be a resilient and assertive factor in a teacher's make-up. Most experienced members of the teaching profession have developed techniques of assertiveness for use with classes of pupils, but they appear less assured in their dealings with colleagues in the staffroom, where they do not have the authority of the school to back them. This skill of constructive assertiveness in relation to colleagues must be clearly distinguished from the more emotional show of aggression by a teacher in controlling classes. If transferred to the adult-adult situation it will have destructive effects on individuals' relationships with their colleagues, and indeed have repercussions throughout the whole organisation. The destructive effect of aggression is based on the fact that it intrudes into the life-space of others and may produce one of two major responses. The complementary reaction to aggression is submission in which people concerned subjugate their own spontaneous reactions, and 'give in' rather than risk the anxiety produced by open conflict. The other response, of course, is to react with increasing aggression and self-justification; the differences between the two parties then escalate without much hope of restoring good relations. Assertion can be thought of as the mid-position on a continuum with submission and aggression as the two extremes (Fig.7.3).

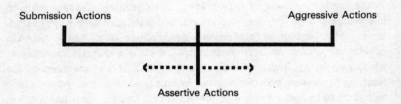

Fig. 7.3 The Submission – Assertion – Aggression Continuum

Some of the non-verbal, verbal and emotional aspects associated with these behaviours are shown in Fig. 7.4.

From Figure 7.4 it can be seen that the balance of energy between any two people involved is uneven and unstable, with the consequent dangers of the build-up of smouldering resentment afterwards. There may also be subversive attempts at revenge by personnel who see themselves as defeated in the 'win-lose' situations created. Further attempts at resolving the difficulty may only result in additional enactments of the scenario, until, in transactional analysis terms, the submissive person collects enough 'brown stamps' to feel justified in trading them in for a dramatic

EFFECTS	SUBMISSION	ASSERTION	AGGRESSION
Emotional	fear, guilt, internal tension associated with 'under-reaction'	tension at a constructive level	Anger turned outwards, 'over-reaction'
Nonverbal	self-effacing, dependent, withdrawal, 'flight response'	independent, firm, fairly detached, self-confident	intimidating, pushy, over-confident, 'fight response'
Verbal Language	uncertain, vacillating	co-operative, empathic, speaks with conviction	threats and insults, increase in intensity and pitch of speech

Fig. 7.4. Summary of Types of Behaviour Associated with the Submission-Assertion- Aggression Continuum.

confrontation (see below) and 'the worm has turned'. In assertion, the attempt is made to equalise the balance of power and avoid the potential dangers of the 'win-lose' situation.

However, despite the most careful approach, assertion messages carry an inbuilt criticism of the receiver's ideas and/or behaviour, and it must be recognised that a 'push-pushback' response is inevitable. It is this phase which must be handled carefully since any resulting argument can lead to escalation as both participants strive to defend their positions. The emotional discomfort of the receiver must be given time to dissipate before constructive dialogue can be resumed. Bolton (1979) has developed a six-stage process of assertion which he summarises as follows:

- preparation
- sending the assertion message
- being silent
- reflectively listening to the defence response
- recycling the process
- focusing on the solution.

Assertiveness can be seen as an amalgam of attitude and social status as well as social skills: senior members of staff will probably find the head to be more assertive than their colleagues. Reasons for avoiding an assertive approach include fear of arousing hostility and reaction, fear of not being able to see the issue through and sometimes the lack of inclination to become involved in face-to-face conflict. However, in reality, assertive behaviour can be regarded as the application of a group of those personal qualities thought desirable in an individual, as outlined earlier. Assertive teachers will be approachable, considerate and genuine in their efforts to understand the point of view of other people. They make no **pretence** of empathy and rapport since they recognise that such ulterior pretensions can quickly lead to accusations of manipulation with consequent loss of trust. This may jeopardise future successful interaction with that particular person and possibly others. Assertive teachers will also make sure that the issue is clearly specified, and that is the issue which is at stake, and not a personal battle, recognised or unrecognised, which can only be resolved by a 'win-lose' situation. They therefore avoid all 'ad hominem' arguments. The need for clear communication, an indication of the position taken and the degree to which the issue is open to negotiation is vital at the outset, and a determination to carry through the issues to resolution must be apparent, so that there is no 'unfinished business', in the Gestalt therapy sense (Perls, Hefferline and Goodman, 1972), at the end of the discussion. Assertive teachers will acknowledge other viewpoints but will continually return to their own, and be aware of the subversive nature of the 'flak' which is directed at them to relieve the pressure felt by their colleagues, as their position becomes more clearly defined. Crucial to the climate in which this takes place is the avoidance of confused emotions which can quickly lead to confused ideas and the development of prejudiced and biassed stances. At no stage should threats regarding the consequences of non-agreement with the teacher's ideas be used to coerce colleagues into agreement. The link between coercion and alienation has been referred to earlier in a slightly different context. Finally, it should be possible in the later stages of the discussion to acknowledge mistakes and errors on both sides without feelings of malice and inadequacy, and thus pave the way for future constructive dialogue. It is no use winning the battle but losing the war.

The process of self-management

All teachers have developed predominant images of themselves which persist throughout various changes in mood, activity and circumstances, as they go about their organisational tasks. This self-image is constructed mainly from perceptions of the outside world and the treatment to which the teachers have been subjected, and many teachers adapt their behaviour in ways calculated to establish control over these external factors. That is, they seek to develop processes of self-management in order to evoke favourable responses from others and to raise their own self-esteem (Goffman, 1969). The 'good teacher' self-image, for example, can be built up over a period of years and remains with those promoted teachers whose work now takes place mainly outside the classroom. Indeed, the ability to teach well makes a considerable contribution to the credibility of secondary headteachers, and one reason they frequently display their classroom skill is that this contributes to the self-respect they gain from the approval of their colleagues who may not be so competent. The knowledge of other teachers' perceptions of themselves is a vital prerequisite for self-management. The power of situational knowledge is also frequently used as a means of pre-empting responses from others which add to the favourableness of the self-concept.

Self-management activities can thus be regarded as comprising those behaviours which develop a positive attitude towards abilities and powers in such a way that they can be used to advantage in the organisation, with the consequent satisfaction of the self-esteem and self-actualisation needs of the individual. Such personal abilities include creativity and originality of thought linked to the generation of ideas to assist in problem-solving situations as well as the more organisational aspects of power associated with role definition. However, in the school perhaps the most important personal power which is linked to self-management lies in the ability of senior members of staff to manage the finite amount of time available to them. From this it follows that one of the most fundamental aspects of self-management is the effective management of time; if the time available is not used wisely, pressures will build up as demands increase and the stress symptoms will become apparent as the job's demands intrude into leisure time (Austin 1979). The balance between work and personal activities may then become disturbed.

Apart from ineffective distribution of tasks which could be more appropriately carried out by others and failure to plan and meet time schedules, the main cause of time dissipation by senior members of staff is when they allow their time to be structured by others. This often takes place in ways which satisfy mutual 'structure hungers' but which have little application to personal or organisational problem-solving. In transactional analysis terms, this unspoken agreement to structure time may take one or more of the following forms:

Withdrawals - During the course of a meeting or discussion both the senior members of staff and their colleagues are physically present, but some, at least, prefer not to be in the face-to-face situation and simply 'shut off'.

Rituals - It is easy for any group of individuals to develop a predetermined pattern of interaction which enables their time together to be structured superficially without confronting any major issues. After several of such meetings the more task-minded individuals tend to question the value of continuing in this way; whether their 'protest' succeeds or not often depends on the attitude of the senior members of staff present.

Activities - Time is structured by discussing, often readily and with great animation, any external issues which may be interesting, but irrelevant to the 'here and now' needs of the organisation.

Pastimes - These consist of superficial complementary transactions (see below) which are usually pleasant but leave those present with the uncomfortable feeling that they have somehow not got the most out of the meeting.

Games - The discussions quickly develop into a series of complementary ulterior transactions progressing inevitably to a well-defined ulterior outcome - 'the pay-off' - usually unconscious or unrecognised. The participants accept the 'pay-off' as the true conclusion, rather than the reaching of a decision. A classic example of this is the game of 'sabotage' which can quickly develop into a time-wasting script for future transactions.

In order to avoid the pitfalls of time structuring, the senior members of staff must be aware of their existence and seek to avoid being drawn in, if they are to manage the use of their own time to the best advantage.

The TA Perspective

It is quite natural for individuals to operate under the assumption that they perceive and observe others in a 'correct, factual, unbiassed way' (Ichheiser, 1970), but as the transactional nature of communication proceeds and working relationships develop, initial perceptions become modified through a greater familiarity with styles of behaviour used by different people or by the same person in different circumstances. Transactional analysis (TA), derived from Freud's psychoanalytical theory of personality, provides relatively simple and effective ways of considering individual and organisational behaviour and interactions in a form readily applicable by teachers. As such it is especially valuable to those with managerial responsibilities but who have little time for more sophisticated theories of personality and social interaction. TA has the advantage that it can be used to help teachers influence situations positively, without the danger inherent in manipulating the responses of others during interactions. Its main application in schools therefore is to help all teachers to appreciate more fully the influence of personal interactions within the school organisation (Jongeward, 1976).

Berne (1964) suggested that the personality of an individual can operate in one of three 'ego-states', each of which is characterised by a related set of behaviours and attitudes - Parent, Child and Adult - and defined an ego-state as a 'consistent pattern of feeling and experience directly related to a corresponding consistent pattern of behaviour'. The ego-state should not, of course, be confused with real parents, adults or children. Berne's structural concept of personality is summarised in Figure 7.5.

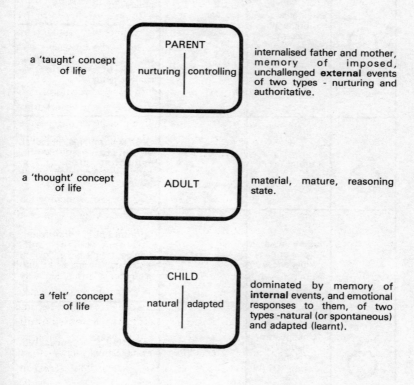

Fig. 7.5 Summary of the three ego-states suggested by Berne

Figure 7.6 indicates the main features of these states.

EGO-STATE	DERIVATION	VARIANTS	CHARACTERISTICS
Parent (P)	External sources primarily parents	Critical/ Controlling	Setting standards, ready use of power and authority accepting responsibility, making value judgements, controlling others, readily prejudiced.
		Nurturing	Caring, loving, protective, proud of subordinate's achievements.
Adult (A)	Current reality	-	Objective, rational, practical, organised, adaptable, estimating probabilities, gathering information, reality testing.
Child (C)	Natural impulses 'Tapes of early experiences'	Natural/Free	Spontaneous, emotional, curious, selfish, self-indulgent, pleasure loving, rebellious, aggressive, self-centred.
	Uneducated wisdom of childhood	"Little professor"	Intuitive, creative, manipulative.
	Early responses to experience	Adapted	Compliant, polite, withdrawn, procrastinating.

Fig. 7.6. The Characteristics of the ego-states.

Although there is no correct state it is clear that the Adult state is the most appropriate for teachers in their managerial roles, since in professional interactions with colleagues this state will prove most constructive. However, the Child state will have much to contribute to relaxation in the staffroom. The intellectual ability of the teacher, of course, is quite independent of the ego-state; an important part of the significance of Berne's work for teachers in management positions is that an appreciation of ego-states may indicate preferred ways of working and suggest ways in which different teachers will structure their jobs if the opportunity is provided. This can have significant effects in the organisation as a whole when new people are appointed whose ego-state structures differ from those of their predecessors. This follows from Berne's application of the ego-state to the types of interaction between people since he suggests that such social encounters take place primarily between the ego-states of the people concerned. Some examples of possible types of transaction are given below.

Complementary Transactions

The first statement is sent from one ego-state and receives the anticipated response from the specific ego-state of the second person - a 'healthy' response.

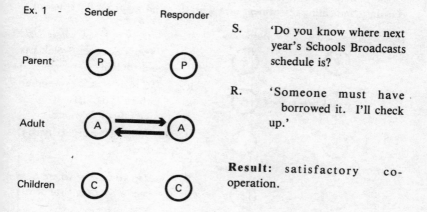

Ex. 1 -   Sender   Responder

Parent

Adult

Children

S.   'Do you know where next year's Schools Broadcasts schedule is?

R.   'Someone must have borrowed it. I'll check up.'

Result: satisfactory co-operation.

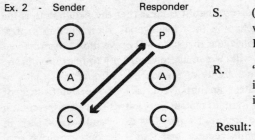

Ex. 2 - Sender   Responder

S.   (worried) 'Do you know where next year's Schools Broadcasts schedule is?

R.   'Someone must be using it. Don't worry, I'll chase it up.'

Result: satisfactory, supportive.

Ex. 3 - Sender   Responder

S.   (angrily) 'Where the devil is next year's Schools Broadcasts Schedule?

R.   'I'm sick of hunting for it. Some people never bring things back. I'll have another look.'

Result: satisfactory - agreement that it is the fault of others.

Crossed Transactions

The original statement evokes an unexpected response from a different ego-state, indicating resentment or a wish to withdraw from the situation.

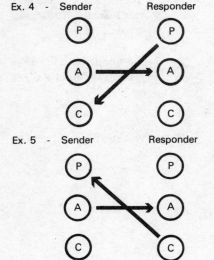

Ex. 4 - Sender   Responder

S.   'Do you know where next year's Schools Broadcasts schedule is?

R.   'Can't you remember where you left it? It should still be there.'

Result: unsatisfactory -criticism, a "put down".

Ex. 5 - Sender   Responder

S.   'Do you know where next year's Schools Broadcasts schedule is?

R.   (whining) 'Why ask me? I never use the thing?

Result: unsatisfactory - excuse to avoid confrontation.

Ex. 6 - Sender   Responder

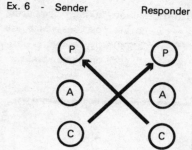

S.   'Please help me to find next year's Schools Broadcast schedule. I'm dead tired.'

R.   'I'm tired too; I was late getting in last night.'

Result: unsatisfactory - both asking for help or sympathy to the exclusion of the issue.

Ulterior Transactions

There is a hidden message behind the overt transaction which is recognised by both sender and receiver.

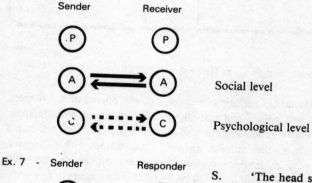

Ex. 7 - Sender   Responder

S.   'The head said he wanted to know whenever this occurred again. We'd better tell him.'

R.   'No, there will only be trouble if he finds out.'

Result: social level - apparently satisfactory as the issue appears to have been resolved.

Psychological level - unsatisfactory as there is an implied conspeiracy against the head.

129

As a result of many thousands of such transactions taking place during and after childhood, all people develop certain life positions which are described by Harris (1978) as the basic OK and not-OK psychological positions. These life positions can have a great influence on human transactions within the organisation (Fig.7.7).

1 I'm OK - You're OK	**2** I'm OK - You're not OK
3 I'm not OK - You're OK	**4** I'm not OK - You're not OK

Fig. 7.7. The Four Life-positions of Harris

It is suggested that OK feelings are associated with a sense of self-respect, capability and well being, and not-OK feelings represent weakness, insignificance, self-doubt and anxiety, and that similar feelings are attributed to colleagues. During the course of a series of transactions with colleagues, the life positions taken are reinforced as they appear to coincide with reality. The following life positions will be recognised in colleagues in any staffroom.

I'm OK - You're OK - 'the success disposition'
This position results from effective relationships with others and is characterised by independence and self confidence. Trust is communicated to others and makes for relaxed openness in communication and action.

I'm OK - You're not OK - 'the smug disposition'
In this position teachers find it very difficult to delegate responsibility as they believe that others have little to contribute, and may even be untrustworthy. The feeling that problems are always the fault of others suggests arrogance and this makes such teachers hard to relate to, and the tendency to exaggerate the value of their own contributions gives an impression of over-confidence.

I'm not OK - You're OK - 'the failure disposition'

In this position, teachers are always prepared to accept the authority of and evaluation by others regarding their ability or influence. Since their own confidence is low they tend to withdraw quickly and, as their views lack conviction, they are unlikely to make much contribution to the work of a school management team. It is unlikely that they will take the initiative in case they are seen to 'fail again'. They always appear to be under stress.

I'm not OK - You're not OK - 'the suicide disposition'

Lacking the energy or motivation to assert themselves, such teachers appear depressed and constantly oriented towards failure. Their work is characterised by low creativity and they generate negative relationships: 'a third rate teacher in a third rate school'. They are waiting for retirement .... or something.

An awareness of the positions which colleagues are likely to take, as well as a knowledge of individual teachers' own preferred positions, can be of value in moving themselves and others into more healthy positions, and thereby improving the climate in which teams of teachers can work. This is important, since people build up systems of interacting with those with whom they work most often, and systems of interacting can result in the substitution of games, pastimes and rituals for honest discussion and progress. The term **'rackets'** has been used to describe habitual ways of feeling bad which can result from the actions of parents or substitute parents, and these can inhibit the taking of constructive action.

One positive form of interaction which can go some way towards compensating for unhealthy life positions is that of 'stroking'. A **stroke** is an act by one individual which implies recognition of another and can be either positive or negative, and which can be regarded as a unit of recognition which accompanies a transaction. Thus strokes can affect job satisfaction and also the satisfactoriness of jobs, and effective teachers will be conscious of these as incentives in their desire to encourage both colleagues and pupils. Most teachers, of course, have used this technique very effectively with pupils, but find it difficult to demonstrate their appreciation of their colleagues without feeling self-conscious. The storing up of good and bad feelings has been likened to 'stamp collecting' in which 'brown' stamps represent bad feelings such as insults and 'put-downs' whereas 'gold' stamps are symbolic of good feelings, such as compliments. These stamps are stored and then 'traded in' for a sudden expression of emotion, involving some form of catharsis of stored feelings. As a result people may feel that they have a 'right to be angry' having put up with a series of minor irritations over a prolonged time. Then a fairly sudden and apparent over-reaction may occur, inexplicable to all who are involved.

Individual Life Scripts

According to TA, individuals develop 'life scripts' which are life positions based on the interaction between personal self-concepts and the environment. These life scripts represent an outlook on life, in which the individuals appear predisposed to react in fairly stereotyped characteristic ways, which have either stood them in good stead in the past, or which they have found give them some kind of satisfaction (the 'pay-off'). The following table (Fig. 7.8) indicates such personality style types and was adapted from Mosak (1971) to fit the school situation.

Teachers will be able to relate many of their colleagues' personality style types to these ten extreme positions and recognise that interactions between the bearers of certain life scripts can have far-reaching effects upon the managerial tone of the school. By acting out their 'life styles' in repetitive and self-reinforcing manners, individual teachers eagerly accept organisational roles that fit them and are reluctant to accept those roles they find uncomfortable. Thus each teacher's chosen personality style becomes a self-fulfilling prophecy. It is one of the prime functions of the senior members of staff to recognise these self-determining paths in themselves and in their colleagues and so help the organisation to avoid the destructive games and rackets which may develop as the result of the enactment of such life scripts.

Organisational Scripts

Jongeward (1976) uses the work 'script' with the sense of 'prescriptive practices'. She argues that organisations develop scripts in the same way as do individuals, in which issues are prejudiced, attitudes formed and the organisation given its identity through the social transactions adopted by its members, the formal or informal communication patterns and the traditions of the establishment. The organisational script for a school is frequently established by a revered former headteacher who adopted strong nurturing and critical **Parent** roles, frequently with the best motives and with beneficial effects. Such **Parent** messages, however, are felt to be restrictive and controlling by those teachers once the situation has changed, and yet it would almost be heresy, a 'betrayal of tradition'. ('old so-and-so would turn in his grave if he knew what was happening .....') for them to be challenged as inappropriate. Changes in personnel and even the current leadership have little effect on the '**Parent** tapes' handed down as school policy, and much effort is wasted and anxiety generated in attempts to overcome a scenario or management style which has become enshrined in the organisational script, however inappropriate this may now be. Under conditions of teacher redeployment and the amalgamation of schools,

INTERPERSONAL PERSPECTIVES ON SCHOOL MANAGEMENT

Personality Style Type	Probable Behaviour in the School Situation
1. The Driver	The 'workaholic' collects more jobs than can be done properly, in order to prove competency and compensate for feeling of inferiority; as over-achiever and difficult to work with.
2. The Controller	All aspects of work meticulously organised; planned path must be followed to avoid being blown off course by unexpected events; dislikes uncertainty or human error, own or someone else's.
3. The User	Personal work or section (department, house, school) is of prime importance and colleagues are pressed into helping to develop this.
4. The Aginner	Delights in the role of 'devil's advocate' with regard to other people's proposals or ideas and can always find justification for own destructive behaviours.
5. The Victim	To whom everything happens; actively or unwittingly pursues disaster, often aided by colleagues.
6. The Martyr	Collects injustices and is often prepared for self-sacrifice for a cause - up to a point.
7. The Inadequate One	An under-achiever who gives the impression of always working to the best of ability; from whom nobody can really expect much: anticipates failure before it happens - and it does.
8. The Excitement Seeker	Bored by the dull routines of school procedures and feels it necessary to inject novelty into a stable situation. In difficult circumstances efforts may be supported, tolerated or even despised by his colleagues: disturbing influence.
9. The Right One	Makes every effort to avoid mistakes in own work but delights in pointing out apparent errors in others; will rationalise own real errors ad nauseam, clouding the issue with outbursts about the frailities of others.
10. The Good One	Constantly reminds others of own high moral and professional standards and constantly records the short-comings of others.

Fig. 7.8 Probable behavioural characteristics of teachers' different personality style types.

there often results dissonance between rival scripts operating in the 'hybrid' institution particularly if one of the schools is now acting as, say, the lower school for the new establishment. Shenton and Dennison (1978) have shown how different organisational scripts can develop under split-site conditions in the same school, with accompanying anxiety and frustration and consequent loss of organisational efficiency. It is by evaluating organisational scripts that self-renewal can be achieved; organisational development must therefore be accompanied by changed scripts for the organisation and for most of the individuals in it.

Organisational scripts result in the continual re-enactment of games and rituals such as 'Nothing to do with me', 'See what they made me do', 'Let's you and him fight' and 'I'm closer to the boss than you' and, of course, hierarchy games. These games direct energy from the constructive development of the organisation or the individual into less honest, devious actions, in which 'stamps' can be collected and 'pay-offs' achieved which reinforce the **'Child tapes'** still operating. It is by understanding these games and focusing on Adult-to-Adult transactions that the repetitive and destructive nature of these games can be recognised, minimised or even stopped. Since these games are often played unconsciously and to everybody's satisfaction, it is clear that only a major reappraisal can focus attention on the true issues. The senior members of staff have a great part to play in this reappraisal.

There are few situations in school when attention is focused directly on the processes of interaction itself. Usually interactions are only incidental to the instrumental requirements of the organisation. However, there is one type of situation in which interactive competence is becoming increasingly recognised as the major determinant of the successful outcome of the exercise. This is, of course, the formal or informal interview situation.

Dyadic Communication - the Interview

The principle of the 'interview' is that a two-way channel of discussion provides for interchange of information as a basis for decision-making or behaviour modification. As such it differs fundamentally from 'task' meetings, such as those with union or safety representatives, although there may be certain features in common. Communication takes place on a person-to-person basis and, although organisational issues may well be discussed, the main emphasis is usually on the needs, problems and aspirations of the individual who has initiated the interview. Since senior members of staff spend a great deal of their time in such personal interactions, much of their effectiveness depends on their ability to recognise and respond quickly to the types of situation in which they find themselves. Honey (1976) argued that 'behaviour is critical in human relationships precisely because it is the bit of us that is readily evident to other people.'

'Interactive competence', therefore, though difficult to define adequately, must be worked at conscientiously by all those involved in face-to-face encounters because it is directly related to the achievement of the purposes of particular interactions.

There must be a consciousness, not only of the words and messages which are being exchanged between the individuals involved, but also of the nature of the social relationship which exists. This is seldom actually verbalised but is constantly being reinforced throughout the interaction by a series of non-verbal cues which help to establish the parameters of the interaction. Aspects of non-verbal communication are discussed in Chapter 8, but knowledge of the importance of interpersonal distance, posture, gaze direction, movement, room settings, and 'paralanguage' (rise and fall in voice pitch, stress and loudness of speech, as well as timing and hesitation) (Danziger, 1976) are vital for teachers who wish to maximise their interactive competence under interview conditions as well as in classrooms and in less formally structured interactions. Most types of formal interview fall into well defined categories although in some cases the actual interaction which develops contains elements from one or more of the classifications described.

Selection Interview: The declared purpose is to identify or select candidates for positions in a school. Usually the individual teacher has only a subsidiary role to play in the final decision. Even the headteacher (usually in a selection panel with governors and LEA officers) can only recommend to the Education Committee of the LEA, as it is the employer. In practice there is great variation in the degree to which the head or any teacher may influence such decisions. There are also a wide range of practices in arrangements for selecting headteachers (Morgan et al, 1983). However one way in which the school staff can contribute to the final choice is that when the candidates visit the school they can be helped to decide whether or not the particular post or the particular school will suit their particular abilities and motivations. Frequently information gained by those conducting candidates round the school is fed back to the appointing panel.

Since virtually all selection and promotion procedures in schools involve formal interviewing there is a need to recognise the opportunities and limitations inherent in the process. It is unlikely that those involved in conducting interviews for posts in school will have had adequate and appropriate training and had the opportunity to develop skills by supervised practice with feedback and self analysis. Indeed, those concerned in the process could resent the suggestion that such training is necessary. Likewise the importance of the need for sustained concentration on the part of the interviewer in order to maintain the atmosphere by continuous minor readjustments and other aspects of 'active listening' are seldom recognised (Bodley, 1983). Indeed, the interpretation of body language (Bolton, 1979) is a skill not acquired without considerable practice, and yet judgements based on such interpretation often form the basis of the decisions made. Judgements are made more difficult by the stressful nature of the situation away from the actual job-context, and by the temptation of some individuals to display behaviours which they think the interviewer might wish to see.

Thus, by itself, the selection interview is usually inadequate and Eysenck (1953) only grudgingly accepts that it can be used to supplement information gained in other ways. By contrast it is claimed (NUT, 1981) that valid and reliable information can be gained on the following:

> appearance and general manner
> verbal and interpersonal skills
> skills and attainments where the interviewer has professional knowledge and expertise
> attitudes to jobs, other people and experiences
> social ability
> limited aspects of motivational drive and energy
> emotional make-up
> personal motivation and clarity of self-image
> aspirations.

This view must be treated with caution, as little work has been done to analyse the interview skills and clarify the role of the interviewer in school appointments. There is much that might be learnt from the practice in industry and commerce.

Important aspects of health, integrity and leadership cannot be evaluated at interviews; nevertheless, interviews are, it is claimed, better predicters than tests where higher administrative skills or personal qualities are involved. Although interviews will continue to be used as key instruments of selection and promotion procedures, it is a fact that the interviewee's skills and responses in the interview situation create an artificial picture of his ability to do the job itself, and this gives rise to the considerable misgivings felt by teachers about the interview as a major determinant of their promotion prospects and career development.

Contact Counselling: This is the name given to the attempt made by senior members of staff, in the short period of time available, to help colleagues with problems of all types, without setting up prolonged or elaborate counselling procedures. The main stages in the process are identified by Sperry and Hess (1974) as **L**eying (identifying meanings in people's behaviour) **responding** (communicating understanding) and **guiding**

(finding ways in which the person concerned can be motivated or helped). This is probably the commonest form of interaction between the senior member of staff and his colleagues.

Performance Appraisal Interview: This takes place when standards of performance are discussed with teachers on a systematic and formal basis. Until quite recently such interviews were a comparative rarity in schools (Turner and Clift, 1983) except in the case of probationers and student teachers. The potential role of such interviews within broader appraisal arrangements, as part of staff and school development procedures, are considered in Chapter 9.

Research Interviews: These may be used in schools to accumulate preliminary information for institutional self appraisal, for example the GRIDS project (McMahon et al., 1984). An interview schedule is often administered to a number of individuals and a standard script may be employed so that responses may be collected in a standard form. External enquiries by HMI and LEA Inspectors are often carried out in this way to standardise information gained in surveying regional or national issues. A vital and appreciated aspect of the research interview technique is that final feedback of replies should be provided for those who have contributed their time and effort to the survey.

Disciplinary Interviews: These are designed in order that transgressions from agreed codes of conduct can be discussed to prevent repetition. In most situations a code of conduct has been informally arrived at over a period of time and relates to what is regarded as appropriate professional behaviour. Less frequently a more formal code of conduct seems to have been broken. Action against a teacher is initiated by the headteacher, who must take care to follow the Code of Practice agreed locally, between the LEA and the teacher associations: the headteacher acts as the employer's agent in these circumstances. Any teacher involved must remember that the function of such procedures is to assess the root cause of the difficulty and obtain the commitment of both parties to the agreed solution. Attempts to censure and criticise people's motives as opposed to their behaviour will only make the problem more difficult to solve. Formal disciplinary action should always be immediate, consistent and impersonal and taken only after clear advance warnings have been ignored.

Grievance Interviews: The initiative here comes from a dissatisfied teacher who has perceived a situation in which unfair treatment has been meted out or conflict remains unresolved. Even if the situation cannot be corrected quickly, the aggrieved teacher must be seen as a matter of urgency, and the problem discussed promptly; the teacher and union representative must not be left to 'cool their heels' while more senior colleagues appear to be given time to prepare their case. Indeed, consultation with the teacher's union representative is usually advisable at an early stage, and the LEA Grievance Procedure must be strictly adhered to if the issue cannot be resolved. Again it must be remembered that it is a problem-solving situation in which a number of people are involved in assessing the issues from several points of view, with the purpose of gaining commitment to the solutions found.

Exit Interview: This can take the form of an expression of thanks for services rendered, a smoothing out of former differences and the mutual expression of best wishes for the future. However, some exploration of the underlying reasons for the teacher's decision to leave can enable the headteacher, for example, to make changes in the job description for the replacement, or other constructive modifications for the future. It may be that some factual discussion regarding pension rights or maternity benefits will be welcomed by the person leaving, and, if conditions permit, agreement to remain in contact for the continuing exchange of ideas can lead to the establishment of productive dialogues with other establishments.

A constraint placed on most formal interview situations is that one of the persons present - the interviewee - is given the impression that not only is the case being presented, the individual is also under close scrutiny. In these circumstances there is pressure on that person to produce a performance incorporating and exemplifying the officially accredited values of the school as a society - a performance often inconsistent with the person's behaviour under normal circumstances (Goffman, 1968). The difficulty for the interviewer is to 'normalise' the atmosphere as far as possible in order that constructive interaction may take place. Hackett (1978) has suggested seven possible strategies which can be used in interview situations:

Frank and friendly strategy: 'Sit down, Chris, and tell me all about it' - headteacher moves away from his desk and draws two armchairs close together.

Joint problem-solving strategy: 'Let's see how we can sort it out' - optimistically and business-like.

Conspiratorial strategy: 'You can tell me, we'll keep it unofficial' -winks and lowers voice.

Stress strategy: 'Now, what's all this I've been hearing about .....?' -aggressively and from behind desk, no invitation for teacher to sit down.

Sweet and sour strategy: a 'two-man' approach in which one interviewer takes a hard line and the other a soft line, in the hope that the 'victim' will 'crack'.

Tell and sell strategy: 'You know that you can't teach unless the pupils are kept in order. Get in there and sort them out. I know you can do it' - aggressively encouraging, but without sincerity or conviction.

Tell and listen strategy: 'You did realise when you came into teaching that you would have to mark books didn't you?' - the senior member of staff confines remarks to scoring points and destructive criticism.

Of these strategies only the first three seek to reduce the power differential between the individuals present and establish rapport, and the third only in a way which is remarkably akin to an ulterior transaction in TA and therefore 'unsatisfactory'. Any of the remaining strategies if used could only serve to produce resentment and alienation. Two further lessons can be drawn from the above list of 'techniques'. In all cases of interviewing in schools, formal and informal, there is a need for the interviewer to provide honest feedback and maintain reciprocal and complementary role patterns in order to encourage and facilitate smooth interaction, if the purpose of the interview is to be achieved satisfactorily. Moreover, any semblance of interpersonal manipulation, deliberate or unconscious, should if possible be avoided. Where the power difference between the two persons involved is great, there is proportionate sensitivity to such manipulation - which may therefore be extremely effective. Personal interactions, satisfying or otherwise, amongst members of staff can rapidly affect the school climate and determine the perceptions of staff other than those directly involved. These effects can spread thoughout the school and beyond and influence the whole social system in which the school operates, and lead naturally into the study of the communication networks by which the various activities of the school are integrated.

CHAPTER 8

COMMUNICATION OR CHAOS?

Types of communication

A great deal of staff non-lesson time in schools is spent in communicating and this takes place on various levels: interpersonal, interdepartmental, intra-departmental, interorganisational, between the school and its environment and in other ways which defy simple classification. The key role of communication in organisations is well described as follows:

'Communication is the life-blood of an organisation: if we could somehow remove communication flows from an organisation, we would not have an organisation'.

(Roger and Agarawal-Rogers 1976, p.7.)

However, the professional bureaucracy of the school exerts a great influence on the ways in which communication takes place. Every distribution of tasks within the school produces another link in the communication process and, with it, another channel of communication; hence the larger and more complex schools become, the more complex is the communications system. Basically the administrative, pastoral and academic needs of the school determine what needs to be communicated.

Most communication takes place in one of two ways:

oral - involving the spoken work and which usually shows spontaneous adjustment to the receiver's responses; and

witten - involving more permanent, carefully prepared statements.

Oral communications are accompanied by unconscious non-verbal messages, often referred to as 'body language' which may either support or contradict what is actually being said.

Albrecht (1977) has developed the Multi-channel Communications Model to illustrate that feelings, values and opinions are often mixed with facts, especially in dyadic communication - a term used by Wilmot (1975) and others to describe face to face communication between two people. The result may be that the facts themselves are 'blurred' by being associated with non-objective 'noise', or that the unrecognised messages may exert subtle pressures on the receiver of which both he and the sender may be only dimly aware. 'The face-to-face dialogue is at the heart of effective communications, and if one person cannot see the other, something is already lost' (Honey, 1976). However, within schools, information flows develop in such regularised and controlled ways that they are often referred to as communication systems or networks. Communication relationships imposed on a group of teachers, as when organisation charts are produced and job specifications formulated, are commonly described as **formal** networks; networks which emerge as the result of the needs and preferences of teachers are considered to be **informal** and often referred to as the 'Grapevine'.

Curricular and pastoral sub-systems of management in schools have their own access to information from external sources as well as from their status in the formal communications system, and, because of their positions in the operating core of the school, they are likely to be distinctly effective in coping with their own problems. There is, of couse, no clearly defined set of problems common to all sub-systems in the school and therefore an ideal management structure should recognise this and place no obstacles in the way of the development of the flexibility needed. Teachers such as deputy heads who occupy central positions in the organisation may have initial reservations about the freedom and autonomy inherent in this situation, and have a fear of being by-passed, but they need to appreciate that such informal networks arise precisely because of need and not to subvert the objectives and goals of the institution. They develop, rather, to make up for the inherent deficiencies of any hierarchical information structure which takes little cognisance of the fact that centres of management are diffused throughout the school organisation. For example, a head of department not only needs to initiate and control communication but also has to ensure a flow of information throughout the department. Provision for effective communication upwards, downwards and laterally must also be made. There are obvious dangers inherent in a system which allows this decentralisation to take extreme forms. For example, the 'unofficial' establishment of a Departmental or Faculty Staff Room would indicate to the deputy head that perhaps autonomy has gone too far and that fragmentation and clique-formation are dangerous possibilities.

Most recent communication process models are typically cast in the image of electrical transmitters and receivers, represented diagrammatically as a series of shapes (Fig. 8.1.).

This obvious over-simplification has advantages in that it allows each stage to be examined critically, but it must be remembered that actual communication is far less logical than the models would suggest. Such a model can be related to the school situation as follows. The originator (or **source**) of the message has the major responsibility for preparing the content suitable for a particular form of transmission. It must be remembered that

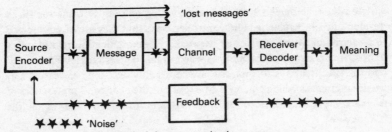

Fig. 8.1. Generalised model of the communication process.

what is said in schools is often less important than who says it, and consideration must be given to the appropriateness of the sender in relation to the material to be communicated: thus, the headteacher will often be, or be understood to be, the source of the staff bulletin.

The **message** must be communicated in a form which has meaning for both source and receiver, implying shared points of reference. Clarity of purpose is as important as content, since it must be clear to the receiver what type of response is expected (commands, requests, giving information, inculcation of correct attitudes, idea stimulation etc.) and some indication should be given of the required reaction. The content of such a message can be conveniently considered to fall into two categories:

- **motivational:** emotional climate, attitudes, hostilities, appreciation/rejection
- **cognitive:** information, problems, ideas, suggestions, policies.

Disturbances in the message may be produced if the **channel** chosen is inappropriate to the content. Awareness that distortions may occur in either oral or written channels and alertness to these effects on the part of those using them are vital aspects of the communication process in all organisations, but particularly in professional bureaucracies like schools where there is no steep hierarchy and most communication is informal.

For example, the use of pupils as messengers is common practice in many schools to provide 'rapid' channels of communication. Unless there is a genuine emergency, the interruption to the pupil-messenger's own learning, and that of the interrupted classes makes this undesirable. Also, someone interrupted during teaching has not enough time to consider the meaning of the communication especially when asked to 'Please read, and initial.' Furthermore, a message sent in this way is very liable to distortion.

The most important single element in the process is the **receiver,** the teacher, pupil or parent who may show changes in knowledge, attitude or overt behaviour after interpreting the communication as it appears to him. The **meaning** of the message is established in the context of the receiver's circumstances, interests, personal and professional needs and current attitudes. The response by the receiver provides the final element in the process, **feedback,** and confirms the two-way nature of the communication exercise. In seeking to develop the 'Management by Objectives' perspective Drucker (1974) has drawn attention to the following aspects of the process of communication:

- 'Communication is perception': the viewpoint of the 'percipient' must be taken into account in any communication process;
- 'Communication is expectation': receivers tend to fit new information into their established frame of reference;
- 'Communication makes demands': unlike social communication, communication in organisations requires to be worked at and developed to maximum efficiency;
- communication and information are different and indeed largely opposite.

'By shifts in stance, facial expression, the velocity or duration of the movement of the salutation, and even in the selection of inappropriate contexts for the act, the soldier could dignify, ridicule, demean, seduce, insult or promote the recipient of the salute.'

(Birdwhistell 1972, p.79)

In the above quotation Birdwhistell illustrates the way in which a 'standardised' action is performed in order to convey a variety of quite opposite meanings to those witnessing it. There are several aspects of such 'body language' (Fast 1970) or 'kinesics' (to use Birdwhistell's term) which are of more importance to the teacher who seeks to interpret non-verbal communication. Non-verbal messages result from the use of various body postures and movements in relation to people and events taking place around them, and are often accompanied by changes in the direction of gaze and eye contact. Such messages are considered to express attitudes held in relation to the presence of others or to activities going on. Even though little oral communication may be taking place, significant meanings can be transmitted by gestures and facial expressions (Morris, 1977).

In the presence of other people, patterns of behaviour emerge in individuals depending on the number, the physical attributes of the persons present, the noise level and the social or organisational setting in which the interactions take place (Davis 1969). The arrangement of the physical environment has an important effect, and head teachers and other staff with their own rooms often rearrange the furniture in order to manipulate the physical setting to their own advantage. Some teachers, parents or pupils may be interviewed across a desk, others may be invited to sit in easy chairs (of the same height) set alongside one another, and so on. The physical distance separating the individuals also has a considerable influence on the interactions which take place, and the concept of 'proxemic zones' has been developed to describe the social significance of the space surrounding a person's body. These zones are described as intimate (15 to 30 cms.), personal (up to 1 metre), social (2 to 4 metres) and public (beyond 4 metres); inappropriate intrusion, even by accident, can cause acute discomfort to one or both of the individuals and this will clearly affect the nature of the interactions. It can happen that people deliberately re-arrange furniture in order to manipulate, but often the arrangement of furniture reflects management style. For example, the willingness of the headteacher to communicate on a basis of equal worth may be expressed by leaving the desk and going to chairs placed informally for any discussion.

Argyle (1974) has drawn attention to the non-verbal aspects of speech (timing, emotional tone, speech errors and accent) which can also convey messages quite independent of the words used - and sometimes quite unintentionally. In some cases the non-verbal communication may contradict what is actually being said and the recipient may well have difficulty in reconciling the two different messages. This can contribute to the 'noise' described previously. Of particular importance to teachers is the concept of 'postural echo' (Morris 1977) which suggests that individuals synchronise their movements as they talk; the similarity of body postures gives an indication of the agreement and companionship between the people concerned. Postural echo may be used (possibly unconsciously) by a senior member of staff, such as head or deputy, to make more junior colleagues feel at ease during informal interaction. If the intention is to prevent informality, the senior member of staff may adopt a posture which is considerably different in order to illustrate a wish to dominate the situation. In discussions involving several teachers the postural echoing which takes place may indicate the taking of sides, since teachers tend to echo the posture of those with whom they agree, and take up quite different physical positions from those with opposing points of view. As has been indicated, the importance of such non-verbal communication is that it always occurs alongside the spoken word and the face-to-face encounter and may enhance or confuse the perception of the receiver depending upon the circumstances.

Barriers to Communication in Schools

Despite the well-intentioned efforts of senior staff there is often great concern in staffrooms over the ways in which communication takes place in schools. 'Staff Guidance Notes' are issued, notice boards appear crammed with paper, pigeon holes are filled daily, and yet the complaints are still heard. Why does this situation persist? As a partial answer to this Jackson (1977) suggests that there are four problems within organisations which people must solve:

- the problem of trust or the lack of it, which allows for content to be more freely communicated;
- the problem of the indentification of common goals, and how the members should act together to achieve them;
- the problem of distributing rewards fairly, so that people's needs are being met;
- the problem of understanding and agreeing upon the social structure of the organisation.

Whilst these issues have implications wider than communication problems, it is clear that the degree to which they are satisfactorily solved will create a suitable school climate within which communication difficulties can be improved. The majority of such difficulties can be classified into two types - organisational and interpersonal - although some problems are outside this classification.

Organisational Barriers: These are problems created by the very nature of the organisation in which the teachers find themselves.

1. Physical distance McLeary's (1968) study of communication amongst principals of large secondary schools indicates that departmentalisation and specialisation into curricular and pastoral subsystems are necessary features of large schools. This increases the difficulty of coordinating information through meetings or nonverbal media, and formalised systems need to be established. Specific problems are caused by teachers having working areas away from the staffroom, a situation which occurs in multi-site schools, or in single-site schools where the teaching areas are widely dispersed.

2. Technological barriers Telephone calls and other interruptions may disturb face-to-face discussions; extensions may not always be in appropriate places.

3. Cost barriers may result from shortage of materials, facilities or time.

4. Status-authority barriers People of the same status communicate more with one another than with those at different levels. They tend to direct their communications to those who can get things done, make them more secure, or as a means of improving their positions, and will abstain from communicating with those who will not assist them. Smith (1966) has pointed out that the greater the number and types of status within an organisation, 'the greater are the barriers to communication within it'. Thus, the professional bureaucracy may contribute to a diminution of the error-correcting function in communications, since the steeper the status pyramid, the greater is the inhibition of upward communication. Within such a hierarchy there are 'gatekeepers' who sit at the junctions of communication channels and are in a position to open and close communication channels and so may collect, combine and regulate information. Such gatekeepers, for example union representatives, may have multiple sources of information that are denied to their superiors. Other members of staff may enjoy considerable personal status because of their activities in the community outside the school, for example, as JPs, staff governors, members of the Education Committee, indicating an 'unofficial staffroom hierarchy' independent of the 'official' organisational tree diagram. When junior members of staff communicate with more senior colleagues they are occasionally selective in what they say, and at the same time senior staff may also hold back certain facts which they regard as privileged information.

5. Job-specialisation barriers In secondary schools many groups of staff are more used to communicating among themselves than with members of other groups: the 'people-specialists' of the pastoral team may have a completely different viewpoint and language from their more task orientated 'academic' colleagues - a further example of formalisation discussed in Chapter 4.

Inter-personal barriers

These problems are often created by the conflict between teachers' perceptions of the role expected of them by the organisation and their own individual attitudes. They are of four main types:

- **Value and attitude barriers.** These may stem from different age groups, or different interest groups on the staff who have different values and role-expectations from their colleagues.
- **Personality barriers.** Personal jealousies and resentments can be most injurious to smooth communication, as can friendship groups when they assume more importance to those involved than the organisational goals.
- **Knowledge and credibility barriers.** The credibility of the sender of information influences the value placed on his communications; similarly the greater the difference in background knowledge between sender and recipient the less likelihood there is of the impact of the message being completely understood.
- **Lack of complementarity of ego-state of sender and recipient.** The importance of processing information from the

proper ego-state was considered in Chapter 7. When communication takes place the ego-state of one person engages with that of another, and the most desirable communicative state is adult - adult which requires extensive use of data-processing and information-sharing, as opposed to dealing in emotions and attitudes (Berne 1974). 'Crossed' or 'ulterior' transactions may involve more than two ego-states, cause communication to veer from its anticipated and productive path and are a frequent source of difficulty. Written communications can be misinterpreted, and spoken communications depend upon a great interplay of personal factors.

Other miscellaneous barriers

Timing is essential for the co-ordination of messages by a receiver who may have to respond to demands from several directions at once. Junior members of staff often have this problem, while at the other end of the scale headteachers may have equally little control over the urgency of the demands made on their time. Another issue emerges when particular information has to be transmitted to a number of colleagues - who first? A wrong answer to this can provoke the answer, 'I'm always the last one to be told', at all levels in the organisation. There is also the problem of **immediacy** in that a more recent communication may drive out former commications. Thus discussion can displace written communication.

There are limits to the amount of information which can be effectively handled by an individual without resulting in **overload**. Although timing is clearly involved in this issue, problems are frequently created by senior members of staff who feel sincerely that increasing the information available to all members of staff would facilitate the solution of the communications problem. Simon (1957) has warned that there is a finite capacity in individuals to deal with all the information that the environment can generate, and there is no advantage to be gained in exceeding this limit; Miller (1968) has identified seven maladapted responses to overload:

(i) omission - simple failure to deal with some of the information received

(ii) error - there is too much information to be processed correctly

(iii) queueing - delaying processing of information during periods of peak load in the hope of catching up later during lulls

(iv) filtering - neglecting to process certain types of information according to some scheme of priorities

(v) approximation - cutting down categories of discrimination

(vi) employing multiple channels, using parallel channels or decentralisation

(vii) escaping from the task by ignoring it completely.

In attempting to avoid the communication problems described, many senders may feel that the only certain way of keeping colleagues informed is by **written statements**, but even these may pose problems. There is a possible **lack of clarity** in that what is obvious to the sender may be subject to misinterpretation by the recipient whose perception of the situation may be quite different, and who may place the information in a different context from that in which it was produced particularly after a lapse of time. This difficulty may be aggravated by problems of **semantics**, and confusion may arise over imprecise definition, 'in' jargon and circumlocution.

There are, of course, occasions when individuals deliberately resort to **omission** and **distortion** in order to protect their own positions. This may also take the form of **filtering** in which the content is manipulated to colour events in such a way as to benefit the sender. Similar intentions may lie behind **information-hoarding** in which positional power is used to keep information secret instead of sharing it. Considerable difficulties may also arise when one or more persons in an established vertical or horizontal communication system are left out - either accidentally or deliberately. Colleagues who are **short-circuited** in this way can quickly become frustrated and resentful.

A final problem in communication is that of **whistle blowing** which takes place when individuals within the organisation attempt to disturb the smooth running of the bureaucratic structure by stressing organisational problems (Parmelee et al, 1982) - even suggesting their own solutions - in an attempt to pose a threat to the authority of, and constraints imposed by, the school hierarchy. Quite senior and respected members of staff may act in this way in order to resist the degree of control to which they feel subjected. The school management team may respond to these tactics in the following ways:

(i)   the complaints may be investigated and positive steps taken to remedy the problems indentified, in a spirit of co-operation;

(ii) sanctions against the whistle-blowers may be employed in order to punish them for their 'awkwardness';

(iii) complainants may be given the impression that action is being taken in response to their activities, but in order to avoid further trouble their ideas are merely shelved;

(iv) those at whom the complaints are directed simply refuse to co-operate, recognising that the whistle-blowers' motives are such that they do not really wish to take part in the true give-and-take of genuine negotiation.

The danger of course is that future processes of involvement and participation are undermined and interpersonal relationships may well suffer if the problems and responses to whistle-blowers' activities are allowed to become superimposed on the organisational, interpersonal and other barriers which affect communications in all schools.

Direction of communication

Although communications may appear to have a dominant organisational direction there must be a cyclical character to all communication activities, in order that feedback may be encouraged. There are two directions of formal communication, vertical and horizontal. The former can be upwards or downwards communication. Katz and Kahn (1978) have identified five basic types of downwards communication which take place from a superior to a subordinate. Each type can be recognised in the school situation:

- specific task directives such as job instructions, duty lists, standards expected, syllabus objectives and schemes of work.

- information designed to produce understanding of the task and its relation to other organisational tasks or job rationale. Since there may not always be complete accord between teachers as to their individual places in the 'scheme of things', discussion in ' this area may well stimulate conflict; such conflict may of course be constructive, but senior members of staff must be prepared for it. Experience suggests that many teachers are content to be classroom practitioners and, in order that they can avoid feeling committed to it and retain their right to criticise, do not wish to be involved in general discussion of school philosphy.

- information about organisational procedures and practice. Most secondary schools produce a 'Staff Handbook' outlining guidelines, obligations, entitlements and limitations in an attempt to produce cohesion of standard practice among the members of staff. The task of senior members of staff in the professional bureaucracy is thus to help their less experienced colleagues to interpret this code of procedure in the light of particular circumstances, and even to suggest changes in it as a result of experience.

- feedback to a subordinate about performance. Informal appraisal of department staff has always been the basis of the constructive help and support given by heads of department, for example. Suggestions regarding teaching skills are usually welcomed by the receivers and taken as evidence of the interest shown in their professional development. However, when such appraisal is carried out by teachers who are more than one step above the person concerned in the hierarchy, discomfort and unease may well be the result, since it seems more 'official'.

● information of an ideological character to create a 'sense of mission', motivation and commitment. Unless great care is taken, this type of communication is liable to be interpreted as simply a general exhortation to work even harder, or worse, it may be regarded by those teachers who suspect the sincerity of the sender as indoctrination or propaganda.

Much of this information, however, is not disseminated directly from originator to final receiver; intermediary channels and communication loops are often used. The size of such loops is important and varies with the nature of the communication , but hierarchy levels are often used to pass the information down. However, such is the nature of intermediate communication that the original message becomes modified and re-interpreted at each stage in the process. The following example indicates how a general message 'from the top' may become translated into terms appropriate to the hierarchical level at which particular communication is taking place. It concerns the implications that follow the introduction of such innovations as the General Certificate of Secondary Education or Certificate of Pre-Vocational Education.

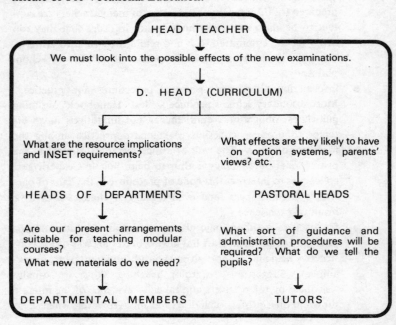

There are a number of issues illustrated by this example:

- All pastoral heads have teaching duties and are members of at least one academic department. Thus they are likely to receive at least two apparently independent requests for views on the possible innovation. These two requests are likely to be made at different times, with the result that the subordinate teachers feel that their superordinate colleagues are not really organised.

- The types of feedback taking place along the two different paths will be quite different and will have to be coordinated.

- The original general message has been reduced to a series of basic questions which have been considered relevant to the people at different levels in the hierarchy. The danger of over-simplification of the general message is that something will be lost, unless it has been 'picked up' by those who have 'sliced up' the communication into what they consider to be the appropriate component parts.

- Small network groups tend to emerge, based on job interests, personal interests and professional background and though these networks are 'ad hoc' and informal, they may well influence the decisions and views of more formally constituted groups.

- A headteacher may communicate verbally with deputies about issues like the one described; they in their turn may communicate in writing via the notice board, or to appropriate groups of staff. Thus, the nature of the channel changes as the message travels 'downwards', as well as the content of the message itself.

In relation to upward communications, there are three main reasons why junior members of staff seek to initiate communication with their more senior colleagues:

- As indicated above, teachers seek to discuss their own problems and performance with their more experienced and successful colleagues. They also look for opportunities to discuss the problems of colleagues which affect them.

- There is always a strong desire for teachers to express their feelings about policies and practices, especially if these have been formulated without reference to them. The context in which these views will be expressed will depend on the school's arrangements for consultation and participation.

- Teachers also like to express their views about what needs to be done and the methods by which desirable outcomes can be achieved. Teachers' experiences in other schools provide a valuable resource of successful and less successful ways of proceeding in their present institution.

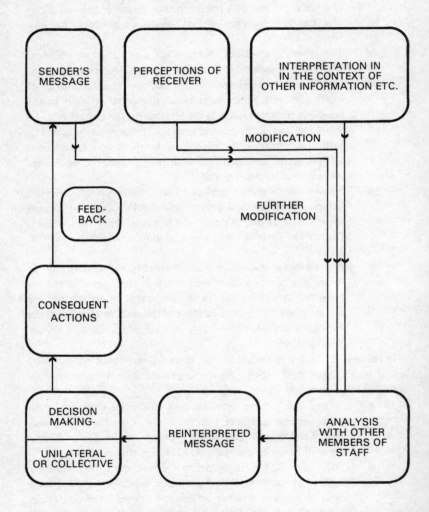

Fig. 8.2 shows how the simplified diagram of Fig. 8.1 has been modified in the light of the practical problems described.

Despite considerable research on methods used by managers to obtain compliance through downward influence, research on strategies used by subordinates to influence their superiors is rare (Schilit and Locke, 1982). The methods of exerting upward influence have been characterised as follows:

> logical and rational presentation of ideas;
>
> informal or non-performance specific exchanges including praise for the supervisor;
>
> formal exchanges;
>
> adherence to rules;
>
> by-passing of immediate supervisor through upward appeal;
>
> threats or sanctions;
>
> manipulation - when the supervisor is unaware of being influenced or used;
>
> formation of coalitions;
>
> persistence of assertiveness.

However, during discussions in which there is considerable variation in the degree of status of those involved, care must be taken that differences in perception of the issues are clarified and do not obstruct objective discussion.

There are few organisational provisions for formal **horizontal** communication in schools. There is ample opportunity in staffrooms for conversation which may provide satisfaction for individuals by giving emotional and social support, and although such discussions may transcend functional issues they are often highly task specific. However, in staffs in which there are pronounced age, sex, and background differences between groups, such lateral communication may merely encourage exclusiveness and the inbreeding of ideas. Lateral communication may even become a method of controlling people in the organisation since groups of senior staff may have in common and seek to perpetuate ideas and beliefs which are 'in-group' property. Members of such a group are sometimes unwilling to pass information upwards or downwards, either using it to punish subordinates or to 'get their own back' on superiors.

The provision of rooms for groups of senior staff is fraught with danger. It should enable individual senior managers to discharge their duties more efficiently, but exclusive group rooms can lead to difficulties because they may assist in increased specialisation in loosely-coupled areas. There also is the danger that organised activities will be planned by the small group in isolation with the result that other teachers may distance themselves from the event or decision on the basis that, since they were not informed and did not participate in the planning exercise, there is no need for them to participate in the event.

Informal Communication (the "Grapevine")

As has been described previously, the grapevine appears to originate to compensate for senior management's inability to recognise that the centres of management are diffused throughout the school, and that there is no formal communication network to link them. It arises as a more spontaneous form of expression and hence is more intrinsically satisfying than the formal channels, and is certainly more rapid in operation. It is also flattering to a teacher's ego to know more than colleagues and this can only be proved by communicating this knowledge. In less exalted circles it is called gossiping. Finally, on certain topics where official censorship and filtering take place, it can be more informative. This sometimes leads to the fear at senior level that formal communication patterns are being undermined, since there is no doubt that erroneous information and rumours are transmitted as 'noise' along with the facts. Impromptu meetings and discussions often feed the grapevine with titbits of information which are frequently linked together before being transmitted. A typical example of this would be provided by a group of teachers from different departments and varying status who travel to school together by car. Thus the informal network tends to be person-centred rather than goal-oriented and relies on the interpersonal trust inherent in friendship structures. The grapevine differs from the formal lateral communications system in that it depends upon the interests and personal concerns of the members and their opportunities for discussion, rather than the interests of the organisation.

However, there are many advantages of the grapevine network when it has developed. Information can be passed on when the sender does not wish the issue to be treated formally, and a problem situation may be defused in this way. Morale is maintained, as teachers learn to form good and valued relationships. Also the informal opinion-leaders in the staffroom can be indentified and used positively to transmit information to others, possibly with the attendant emotional overtones, and feedback can be solicited. In this way tensions can be recognised and possible trouble can be averted.

The main disadvantage is that grapevine networks that arise spontaneously are less structured and therefore less predictable than formal systems. Consequently there is the danger that members of such groups could be influenced to hold back important information or distort it for their own reasons. There are also opportunities for opinion-leaders and gatekeepers to work against organisational goals, thereby encouraging hostility to the administration. But perhaps a more realistic criticism is that the formation of cliques, rivalries and dissension is more probable than in the extreme instances of out-and-out opposition to the official activities of the school communication system and what it is hoped it will achieve.

Effectiveness of the Communication System

Barry and Tye (1972) pose three deceptively simple questions about the effectiveness of communication systems in schools:

'Who ought to know what?

How do they know?

How do you know they know?'

In so doing they raise crucial queries about the nature of senders and receivers, the channels used and the question of feedback. McLeary (1968) has developed a more detailed process of communication analysis involving seven issues.

Nature of the uncertainty and value of the communication devices

The 'open door' policy adopted by many headteachers apparently gives freedom of access to all staff, but in practice an unfair system is created since not all teachers have equal opportunities of discussing problems fully with their headteacher, even if that person were the most appropriate member so staff to deal with all the problems which are brought to his notice in this way. While such discussions undoubtedly have value, problems of 'fencing' and 'hidden agendas' often leave both head and assistant teacher with vague unease after the discussion. The difficulty of establishing empathy where such a power difference is involved casts great doubt on the value of what can be achieved on a task level under these circumstances. As an exercise in interpersonal relations of course it may well be worth the time spent.

Judgement of the communication devices in use on the basis of fidelity required

If there is only a limited range of communication devices in use, key people may remain quite uninformed about many facets of some problems. Thus decisions may be made on the basis of information provided by people only partly conversant with the facts of particular cases. Reports on pupils prior to parental interviews are particularly vulnerable. These are often produced after requests for information have been made to all the staff who have been involved with such pupils. When these have been completed they may then be compiled into a 'Special Report' by an appropriate member of staff. It is frequently observed that many of these reports 'tell you more about the teachers filling them in than about the pupil they refer to'. Since the final consolidated report is only as good as the information supplied, it is necessary for attention to be drawn to the types of comment that are expected and can be made use of, rather than leave it to the judgement of each teacher concerned. The 'tightening up' of such internal circulars and reports over a period of time is a natural consequence of the need to reappraise these communication devices in order to improve the accuracy of the information received.

Wide band and narrow band devices

General guidelines are often easier to produce than narrow band aids which give maximum information on specific questions. Provided that teachers are encouraged to interpret these general guidelines freely at, say, head of department level, this is satisfactory. For example wide band devices are used by the headteacher to communicate with the staff as a whole, coupled with narrow band devices used in departments in order to comply with the general instruction. However, the dangers inherent in a policy of 'delegate and forget' must be recognised and countered by planning for feedback.

Appropriateness of the use of wide and narrow band devices

It is not always easy to distinguish in advance situations where a quick marshalling of factual information is called for, as opposed to those where opinions need to be sought from as many people as possible, and genuine wide consultation is desirable. Inappropriate use of wide-band devices can quickly lead to information overload with the problems discussed previously.

Accuracy of the information provided

Subjective judgements of pupils, and appraisals of staff, are often made in the school situation on the basis of very little hard evidence. The degree of finality of a decision should be proportional to the accuracy of the information upon which it was based. This is particularly important in the drawing up of pupil profiles, for example, but perhaps one of the greatest areas of concern lies in the production of a set of Staff Guidance Notes. Curricular developments, staffing contingencies etc. may well have rendered the contents out-of-date while they are actually in circulation. Frequently such documents contain instructions on procedures which have subsequently been modified in the light of experience, but the printed instructions have not been amended. Clearly, continual and continuous review of such documents is essential.

Continuity and accuracy of feedback

Minutes of staff or departmental meetings made available to all interested staff provide information in a written form, which can be checked and acted upon. The processes of organisational and curriculum innovation require feedback sufficiently quickly to enable monitoring and possible adjustments to be made: such developments often take place in small centres of activity in the organisation, and those teachers not directly involved know little about the significance of the changes until the ripples affect them. It is also important to acknowledge the need for feedback in both upward and downward directions. Continuity and accuracy of feedback, particularly where problems are emerging, can go a long way to obviating the need for 'crisis management' and 'ad hoc' decisions. No headteacher likes to be faced with a major confrontation which has resulted from a steady and possibly imperceptible deterioration over a period of time.

Sensitivity of communication systems

The various channels of communication in use should be able to transmit information in appropriate detail to enable accurate decision -making at all levels in the organisation. When it is found that decision-making is being affected, it is important that the communication system is examined and refined, in addition to any corrections which may be made to the information received.

Analysis of a school's communication system along the lines indicated above suggests that there are a number of ways in which the organisational communications can be made more effective:

- the use of **repetition** through multiple channels to ensure that blockages in one channel do not prevent free communication flow;

- **verification** that messages have been received will clearly help, but may overload the receiver, producing boredom or indifference if used too frequently.

Deliberate **redundancy** involves the duplication of reports for verification while adding to the flow of paper and other media on the basis that more people are allowed access to information and to respond to it. Repetition of words and phrases might enable more chances of understanding, since there will be other elements in the communication that will carry the same point. This, however, can be a dangerous practice since repetition leads people to expect more repetition, and is self-defeating in that attention may not be paid first time.

As well as removing any blockages which may become apparent, positive steps can also be taken, such as adopting well designed practical and simple procedures to control paper work (Bentley 1976), encouraging two-way rather than one-way communication, keeping linkages in the communication chain to a minimum and using more than one communication network (Handy, 1985). An increase in the effectiveness of liaison with individuals, more attention to inter-departmental communication and a recognition of the real function and value of the school grapevine (Davis, 1977) are further ways in which the effectiveness of school communications can be improved.

Types of meetings held in school

There are a number of quite different reasons for calling meetings in school and it is important for the senior member of staff to have a clear idea in his own mind why his colleagues should be asked to give up their own time to attend: very few meetings can actually be arranged in school time, of course. Having established the reasons for the meeting the chairperson must ensure that those attending know exactly why the meeting has been called and what level of participation will be expected. The main types of school meetings are summarised below:

- **The Information Sharing Meeting.** This is intended to provide a common flow of information throughout the school organisation, in order to keep teachers aware of what is going on. Full staff meetings and departmental briefings come into this category. Little opportunity is provided at the meeting for discussion although reports may be accepted. Documents are often circulated and explained but there is always the danger of a 'fait accompli' response.

- **The Diagnostic (fact finding) Meeting.** This type of meeting rarely occurs in schools except as a phase during the course of a more general meeting. However it is arguable that more opportunities should be created by calling special meetings to identify problems, establish priorities and generally 'take the pulse of the organisation' or of some of its component parts. This type of meeting probably only takes place on a regular basis between the head and deputies, although there is a good case also for 'ad hoc' meetings with other members of staff in crisis situations.

- **The Ideas Meeting.** This should be separated from the decision-making meeting in order to allow new ideas to be developed before they are stifled by being subjected to critical review too early. Several techniques are available for the generation of new ideas.

- **The Decision-Making Meeting.** This is called specifically to consider alternatives and consequences of possible actions and then to arrive at a decision on the basis of the discussion. It does not by any means follow that the meeting at which the decision was promulgated is the one at which the decision was reached. Although this situation is at times inevitable since there may be factors affecting the making of the decision that lie outside the control of the meeting, nevertheless senior staff must be alert to the possibility that they will be accused of 'pseudo-consultation'

The terms of reference of any decision making meeting should always be clearly stated from the outset, and re-iterated, with any necessary modification or gloss, at the conclusion.

- **The Planning Meeting.** This type of meeting seeks to find ways of implementing the decisions made. A time-table planning group, or a school management team would be a typical example.
- **The Co-ordinating and Monitoring Meeting.** Delegation and accountability are key aspects of the school organisation and senior members of staff need to be able to conduct well-organised and well-executed periodic meetings to review the work of the curricular or pastoral groups or even the school as a whole.
- **The Ongoing Business Meeting.** This is the most frequently held type of school meeting. Regular committee meetings such as management meetings, and heads of section meetings are concerned with the maintenance of the school as a system. The participants are usually relaxed and cooperative since they have established fairly standard routines for achieving the business of the meeting.
- **The 'ad hoc' Meeting.** Working parties, study groups, and staff conferences are sometimes set up as change agents or to study particular areas of concern which have been identified. The implication is that the formal organisation is not capable of responding to, or initiating, change, or dealing with other serious flaws that have become apparent in the institution or its method of functioning. The establishment of such working parties may help to produce answers to specific questions, but it leaves the major problem, that of deficiencies in the formal system, untouched. The disadvantages of setting up such temporary systems are discussed by John (1980). However, it may be that the 'tight' structured meeting does not necessarily respond to the needs of the dynamic organisation. The possibility of the 'ad hoc' meeting gives the opportunity to 'brainstorm' new ideas. It **never** replaces routine, decision making mechanisms.

Problems with Meetings

Even with the most careful preparation, meetings in school rarely run smoothly and to the satisfaction of all those involved. One of the main reasons for this lies in the perceptions of those taking part as to the real purpose of the meeting. If the intention behind the inclusion of an item on the agenda has not been made clear, ambiguous responses may result. For example an agenda item 'The School Speech Day' may be thought by staff to be an opportunity to propose new ideas, or to be the occasion for decision making, whereas in fact it was simply put there so that information could be given about arrangements which have been made. The fault would appear to lie in the chairperson's failure to clarify the issues involved.

Another aspect of the chairperson's behaviour in avoiding ambiguity lies in whether the initiating behaviour adopted is high or low; if low the meeting may be awkward or forced; if too high, emotional overtones may develop and cloud the discussion. In order to avoid confusion as to what is expected from participants on each agenda item, there are advantages in clarifying whether the main thrust is towards a 'filter' or an 'amplifier' approach.

Filter meetings are designed to reduce a number of suggestions to one on which action will be taken. They are characterised by being efficient and unexciting, but produce a low commitment to the outcome, as 'win-lose' feelings predominate. On the other hand **amplifier** meetings tend to produce a higher quality of solution to problems but are more time consuming since more participation is invited and this tends to produce higher commitment to the outcome.

In addition to producing an agenda, then, there is a need to consider the nature of the items and the response anticipated before a decision is made on the optimum length of the meeting in relation to the proposed treatment of topics and the number of people who will be present. The main causes of failure in decision-making meetings include poor preparation, preoccupation with analysis, too large a group and a leisurely chairperson. Meetings concerned with problem analysis may fail because there are too many people present and there are too many items on the agenda for the time available. Where information exchange is the main purpose, selfish use of time and competitive members coupled with unclear objectives and hidden agendas may well hinder progress.

One major difference between written and oral communication in groups is that the latter usually involves a hidden as well as the surface agenda which is ostensibly the basis for discussion. The hidden agenda represents a movement towards unstated goals by at least one of the participants in the meetings. Most teachers have had experience of a meeting at which the discussion of a fairly routine matter, instead of proceeding calmly to a reasonable conclusion, has led to the abandonment of logical thought, wrangling over inconsequential issues and a disproportionately high show of emotion coupled with obstinate refusals to budge from entrenched positions. The final compromise decisions reached are blatantly wrong and if not reviewed or rescinded will form the basis of more unproductive activities. It appears that the 'official' agenda under discussion has triggered off a whole host of conflicting motives, desires, aspirations and emotional reactions of group members and is being used as a channel for the communication of these personal issues, without their having to be 'owned' by the participants. Such a hidden agenda cannot simply be ruled out of the discussion, but, since it gets in the way of task completion, it must be acknowledged and dealt with at a more appropriate time. Surface and hidden agendas may sometimes run concurrently only for the hidden agenda to resurface when discussions have reached a sticking point. Since there are few meetings which do not have hidden agendas, it is important for all teachers to be able to recognise and deal constructively with them.

Prior to the meeting an attempt should be made to forecast the hidden agendas which are likely to be in the minds of individuals and sub-groups; deputy heads, for example, will probably have some ideas about this from their knowledge of the people concerned and their previous reactions to the topics. An invitation to group members to express their views in turn without comment from the others provides a good way of checking on this.

However, it is unreasonable to expect that all hidden agendas can be brought to the surface, since some difficulties may only be dimly recognised by the people concerned: the group can only handle those items which members are prepared to make public, and the expertise of senior staff in committee work is largely determined by their judgement in these matters. They must not allow themselves to be drawn into criticising the group for its failings when progress is slow. Perhaps private discussions with disconsolate members afterwards would provide a sounder basis for future meetings.

Most of the centres of management in a school consist of a section head working with a group of teachers to achieve particular objectives, solve problems and plan courses of action as a result of decisions taken. It is therefore important to identify any built-in mechanisms which may influence the workings of such groups. One such mechanism, the so-called 'risky shift' refers to the phenomenon that individuals who have previously indicated their private decision, having been involved in group discussion, opt for a more extreme and risky group decision (Davis, 1969). It is probable that group members favouring high risk solutions to problems are more active communicators than low risk takers, show more enthusiasm and are more persuasive. Often their ideas have a certain appeal to their less adventurous colleagues who are afraid of being labelled reactionary. This is coupled with the fact that a 'group decision' allows the members to diffuse responsibility for riskier decisions on the basis of risk sharing leading to a 'nothing ventured, nothing gained' attitude by the group.

161

Having made a decision collectively, the members then feel committed to carrying it out, thereby improving the chances of success. Such success reinforces the decision and establishes a more adventurous climate for further meetings of the group.

Handling a meeting of teachers, then, has many features in common with the teaching of pupils in that a knowledge of the participants, processes and content are vital, as is adequate preparation. In any such preparation the senior members of staff should seek to avoid falling into repetitive routines but should plan for variation of activities and experiences. These should be designed in ways which contribute to the goals and objectives of the meeting in particular and the school in general. They must also ensure that the time devoted to the meeting is utilised efficiently by preparing papers early enough beforehand for them to be read before the meeting. Meetings at which time is devoted to reading papers or listening to long expositions are bound to make intelligent people grudge the time spent. Even if the meeting is handled well and matters brought to a satisfactory conclusion, the question 'was it worth all the time?' is perhaps the greatest criticism which can be made of the teacher-manager's performance.

The Role of the School Office in Communication

In using both oral and written communication, the support of clerical and secretarial staff is vital. Good managers pay attention to the proper functioning of the school office and its contribution to effective communication. The value of an efficient and reliable clerical staff, especially when schools are large and the centres of management are widely scattered cannot be overstated. To avoid misunderstandings and friction, the role of the office staff needs to be analysed, made complementary to the needs of the school, and stated with sufficient clarity to remove all ambiguities. In addition, the image projected by office staff contributes to the tone of the school since it is commonly taken to be an extension of the headteacher's attitude and personality. Because of the confidential work they do and their role as 'gatekeeper' to the head and indeed the whole school, there is a danger that office staff may tend on occasions to forget that they are part of the 'technological support' system of the school, and not members of the 'strategic apex' in Mintzberg's terms (Chapter 4). However, since office staff do represent the headteacher on many occasions in a boundary-spanning role, care must be taken to ensure that such representation accurately reflects the headteacher's wishes. It is also vital that members of the office staff understand the formal organisation of the school and the methods of management in order that they can contribute in boundary spanning between headteacher and staff, and also between the school and its environment.

Communicating with Others

Although the aspects of communications described so far are mainly concerned with teachers as members of the strategic apex, middle line and operating core of the school, there is also a vital need to communicate efficiently with colleagues seen as working in the technostructure and support areas of the school. As the permeability of the school boundary increases and the school takes on the characteristics of an open system, greater attention must be paid to communication with those outside the organisation proper. Such communication then serves two main purposes:

- to improve the image of the school in the perception of outsiders, and
- to get things done.

A relatively new development in communication and boundary crossing emerged with the legal requirement to publish certain specific information regarding individual schools (Education (School Information) Regulations, 1981). Most LEAs have evolved a format for the ways in which their schools present the scheduled information, but there is considerable scope for variation in the ways in which schools seek to market themselves. A deliberate and sustained policy of projecting a favourable school image and marketing the school through the media of press, radio and television as well as through the activities of PTA, Community Association and so on, can draw attention to school activities and successes and publicise the contribution that the school makes to the life of the local community, thereby improving relationships with the members of the society it serves. Such efforts, of course, must be based on a good self-image of the school built up painstakingly and deliberately (Poster, 1982).With careful and sensitive handling, these attempts to present the school as an important community institution can also be used to gain recognition of the importance of education in general, and increase the status and credibility of the teaching profession.

Those involved in the technostructure and support areas form distinct and probably isolated groups in the total school staff. Only in relatively few schools are they encouraged to use the staff-room, their hours and conditions of employment are different from those of the teaching staff, and they belong to non-teaching unions. They also have a dual loyalty in that they have as their official superior the Superintendent of Caretakers or the School Meals Organiser; and often these LEA-based supervisors have more familiarity with their conditions of employment and interest in their well-being than do the teaching staff. However it is well to remember that such non-teaching staff are usually recommended for appointment by the governing body in consultation with the headteacher, who is, after all, held responsible for all aspects of the management of the school.

It is therefore important that teachers recognise that the nature of the contracts of the non-teaching staff are very different from their own. Although it is customary to invite non-teaching staff to school functions in order to indicate that they have a recognised and valuable contribution to make to the school, it must always be remembered that they are often paid on an 'hours worked' basis, and are entitled to overtime if they are asked to work outside their prescribed hours. In job-definition, too, all teachers must take care that they do not unwittingly antagonise ancillary staff by asking them to do jobs which they have mistakenly assumed would fall within their list of duties, only to find out later, possibly as a result of union intervention, that a major 'who does what' incident has been triggered off. In particular, lines of communication between caretaker and kitchen staff, and between caretaker and LEA Works Department are particularly difficult for the teacher to appreciate on the spur of the moment when a problem has arisen and a solution is required as a matter of urgency. The freedom of action enjoyed by the teachers as members of the professional bureaucracy gives them a misleading perception of the conditions of service of those working in the technostructure and the support structure.

Good relations between support staff and teachers can thus only be maintained by careful attention to methods of mutual communication. It is often assumed that information has found its way to the ancillaries only to discover later that they remain uninformed about school activities which have a considerable effect on their work. The usual way in which communication is maintained between teachers and support staff is by regularly scheduled informal meetings. This enables day-to-day contact to be maintained with interchange of information. It is usual for a senior member of staff to take charge of liaison with the caretaker and ancillary staff. Certain communications from the Education Office to the caretaker (for example, instructions for heating arrangements) can have such an effect on the physical environment of the school that the headteacher must be kept informed so that the information can be relayed to the staff.

Other major specialist areas in which non-teaching staff can make great contributions are in the science and technical departments of secondary schools. Other specialist non-teaching support is provided by the education welfare service, whose officers act with considerable freedom and discretion as boundary spanners. They frequently have on-going contact with pastoral staff and their access to parents enables them to act in ways similar to Likert's (1961) linking-pins between school and home - clearly a vital part of the school's communication scheme.

Bad Communication as the Cornerstone of Bad Management

The staff of any school consists of a number of well qualified and experienced teachers who are all trained as professional communicators in the classroom. They are often resentful of the 'non-teaching time' of senior staff and are critical of the use which is made of it. Formal communication systems which expand from an informal 'need to know' foundation are unsatisfactory in the school situation, since most of the teachers find ways of keeping themselves informed about the things that affect them most. Resentment occurs when people are not informed through the channels they were expecting to be used. In many cases it is not the lack of specific information which is the source of difficulty, but rather the perceived lack of organisation on the part of those who have information to impart. However, trying to tell everything to everybody is impractical and can only lead to information overload, with the attendant dangers.

Failure to communicate the school's aims, values and achievements to the community it serves would be regarded by the industrialist as failure to capitalise on opportunities for good publicity. While the maintained school is not in a position to advertise its products, apart from the school brochure, there is no question that, at a time when a decreasing number of schools is chasing a faster decreasing number of pupils, a good reputation may even be vital to a school's continued existence. Even where a school is not threatened, the principle of parental choice operates to increase the potential quality of the intake to those schools which have established good reputations, and part of each teacher's job is to communicate successes in his or her own sphere in order that the headteacher can develop a strategy for communicating these successes into the area where market forces operate.

CHAPTER 9

DEVELOPING TEACHERS AND SCHOOLS

Appraising for Development

During the 1980's, in particular, issues related to the appraisal of schools and teachers have become dominant themes. Often appraisal seems to be considered as an end in itself. This may occur because of the practical problems of implementing an appraisal system, problems exacerbated by the political pressures for establishing such a system. Practicalities of appraisal receive little attention in this book, but it would be impossible from a management context to overlook the place of appraisal. Without appraising the activities of teachers and schools efforts directed towards their improvement risk misdirection. Appraisal should provide the targets for development. Until quite recently the main function of appraisal in schools was to identify and prepare teachers for promotion. However, with more emphasis on organisational health (Miles, 1965) and the self-regeneration of schools, a broader view of appraisal has emerged. It seems to have been recognised that the processes and results of appraisal can lead to ways of diagnosing the causes of organisational inefficiency and indicate means of amelioration. Miles's definition of organisational health as 'the school system's ability not only to function effectively, but to develop and grow into a more fully functioning system', and his statement that 'attention to organisational health ought to be priority one for any administrator seriously concerned with innovativeness in today's education environment' are perhaps more apposite now than when written.

In the original context appraisal included two inter-related components. First, it involved the routine monitoring of the work done individually and by groups of teachers. Second, it was seen as a means of reinforcing accountability and increasing the control of the headteacher and senior members of staff over the activities of their junior colleagues in the professional bureaucracy of the school where a well-delineated hierarchy, overt chain of command, span of control etc., would prove unacceptable to many teachers. The process of appraisal also provided the basis for clearer definitions of teacher responsibilities and tasks, and led to clarification of job descriptions at a time of expanding education. The appraiser, too,could benefit from discussion with colleagues and gain a sharper knowledge of both personal and organisational strengths and weaknesses. More recently, with falling rolls and declining promotion prospects, the focus of appraisal activity has switched to issues concerned with job satisfaction and the effective use of resources - including staff. In this context Miles's recognition of problem-solving as the 'master dimension' of effective organisation is very appropriate, particularly his emphasis on communication adequacy ('how easily and accurately information travels in the organisation') and power equalisation ('a collaborative stance towards work, as contrasted with the exercise of arbitrary authority based on position', Schmuck and Miles, 1971).

In practice though most staff appraisal in schools has been informal. Often those appraised have not always been aware that it was taking place. Indeed, whenever two or more staff discuss work it is likely that some appraisal occurs as they attempt to assess one another and other teachers at a conscious or sub-conscious level (French, 1978). The move towards more systematic arrangements in schools, although owing something to a need for more flexible responses to changing demands, has been largely based upon external calls for the monitoring of the performance of teachers. In conditions of strict public expenditure controls and declining rolls the thrust has become inextricably linked in the minds of teachers and the public to issues associated with teachers' pay, efficiency and the sifting out of incompetent performers. As a result, any appraisal system that might be imposed is perceived all too easily as a threat with little attention being paid to the positive effects. To some extent, such perceptions have been exaggerated by the unwillingness of schools in the past to consider anything other than informal and casual approaches. In addition, there is the likelihood that an increase in formal appraisal will take place and with few staff holding any experience of designing and sustaining appropriate procedures there is a risk that schools will borrow from other environments (mainly commerce and industry) where arrangements have become refined over a period of years. This can result in insufficient consideration being given by schools to their own uniqueness; simultaneously, the establishment of some sort of appraisal system will be regarded as a hurdle to be overcome, rather than as providing the school with a range of potential opportunities to improve leadership, motivation and adaptability.

Even from an industrial point of view it is sometimes unclear whether the developmental possibilities of appraisal have been fully realised. For example, Scott and Edwards (1972) offer three aims for an appraisal system:

> to establish current levels of performance in the job and seek ways of improving it;
>
> to identify potential for improvement;
>
> to link salary realistically with performance.

Similarly Stewart and Stewart (1977) suggest a number of functions relating to the selection and induction of new staff (including personnel moved within the organisation to new posts), the identification of individual and organisational training needs, the planning of staffing requirements, and the production of an objective view of the current state of the organisation. While each of these may benefit from appraisal, the procedures which enable this to happen must be performed with caution both in schools and elsewhere. The issue of pay, for example, is totally outside the control of the headteacher whose only input to an appraisal situation in this context might be to assist a teacher to obtain promotion, and yet the importance of teachers being able to express their frustration about diminishing career prospects at a time of financial constraint should not be underestimated. In addition, attempts to judge an individual's potential can be double-edged, helping to show teachers what they might accomplish (usually in terms of career progress) but without any assurance that the frustrations that non-accomplishment might arouse can be ameliorated. There are also problems associated with attempts to predict an individual's potential in anything other than the short term (Drucker, 1955).

The main criticism, however, of these particular approaches is that they do not pay enough attention to what appraisal can offer the individual in relation to fulfilling developmental needs. They tend to represent an organisational perspective, when it is the compromise between organisational and individual interests which provides the dominant rationale. The school benefits by assessing its staff relative to the identification and achievement of objectives; teachers are helped to assess what they can gain from working in the school. Trethowan (1983) suggests a number of topics which a teacher might wish to consider in this context:

- discussion of performance in relation to school, departmental and house or year group objectives;
- co-ordination of job tasks with other staff;
- determination of priorities - within the job;
- assessment of stress in any area of work - its causes and possible means of alleviation;
- anticipation of problems associated with forthcoming tasks;
- changes that may be necessary in any element of task performance - and likely difficulties that could arise;
- minimisation of misdirected effort;
- monitoring of the performance of any staff for whom the teacher has responsibility;
- identification of job-tasks where performance might be improved - and the means to improvement.

- acknowledgement of the contribution to the working group and the school;
- development requirements related to the present job - and a discussion of readiness for, and possible availability of, promotion.

Reported in this way such a collection of targets may achieve little unless they encourage some consideration of teachers' higher order needs for recognition, achievement and personal development, through focusing attention upon such factors as the cognitive-rational elements in job decision-making, and the relation between effort, performance and the desirability of outcomes. Practically, of course, the uniqueness of each teacher's work environment will have considerable influence on perceptions of development. For example, Nias (1980) found that young primary school teachers favoured positive leadership (Chapter 3) which meant in practice a headteacher taking an interest in their development, monitoring their work, setting high professional standards and, while giving a lead in the formulation of school objectives and policy, encouraging and assisting teacher participation. Similarly, Hunter and Heighway (1980) , in their consideration of the problem of job-satisfaction during contraction in middle schools emphasised the need for greater recognition of teachers' work, more opportunities to be involved in the development of policy, and the taking of enhanced responsibility; it was considered that these would raise motivation. In their view, two-way communication would do much to improve job-satisfaction.

Of course, positive attitudes towards appraising for staff development can soon be dissipated if formal and systematic approaches established by a school do not appear to be meeting the requirements of individual members of staff. In addition, the likelihood of satisfying these requirements must be matched by the time and effort which individual staff and the school as a whole must devote to the mechanics of running any scheme. Warwick (1983) suggests a number of determining conditions:

- the positive side of a scheme should relate to the developmental needs of the teacher and school; how these might be satisfied must be reflected in the prevailing attitudes;
- there should be interested observers who ought to be able to see that the school has the capacity to organise an effective scheme and assist in the school's response to changing demands: this requires emphasis as on occasion it may divert attention from the main objectives of appraisal;
- all teachers should be offered the opportunity to perceive that the arrangements constitute an objective self-appraisal

and also cover their whole range of involvement with school activities;
- all teachers should be offered the opportunity to view the arrangements as equitable both between individuals and where all staff are involved, including the headteacher;
- any formal appraisal situation should include a two-way exchange of views;
- the teacher must be assured of confidentiality;
- reviews must become regular and consistent so that they form part of the continuing planning process of the individual teacher and the school.

A number of matters require clarification if the mode of appraisal developed is to provide a framework for staff development. First, it must include much more than self-assessment. While it would be remiss to belittle its importance (indeed Latham and Yukl, 1975 suggest that participation in self-assessment relative to goal-setting produces substantial improvements in performance), comprehensive appraisal seeks to encourage and support self-assessment by utilising the views, experiences and attitudes of others. A sense of achievement related to work and a view that effort is fully recognised cannot be entirely self-generated. Without the assistance of others, teachers may feel unable to satisfy fully their needs and realise their expectations while the school fails to exploit the psychological growth which can accrue to individuals through being able to exercise their skills and talents. It must be added, of course, that even if a strong relationship between job-satisfaction and performance exists for teachers (Sergiovanni, 1976) and if this notion is accepted by all teachers in the school, then introduction of appraisal procedures in an attempt to promote those factors leading to satisfaction, while limiting the influence of those likely to produce dissatisfaction, may not improve the performance of all teachers. Like everyone else, teachers cannot be compelled to be satisfied.

Second, the issues to be considered for appraisal must constitute more than simply a group of targets designed to raise the accountability level of the teacher. They need to relate to what the teachers themselves regard as relevant staff development matters.

Third, the place of classroom performance requires clarification. All teachers are evaluated at least once in their career (on entry to the profession) but by the use of criteria and acceptable standards of achievement which are never formally defined. They do, however, seem to relate closely to classroom performance. Clearly such an arrangement is unsatisfactory. Yet if 'the formal assessment of teacher performance' (CMND 8836, 1983 para. 92) were imposed upon schools there is a good chance that procedures in many schools would be restricted to classroom practice. Given the central importance of the classroom situation in teaching, this may seem hardly surprising but little detailed attention has been given to the factors which contribute to the achievement of teacher proficiency and its assessment (Wragg, 1984). In these circumstances the developmental thrust in appraisal is overlooked all too easily. The headteacher evaluates teacher X as good, and teacher Y as just satisfactory. Activities outside the classroom receive little attention. As a result X becomes complacent and Y may lose confidence unless offered a route towards improved performance. In either case there is a likelihood that appraisal will not be used as a base for development.

The fourth matter is concerned with the skills required by staff, particularly the more senior, who would be mainly responsible for introducing and sustaining any appraisal-based system of staff development. The specific requirements will depend on both the characteristics of the school and the procedures adopted, particularly as no single best system exists, and the suitability of any scheme relies upon the nature of the institution and the conditions in which it functions (Stewart and Stewart, 1977). The real problem is that in schools appraisal will be seen as a punitive measure, to punish the bad teachers and to chide the others into increased efforts. Unless well organised this will be the perception of many teachers about appraisal. The positive side, in which appraisal forms the essential framework around which a staff development programme is assembled requires effective management if it is to become dominant. Nevertheless senior staff must seek such a situation, for without the essential base provided by appraisal much developmental activity for the whole school, groups and individuals will be misdirected.

Staff Development

Schools introducing appraisal schemes report many practical difficulties making the process extremely time consuming (Turner and Clift, 1985). However, policy formulation and staff development procedures in a professional organisation form part of that process, and cannot be brief if the views of staff about individual needs and expectations are to be combined in a way which both incorporates and satisfies organisational requirements. If procedures to discover staff development needs are foreshortened some staff will readily convince themselves that their part in the school has little significance and that they have nothing to contribute to the establishment of consensus regarding the central balance of interest between the teachers and the school. However, in staff development it is worth taking time to establish the rationale for introducing procedures, before moving on to the next stage of implementation, for if the system is well organised dividends will be gained. Teacher activities will emerge from those parts of the discussion which have identified teacher requirements and are then used in the design of individual and group development programmes. The teachers are thus better motivated to commit themselves to developmental activities.

The notion that teachers require some form of in-service training is, of course, long-standing and subject to periodic restatement (DES, 1972) but the emergent strategies have frequently lacked a reliable base. Teachers may wish to develop their professional competence, evaluate their own work, receive assistance in looking towards the changing demands upon schools, and so on (ACSTT, 1974). Indeed, these desires are central to job-satisfaction, but they do not exist in a vacuum. Their satisfaction can only be achieved within the framework of the current job and this is becoming increasingly difficult with contraction and reduced promotional prospects. The function of management must be to assist individuals in defining their development objectives relative to those of the school. Without this, much in-service activity to date has been unco-ordinated, focusing for many teachers around perceptions of their own requirements. Often in an individual capacity (although perhaps supported financially by the school or local authority), many teachers have attended courses provided by a range of agencies (colleges, universities, teachers' centres) which have attempted some systemisation of what can be offered on a regional basis.

Even so, such arrangements tend to allocate scarce resources ineffectively, by concentrating on the product (the provision of courses for those who choose to attend) rather than the requirements of the clients - teachers whose needs have been redefined through discussion. Also, courses are only one of a range of activities which can assist in individual staff development. Other activities include guided reading, membership of discussion groups, observation of other staff, the availability of alternative experiences, the use of mentors and team teaching. Quite properly, such development is best viewed as a form of adult learning, whose main characteristics have been outlined earlier (Chapter 2). In particular the independence and initiative of the teacher as learner, the place of experience, the readiness of the individual to learn and the nature of the motivation, provide the main parameters which determine effectiveness. Teachers cannot be made to learn or instructed to develop. The essential rationale has to be that of self-development so that they want to develop to satisfy needs, fulfil expectations and achieve job-satisfaction. The responsibility of the school, the LEA and the education system as a whole is to provide the conditions and the opportunities, as well as feedback through appraisal, so that teachers find their work sufficiently interesting and rewarding, with the result that developmental activities are viewed as part of a logical progression.

The achievement of a balance between individual, group and school interests represents a new element introduced by appraisal. In effect, staff development in schools has by tradition been limited to self-development. It has been assumed that individual professionals have the competence, awareness and analytical skills to define their own developmental needs to find the means of satisfaction and ways of evaluating what has been achieved. That such assumptions have defects is clear: the impact of changing demands combined with financial retrenchment and reduced pupil numbers have made this increasingly obvious both to teachers and those outside schools. The advent of school-focused in-service education and training supported by the local authority provides a useful compromise between individually-oriented and institutionally-focused developments. The involvement of staff in the planning and organisation of such courses with the resulting commitment ensures that the topics chosen for discussion are relevant and appropriate to the needs of both teachers and institution (Jackson, 1978).

Ideally, the results of appraisal can be used to answer the questions of what, when, who and where posed in relation to management development in Chapter 2. In specific terms: what is the most appropriate development plan for individual staff; when should it happen; who should be included; and where should the formal elements of development take place? The dominant issues for a school, LEA or even DES in finding answers to these questions centre around the design of a strategy which acknowledges and encourages the individuality of the teachers (whether working alone or in groups) while still retaining the elements of an overall plan. If it appears too rigid and unable to take account of the individual characteristics (and perceptions) of each teacher involved, much of the appraisal-development activity will be dismissed by such teachers as staff training exercises in which needs have been identified by the headteacher, perhaps even with Local Authority backing. In effect this could be interpreted as a 'deficit-model' which concentrates upon the skills and attributes the teachers lack in achieving school objectives (Olsen, 1982). The possible conflict between individual and organisational goals needs to be borne in mind when applying published guidelines and procedures to individual schools. McMahon et al (1984) have drawn attention to this in connection with the GRIDS technique. However, there is an equal danger that a strategy determined by the perceptions of different staff members will, in the end, prove to be no strategy at all.

Even in a small school, the scope for individually focused development which can be identified varies enormously, because of the differences in attributes, experience and situational requirements. For example, some staff are justifiably proud of their teaching ability but remain quite unaware that changes are taking place which will make severe demands on their adaptability; other teachers, more aware of the demands, may well require support and encouragement if they are to become involved with new curricular materials or with children of a different age-range. Similarly, perceptions of job-satisfaction or the needs that are being satisfied by the job, vary considerably among teachers working in the same school, even though teaching loads and responsibilities appear similar. One such teacher may be frustrated with many aspects of school activity and experience decisional deprivation; another may be highly satisfied that the work with the pupils meets all job-related expectations. Further analysis may reveal that such differences are related to promotion aspirations as well as feelings of unrealised potential and the relative importance attached to the work being done.

In addition to differences resulting from individual preferences and characteristics there are others which are job-induced. The needs of a headteacher are clearly different from those of a scale 1 teacher, while the requirements of newly-appointed staff rarely coincide with those of more experienced colleagues. In secondary schools the demands are also subject-dependent; teachers of science, technology or vocationally oriented courses require regular up-dating of knowledge in addition to information regarding pedagogical developments. As new subject areas such as health education or pre-vocational activities emerge, an alternative staff expertise has evolved. These changes highlight the problem that a single pattern of staff development cannot satisfy the overall developmental need. Different patterns may be established, possibly based on the initial qualifications of teachers, followed by a period of induction after which staff may be entitled (or be obliged) to attend a certain number of courses, etc., each year throughout their careers. Such an arrangement would undoubtedly stimulate much activity but without individual assessment of needs, the very uniformity of such a system could prevent the development of further effective action.

A more promising approach than specifying a plan for all staff is to identify the possible constituents of a staff development programme (Billing, 1982). Six separate aspects can be suggested, although these are inter-related:

- the maintenance of educational competency, by considering the job and the activities of the school or department, in a wider educational context, particularly in relation to changing demands;

- the extension of pedagogic skill, through considering alternative teaching approaches, the availability of new equipment and materials, extra information on children's learning and other perspectives relative to curriculum design;
- the enrichment of professional knowledge in order to widen the information base and enhance confidence;
- the encouragement of flexibility in relation to teaching and in judgements which relate to the job;
- the fostering of personal growth and improvements in inter-personal relationships as a result of the job and job-related experiences;
- the stimulation of self-awareness and knowledge about the responsibilities associated with the job.

In pursuit of such intentions the necessity of individually designed packages is clear. Although not wholly based upon experiential learning, it is apparent that this mode must provide the main route towards development. Each teacher has certain experiences in the classroom and through discussion with other staff as a result of initial training and so on, is then offered an opportunity for organised reflection, with the intention that a learning cycle can be established (Chapter 2). In essence this consists of a blend of experiences and organised reflection, with time and support coming from a variety of sources - guided reading, membership of working groups, observation of others and attendance at courses (both in and out of school time). Some of the more technical components, changes in subject-content or alternative examining arrangements for example, are probably best learned by more formal means such as lectures or courses; others, such as self-awareness, have to be learned as part of the cycle. Further elements must therefore be added to any discussion relating to development as the most appropriate learning arrangements are identified and matched to the preferred learning style of the teacher.

The centrality of learning in staff development raises many issues, more so for teachers than members of other occupations. Many teachers for example, will have little awareness about their own learning needs or the most effective means for their satisfaction. Their job is to promote learning in children, but the nature and demands of that job can often inhibit their own learning. According to Hargreaves (1980) they often become bad learners, because their work as teachers concentrates upon a pedagogic learning mode. Only rarely do they give much attention to the concept of andragogy related to the self-directed independent learner. Yet if staff development strategies are to attain their objectives a new approach to teacher learning has to be appreciated and refined, and it will bear little resemblance to the learning arrangements found in many classrooms.

The attitude of senior staff towards this transfer of attention from pedogogic to andragogic learning is vital. They have to convince other members of staff of the benefits that can accrue to them as a result of being concerned about their own development. They are also in a position to persuade, advise, support or even cajole individuals into realising the potential gains which can be made. Perhaps in small primary schools this facilitating role will be limited to the headteacher (Southworth, 1983). In such circumstances this process of facilitation represents the single most important managerial function, and to discharge it competently requires the skill to apply considerable knowledge of the management processes discussed earlier. The function of the headteacher, and senior staff in secondary schools, can appear deceptively simple; it is basically to sustain a climate in which teachers wish to find out their own developmental needs in relation to the changing demands upon the school so that the satisfaction they seek from their work appears to be attainable and their promotion prospects increased. In practice such a climate is not easily maintained. Nor will it continue if teachers on a school staff decide they have no wish for developmental activities, for, as teachers have discovered with pupils, individuals cannot be made to learn. Attempts at direction, without acceptance, lead to disruptive behaviour by the would-be learner and misdirected efforts by the teacher or facilitator. A staff development arrangement for a primary school, for example, must rely on voluntary commitment for its success. In striving for an appropriate climate, of course, the headteacher aims for a situation where no staff wish to be excluded.

For success, however, voluntary commitment must be accompanied by some degree of formalisation in procedures. If development is based upon interviews then these need to be regular, well-planned, follow a consistent form and lead to a clear outcome; a chance meeting or conversation between headteacher and scale 1 teacher will not suffice. At its best the outcome will be an agreement about the developmental activities of a teacher (either individually or as a group member) in relation to the support available in the school and the LEA. Undoubtedly the agreement will require modification at later discussions. Within a framework of matching school to individual needs as circumstances and demands change, these agreements provide for a performance review, not only of the work of teachers involved, but also of the broader school situation. The process ought to be two way. The teachers need the opportunity to reflect and review the ways in which the school and sub-unit affect their performance. If the teachers allow their development needs to be influenced by school requirements, they have the right to expect reciprocation by the school. Any agreement between the individual and the organisation must be based upon trust. The skills of senior staff in shaping such agreements is crucial. As a result satisfying their own developmental needs becomes a dominant issue, particularly because of their responsibility in establishing a climate supportive of development. Senior staff are not well placed to advise other staff about learning needs and preferred styles without knowledge of their own, and it is difficult to see how this can be achieved without spending some time considering their own developmental requirements, following review of their performance.

Team Membership

The question of the suitability of venues for staff development activities has received only oblique mention so far. The most appropriate location for experiential learning must clearly be the school, while time for organised reflection is probably better spent in different surroundings, with access to a tutor or professionals from other institutions for group work. Escape from the day-to-day demands of the job can be of great value in the latter circumstances, provided that the time allowed does not reduce the impact of direct experience which may cause the learning to become blunted. In fact, when staff development consisted almost entirely of the individual activities of self-directed professionals it was assumed that all such development took place away from the school. Most in-service activities, full and part-time, were organised in colleges, universities, and teachers centres. When staff attended as individuals, normally only one member of staff of a particular school was able to attend. During the 1970s a trend towards more school-based activities emerged (Elliott, 1983).

A number of factors have contributed to this reorientation. First, it appealed during a time of increasing financial constraints, because of its relative cheapness. There are potential savings in organising a one-day course for the 20 teachers of one school as compared to, for example, supporting the equivalent of 20 days attendance at a variety of courses. Second, not only does the possibility of savings seem attractive but it is reinforced by the ease with which greater concern for cost-effectiveness can be demonstrated by such arrangements. It is far easier to convince governors, the LEA, or parents that school-based work intends to concentrate on the satisfaction of school needs, rather than the more nebulous results which can be portrayed as emerging from programmes apparently designed or selected by individual members of staff for their own, rather than the school's purposes.

A third factor contributing towards school-based work has been the movement of much curriculum development activity away from centrally determined projects (with schools viewed as passive recipients of ideas, materials, etc.) produced elsewhere, to the provision of more flexible material which emphasises the ability of the school to adapt it to its needs. Schools now accept curricular packages on the understanding that the teachers themselves will determine the most appropriate use for the materials. Simultaneously, such teachers are most likely to be generating and refining projects and schemes of their own in response to changing demands, and these also tend to create developmental needs common to a number of teachers. Fourth, with teachers remaining longer in the same school there is more opportunity to identify learning requirements across the whole staff of a school or department, and a greater likelihood that school-based developmental activities will prove beneficial before staff move on to other posts. With skilful management, issues relating to a school problem such as the introduction of a pre-vocational course or the establishment of a new mathematics syllabus, can be used as vehicles to expedite staff development.

From a management perspective the move towards school-focused developments appears to contradict the concept of the professional bureaucrat working autonomously in the classroom. Interactions among teachers are hurried and usually unplanned. Even with team-teaching - in open plan primary schools for example - the energy and time demands made by the pupils are so great that communication between teachers is 'fleeting' and 'spasmodic' (Southworth, 1983). Such working conditions may direct teachers towards self-reliance, but they are not conducive to team-building. However, in most work situations a group can achieve much more that a collection of individuals since the advantages gained by division of labour, the control of work, increased co-ordination of activities and greater liaison between teachers outweigh the disadvantages. Greater awareness of the potential benefits to be gained through teams of teachers would increase the capacity for discovery, processing and disseminating information and knowledge of the effects of external pressures. The members ought to be well-placed to generate and test ideas for the achievement of objectives; group loyalty and commitment may be produced; analysis of previous and current practices can be better carried out by discussion than by individuals working alone.

However, these benefits will only come if leaders (headteachers, heads of department, etc.) emerge convinced of the superiority of team development as opposed to individual progress. Considerable attention will have to be paid to the training of such team leaders, who will be operating at various centres of management within the school organisation. Many secondary schools have well-established senior management teams which seek to exploit the advantages of the team situation. In these, the headteacher and a few senior colleagues form the main policy-making and decision-making group. The sharing of responsibility duplicates changes which have occurred in other spheres (politics, industry and commerce) with the chief executive as a political leader still accepting ultimate responsibility, but supported by a 'team', 'task-force', 'policy group' or other support net-work. Such developments in schools and elsewhere reflect changing attitudes towards authority with the expectation that even the most senior members of staff should seek to involve others in decision-making, since the complexities of the organisation and its environment are such that all of the management tasks cannot be carried out by one person. It is also recognised that there are social and psychological benefits of group membership in addition to any perceived improvement in management performance.

It would, of course, be naive to argue that a school will necessarily achieve more of its objectives because it evolves a series of teams. Many other factors can also influence effectiveness. For example some schools could do better without a senior management team because other staff feel excluded from decision-making, and withdraw from participative structures. Alternatively, such a team may spend too much of its time on routine maintenance matters and fail to identify new objectives or assist staff in designing alternative curricular and teaching arrangements. More generally a team may lack the capacity to generate new ideas; conversely, it may possess this facility in abundance but is unable to convert ideas into working practices. Any of these deficiencies could arise from inappropriate distribution of team-roles rather than inadequacies in individual members. Clutterbuck (1979) proposes that four such roles are essential - generators, integrators, developers and perfecters. An absence of individuals able to adopt one particular role, or too many teachers wishing to play the same role, will unbalance the team and reduce its capabilities. After a long-term study of performance of personnel working in competitive situations, Belbin (1981) has suggested a more detailed categorisation of eight positive role-types which are found to develop when teams are set up:

- **company worker** - has a capacity for turning plans into practical functioning arrangements through hard work, self-discipline and organising ability.

- **chairman** - has a capacity for making the most effective use of the team's human resources by recognising strengths and weaknesses, welcoming all potential contributions and maintaining concentration upon objectives.

- **shaper** - has the ability to shape the team effort by directing attention towards aims and objectives, through a willingness to challenge complacency and self deception.

179

- **plant** - has an ability to advance new ideas and strategies in relation to major issues, often with a high level of intellect being utilised to assist the team to look at problems from an alternative perspective.
- **resource investigator** - has a capacity to search for additional resources outside the team, and a willingness to negotiate with contacts to make those resources available.
- **monitor - evaluator** - has a capacity to analyse problems and offer hard-headed judgements so that team ideas receive evaluation before decisions are made.
- **team-worker** - has an ability to respond to the needs of individuals and situations. This means that other team members can be supported with potential improvements to communication and team spirit.
- **completer - finisher** - has an ability to see a job through to completion so that the team is protected from error. This is combined with a willingness to search for tasks which require attention to detail.

A self-perception inventory enables individuals to assess their strengths and weaknesses in relation to these categories. In practice each of these role-types is related to a type of personality in a similar way to those described by Mosak (Chapter 7); it is this personality which emerges in a group setting and forms the basis of behaviour. In developing his views Belbin argues that six points emerge.

- The person actually in the chair (headteacher, house head etc.) should have personal attributes not dissimilar to the profile suggested for a good chairman.
- There ought to be a strong Plant in the team - that is, one member who must be both clever and creative, although the latter appears more important.
- A reasonable spread of mental abilities among team members is desirable, with at least one clever member, possibly as monitor-evaluator. The team would be further strengthened if there was one other clever member, as Plant, and a Chairman of above average intelligence.
- There are advantages in having a spread of personal qualities among group members so that the demands of team-roles can be accommodated.
- A good match between the attributes of team members and their responsibilities within the group is advantageous.
- The ability of team members to adjust their roles when imbalances emerge and are realised, can prove an important feature in the behaviour of successful groups.

However it must be remembered that any application of Belbin's ideas to the school situation requires caution. Their value derives from the way in which attention can be drawn to the need for self-awareness in maximising the effectiveness of group work. If circumstances permit, it may be possible to modify the membership of groups in such a way that the weaknesses of one teacher can be complemented by the strengths of others. Woodcock and Francis (1974) have developed a strategy for team-building and have recognised five stages in the development of teams - 'ritual sniffing', 'infighting', 'experimentation', 'effectiveness' and 'maturity'. They suggest that a knowledge of the characteristics of these stages can help the team-builder, and, although teams may sometimes cease to develop under their own natural momentum, any 'blockages' to team maturity can be recognised and must be removed before further development can take place.

The aim of the headteacher and senior colleagues, therefore, must be to convince staff of the advantages of team-building as a contributor to the effective management of schools. Although there may be difficulties in disturbing traditional groups of staff - the school management team, academic board, pastoral committee - the establishment of temporary study groups, working parties and other task-oriented groups should take as much account of the personalities of group members as of the status of the teachers invited to attend the meetings. Since teachers are potentially, at least, members of several such groups, this places special emphasis on the role of senior members of staff in appreciating the balance of team-roles required and also in diagnosing the reasons for the ineffective working of groups in which they may be involved. In a professional bureaucracy the quality of team membership and the leadership that senior staff can give have a powerful influence on the success of the team in contributing to the managerial processes taking place in the school. Francis and Young (1979, p8), in their definition of a team as

> 'an energetic group of persons who are committed to achieving common objectives, who work well together and enjoy doing so, and who produce high quality results',

indicate the potential benefit of active teams within the organisation.

Developing the school as an organisation.

The principle that a balance must be maintained between teacher and school interests through developmental activities underlies all aspects of team-building. In practice, or course, it is impossible to reconcile these interests continuously or in the perceptions of all members of staff. Disagreements about objectives and methods of allocation of resources, for example, are unavoidable. That is why skills of conflict-resolution and negotiation in particular are essential, as they are required even in the most appropriately constructed teams. Indeed a mixture of talents and abilities within a group will probably heighten tension with the consequent need for some members to adopt conciliatory roles. Similarly while headteachers and heads of department may strive to develop a climate in which staff wish to design and participate in group development programmes they may not be supported in this by all of their colleagues. Degrees of commitment vary and there is always the possibility that some teachers feel that involvement in developmental work has little or nothing to offer them. This diffidence may be due to a feeling either that such work is too much concerned with school issues in which the individual teacher has little or no stake, or simply that the teacher concerned has no wish to become involved in the new approaches. In discussing this issue Wallin and Berg (1983) maintain that the level of trust, collaboration and unity required to establish an appropriate climate for this form of participation is unlikely to be attained by teachers in a school.

Without a basic set of values leading to agreement about the detail of what to do and how it should be done, they suggest that the concept of a developing organisation is more realistic for schools. In contrast to organisational development this attempts to take account of the specific behaviour of teachers as they endeavour to satisfy their own needs and those of the pupils. This reinforces the view that organisational development in a school - the formulation and implementation of a plan to make the school more effective - cannot exist separately from the consideration of the developmental requirements of individual teachers. Drucker suggests that 'development is always self-development' (1974, p.447) and that development cannot be other that the responsibility of the individual.

The LEA, school or department clearly has some part to play in this development. The contribution of schools and LEAs in particular to supporting the development of teachers in this way has been limited. In general the view that the independent professional teachers are responsible for their own development has prevailed and few LEAs for example have tried to establish staff development policies preceding changes in school curricula; attempts to link promotion procedures to future staffing requirements are likewise rare. Without a well-developed appraisal procedure only a minority of schools have actually sought to ascertain the developmental needs of individual teachers, while even fewer have tried to match curriculum change in any systematic way to the satisfaction of these needs. Efforts to improve this situation, however, will be wasted if the importance of the perceptions of individual professionals is ignored. Moreover, if any activity seems to them to be concentrated too strongly on organisational needs at LEA or school level then resources will most certainly be misdirected.

While much of this in-service activity may lack systematisation and a balance of personal and individual learning is difficult to sustain, members of staff, and consequently the school, do develop by learning, and the ability to achieve this development, whether by a teacher or a school, represents the dominant feature of growth and self-renewal. The ability to discover and respond to information about themselves and the environment in which they work is vital for both individuals and schools. After years of study of the ways that individuals and organisations increase their responses to this information Argyris and Schon (1978) argue that 'single-loop learning' all too frequently prevails, particularly in relation to difficult problems. According to their definition learning takes place first when an organisation or individual achieves its intentions as a result of a match between goals and accomplishments, and second when there is a mismatch between achievements and intentions but identification and subsequent correction of specific problem areas lead to the conversion of mismatch to match. A state of single-loop learning exists when a match occurs, or a mismatch is corrected without the necessity of reviewing the values basic to the system involved - whether this consists of individuals, groups or whole organisations. Just as the human body has homeostatic mechanisms which detect and respond to changes (e.g. temperature regulation) on a 'too-low' or 'too-high' basis, without querying the reasons for the critical settings, so single-loop learning provides for a response to changes at a relatively low level of consideration (Argyris, 1982). In the context of school management single-loop learning can result in inordinate attention being paid to the minutiae of decision-making, while the major issues remain latent and unexplored. Where examination at a more fundamental level is involved, 'double-loop' learning is said to have taken place.

For a teacher at school to benefit from double-loop learning consideration has to be given to 'governing variables' - the preferences of individuals - when a match occurs or when a mismatch is corrected. For example, a school might obtain an excellent report following a visit from HMI or, alternatively, attempts may be made to remedy deficiencies after an LEA advisory report, but in both situations there is little opportunity for double-loop learning unless the variables which appear to motivate and frame the actions of staff receive attention. In such situations the actions taken by the headteacher or section head are crucial because they govern the responses of other staff. In double-loop conditions action leading to changes which might benefit pupils, or improved curricular arrangements which have resulted from the preparation for, or in the aftermath of, visits or inspections, are more important than the actual reports or the ability of the school to please or satisfy a group of visitors. In effect, double-loop learning assists staff to become accustomed to new reasoning processes and is particularly apposite in the context of school management. More clearly than ever the influence of senior staff must be seen to be not only on making adjustments and corrections to established practice, but also on the values and beliefs which underpin this practice and dominate the attitudes and behaviour associated with the introduction of new ones.

Teachers should be well-placed to refine their own approaches to the analytical processes demanded by double-loop learning. They benefit from a long period of education and so have had the opportunity to develop the associated skills of conceptualisation, observation and abstraction. Almost all teachers profess an interest and commitment to the work with children and are involved with a group of similarly educated colleagues, and, although opportunities for discussion may be restricted by timetable constraints, fundamental considerations of values and practices should be essential features of any teacher's working life. Teachers have the freedom within the classroom to respond flexibly to the demands made upon them. Rarely is any attempt made to dictate teaching style or specify definitively the tasks of a house head and the manner in which they ought to be carried out. If the learning processes of teachers can improve as a result of these freedoms, the school or department of which teachers are members can be further developed during discussion of the differences in interpersonal perspectives which emerge. The individual teachers in a school have different capacities for learning and develop them by a variety of routes and in relation to the influences of the external environment. The opportunities for contact between the staffs of different schools provide occasions for the comparison of perceptions and approaches and for greater appreciation of possible responses to changing external demands, and these strengthen organisational learning (Friedlander, 1983).

This view is extended by Silverman (1970) to the concept that members of staff construct their own unique pictures of the organisation and its relationship with the environment. This may result in the formation of different pictures and lead to conflicting demands upon the organisation and its sub-units. One teacher in a primary school may wish to respond to parental demands for higher reading standards by introducing an alternative reading scheme; a colleague may ignore such demands or even doubt their existence. If a change does take place and new arrangements are introduced and the parental responses monitored an alternative procedure will need to be established for continued monitoring. Thus learning by teachers can be seen to have taken place through an appreciation that opposing pictures of the school have developed from the different values and perceptions of staff. Without a discussion designed to reveal such alternative views the headteacher and other staff would remain unaware of their existence, and the school as a whole would have failed to take advantage of a potential learning situation. Yet if schools have to respond flexibly to changes in demand - through variation in pupils' needs or alterations in other factors which might affect their normal procedures - they must learn how to take advantage of such incidents. This does not imply that every source of pressure must produce a response, but the capacity to be aware of such pressures needs to be developed along with the ability to discriminate between those which require a response and others which do not.

To enable this form of developmental learning to take place the role of the managers in organisational learning is of considerable significance. They have to utilise the different values, attitudes, perceptions and abilities of the school staff through encouraging the establishment of teams and task-groups composed of teachers who have different viewpoints. In doing so however, they must recognise that some of the conflict generated will be almost impossible to resolve. Substantial and irreconcilable differences among the members of staff in a department for example, may accelerate the learning of individual members, but it will be unlikely to aid the department's capacity to design and achieve agreed objectives. The important task, however, of head and deputy headteachers in organisational learning is to help their colleagues to distinguish between 'doing things right' and 'doing the right things'. A school or any of its sub-units has to carry out certain activities which, if left undone or performed inadequately, would lead to fundamental questions being raised about the organisation. These are shown in the centre of Fig. 9.1 as 'Essential Activities'. Within this sphere of activity the organisation learns to 'do things right', and in practice this is much easier than learning to 'do the right things', of which there is an almost infinite number of possibilities to choose from - shown by the large outer area of Fig. 9.1 labelled 'Permissive Activities'.

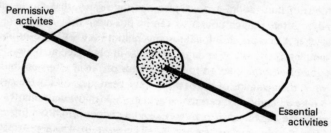

Fig. 9.1. Essential and permissive activities of a school.

185

Within the area of permissive activities lies the whole range of developmental possibilities available to the school or sub-unit, but the extent to which they are taken up depends largely on the capacity and willingness of the organisation to learn. These in turn rely heavily on the ability and commitment of the individual members of staff to develop their own managerial learning. Quinn (1982) has introduced the term 'logical incrementation' to describe management practices which try to ensure that groups of people move together in a dynamic environment. According to Pondy (1983) it includes a union of rational and intuitive behaviour in which incremental processes leading to goal identification and subsequent activities are conscious, proactive and purposeful. By learning logical incrementation, staff and their schools should be better placed to find flexible ways of satisfying the obligations which pupils and society place upon them.

In reality, though, the diagram of essential and permissive activities for the whole school has to be constructed from a series of separate but similar diagrams for each teacher. For the individual roles and relationships have developed around an essential collection of activities. With some junior staff these will relate principally to teaching and directly associated tasks. For many staff, particularly the more senior, a large range of permissive activities will have evolved as a result of negotiating with other individuals and sub-units. Thus many teachers have acquired management responsibilities through interest, ability or opportunism. Not only do these activities contribute to the informal organisation (Chapter 4), but if the focus of the negotiation is on the overall requirements of the school an interlocking jigsaw results (Fig. 9.2.), without gaps and covering as wide an area as possible. The individual teachers, working as a team, then cover the maximum range of developmental possibilities.

Although negotiation between individuals takes place continuously at edges of the pieces of the 'jigsaw', the general configuration can remain fairly stable. However, when roles and relationships become altered under conditions of innovation, certain 'pieces of the jigsaw' may change shape radically. Often a much poorer fit can be produced (Fig. 9.3).

If teacher A accepts additional responsibilities (as a TVEI co-ordinator, for example), there will be an initial decrease in permitted activities during the period of accommodation to the demands of the new responsibilities. Only when the demands of the new job have been met will the teacher feel able to take on additional permissive activities. Meanwhile, other teachers may well have expanded their interests and activities into areas previously considered the domain of teacher A. The ways in which processes of change and accommodation reverberate throughout the school is

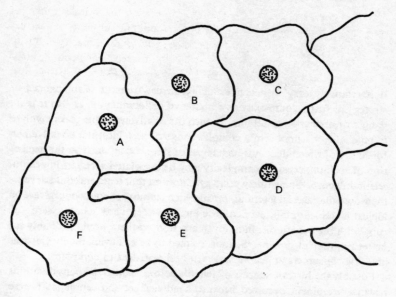

A - F represent individual teachers.

Fig. 9.2. Interlocking permissive activities of a small group of staff

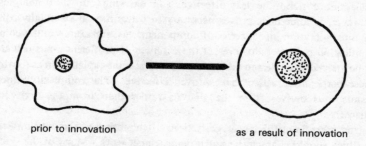

prior to innovation   as a result of innovation

Fig. 9.3. Changes in essential and permitted activities of teacher A

exemplified by such 'jigsaw diagrams'. The propensity of a school to accommodate the pressures which result from such re-negotiated changes is related to its organisational health. The encouragement for individual staff to develop perspectives in which they are prepared to utilise the **opportunities** created by change, rather than see it as producing a series of threats or constraints is clearly a major goal of any staff development programme.

CONCLUSION

It is relatively easy to perceive management writers as participants in a strategy to foster complexity as a matter of deliberate policy. There is the danger of appearing to attempt to turn the relatively simple tasks involved in managing a school into a complex range of activities, the effective performance of which demands high levels of skill. To an outsider the accusation of such unnecessary complexity may be associated with self-interest or self-indulgence. Some thirty years ago, notions that teachers could develop their own managerial learning, or that such learning should concentrate on logical incrementation, evoked little interest. Yet many schools were well run - with the benefit of hindsight, many non-teachers would probably say better run than at present. Schools seemed to be achieving their objectives and few consumers appeared sufficiently dissatisfied to complain.

Possibly the historic success of schools before managerial considerations became prominent occurred because headteachers and senior staff were already using the skills and approaches which now are receiving so much attention. If this is true then all that management writers have achieved is to label certain activities and give them wider publicity. In doing so, they analyse and describe what the best managers seem to be doing and, by implication, criticise the less effective. In carrying out such analyses, however, it sometimes proves necessary to categorise an essentially continuous operation into a series of components, as, for example, the communication process. However, if the practices of proficient managers are to be offered as models to others, there must be some explanation as to why these particular practices have proved effective. The complexity which results thus derives from the analysis rather than from the activities themselves.

Undoubtedly, artificial categorisations often mask the inherent simplicity which should characterise much management work. Many of the skills involved are readily visible in everyday life, particularly those concerned with working with people. Techniques and approaches which might promote good communications, improve motivation and commitment, provide better leadership, or enable staff to accept change more willingly, should not be difficult to understand or explain. Indeed, if they are, or are described in complex ways, the chances of acceptance and successful application are negligible. However, even where the tasks demanded of managers appear to be straightforward, other factors intervene to make excellent management, in schools and elsewhere, a fairly rare phenomenon.

The main factor relates directly to task performance. Although the individual tasks in a particular situation may be none too demanding for the manager, the skills required none too taxing, the real test of successful management lies in the ability to select the appropriate skills for the specific situation, coupled with the capacity to judge timing in their application. Significantly, success will also elude managers unless they have the confidence to use the skills they do possess. Often that confidence derives from their own sense of security. There is no better basis for individual or group frustration than a situation in which a manager knows what ought to be done but lacks the confidence to do it. Frequently, the reluctance to act decisively results from the complexity of the environment and the visibility of the manager's decision-making. No individual can be fully conversant with the multitude of issues which might be associated with a particular situation: there is no certainty that a single action, no matter how well carried out, will produce the desired effect. All management performance takes place in a large, often public, arena, within which numerous personalities, attitudes and interests intersect with the issues. Tasks are thus carried out in environmental contexts, and these can be extremely complex, even in a small school.

Indeed, over the last thirty years, the complexity of the school environment has increased. This has been accompanied by the development of increased scrutiny of the managerial practices in schools by more discerning consumers. Part of this increase in outside interest has resulted from a changing climate of accountability: schools, like all public organisations, are felt to be directly accountable both to the immediate consumer and to the wider audience of politicians and the public at large. Society frequently maintains that many of its problems would be alleviated if changes were made in the ways in which schools prepare young people. If a school is perceived as insufficiently effective, then public criticism will follow from those who feel they have a stake in the school's end products.

Such criticisms, of course, represent thinly-veiled demands, and these are often contradictory. Individuals and groups insist that schools concentrate on widely different priorities as regards teaching methods, the curriculum itself or even pupil behaviour, depending on the perspectives held by the different critics. For example, parents may want a liberal curriculum, excitingly taught (a better process) coupled with outstanding examination results (a good product). The staff of the school may well feel that these demands are mutually exclusive, and the task of the manager is to attempt to reconcile these views to the satisfaction of all concerned. Balancing such contradictions, monitoring changes in demands and attempting to achieve

CONCLUSION

a match between priorities, present an increasing managerial problem; the complexity of the environment compounds the problem. In some schools the issues are never resolved to the satisfaction of the majority; even in those in which there has been an attempt to develop the managerial skills of the staff, there is the paradox that more effective management exposes more problems which demand attention.

One result of this situation is that the number of management tasks is increased while the time available for their completion becomes increasingly restricted. The individual tasks are seldom more demanding. It is the rapidity with which they must be confronted, the problem of having to consider several apparently conflicting demands simultaneously, which raises the level of managerial competence required, and also increases the stress felt by the manager. Since management is essentially a practical activity it is the totality of the actions of a manager which determines effectiveness. The implications for managerial learning are enormous.

A manager can **learn** to become proficient in single, isolated skill areas -motivating colleagues, self-assertiveness, conflict resolution, and so on -but only rarely are these skills **used** in isolation. Any development achieved by an individual has to result from the acquisition of a range of possible managerial activities as a basis for action. A book of this nature would be of little use if it sought only to provide a theoretical framework to guide educational managers: arbitrary divisions of managerial practice must be made for analytical purposes, but the need for integration and synthesis of components must not be overlooked. Similarly, training activities seeking to concentrate attention on small portions of experience, need to be related to the broader range of managerial activities. Success is most likely when the managers appreciate what knowledge and experiential learning are available to help in the work situation in which they find themselves; because management is a practical activity the dominant form of learning must be experiential. The function of this book is to offer insights, supplementary material and explanations to support such experiential learning.

BIBLIOGRAPHY

ACFHE/APTI (1973) *Staff development in further education: Report of Joint ACFHE/APTI Working Party,* London

Adair, J. (1980) *Training for Leadership,* Gower, Farnborough

Adair, J (1973) *Action-Centred Leadership,* Gower, Farnborough

Albrecht, K. (1955) 'What is communication'? in Ayer, A.J. *Studies in Communication,* Secker and Warberg, London

Alderfer, C.P. (1972) *Existence, Relatedness and Growth: Human Needs in Organisational Settings,* Free Press, New York

Aldrich, H.E. (1979) *Organisation and Environment,* Prentice-Hall, Englewood Cliffs, New Jersey

Aldrich, H.E. (1976) 'Resource dependence and interorganisational relations', *Administration and Society,* 7, 419-454

Allport, C.H. and Odbert, H.A. (1936) ' Trait Names. A Psycholexical Study', *Psychological Monograph,* 211

Allutto, J.A. and Belasco, J.A. (1972) 'A Typology for Participation in Organisational Decision Making', *Administrative Science Quarterly,* 17, 117-125

Argyle, M (1974) *The Social Psychology of Work,* Penguin, Harmondsworth

Argyris, C. (1982) *Reasoning, Learning, and Action: Individual and Organisation,* Jossey Bass, London

Argyris, C. and Schon, D.A. (1978) *Organisational Learning: A Theory of Action Perspective,* Addision Wesley, Reading, Massachussets

Argyris, C. (1957) *Personality and Organisation: The Conflict between System and the Individual,* Harper Row, New York

Astley, W.G. and Van De Ven, A.H. (1983) 'Central Perspectives and Debates in Organisation Theory, *Administrative Science Quarterly* 28, 241-273

Atkinson, J.W. and Feather, N.T. (1966) *A Theory of Achievement Motivation,* Wiley, New York

Austin, B. (1979) *Time, the Essence - a manager's workbook for using time effectively,* British Institute of Management Foundation, London

Barnard, C. (1938) *The Functions of the Executive,* Harvard University Press, Harvard

BIBLIOGRAPHY

Barry, C.H. and Tye, F. (1972) *Running a School,* Temple Smith, London

Belbin, R.M. (1981) *Management Teams: Why they succeed or fail,* Heinemann, London

Bennis, W.G., Berne, K.D. and Chin, R. (eds) (1971) *The Planning of Change,* Holt, Reinhart and Winston, New York

Bentley, T.J. (1977) *Information, Communication and the Paperwork Explosion,* McGraw-Hill, London

Berg, L. (1968) *Risinghill: Death of a Comprehensive School,* Penguin, Harmondsworth

Bernbaum, G. (1976) 'The role of the head' in Peter, R.S. (ed.) *The Role of the Head,* Routledge and Kegan Paul, London

Berne, E. (1974) *What do you say after you say hello?,* Andre Deutsch, London

Berne, E. (1964) *Games People Play,* Penguin, Harmondsworth

Bernstein, B. (1971) 'On the classificastion and framing of Educational Knowledge' in Young, M.F.D. *Knowledge and Control,* Collier-Macmillan, London

Billing, D. (1982 *The Role of Staff Development,* SCEDSIP Occasional Paper 6, Birmingham

Bion, W.R. (1961) *Experiences in Groups, and other papers,* Tavistock, London

Birdwhistell, R.L. (1972) *Kinesics and Context: Essays on body motion communication* University of Pennsylvania Press, Philadelphia

Blake, R.R. and Mouton, J.S. (1964) *The Managerial Grid,* Gulf, Houston

Bodley, G.M. (1983) *Interviewing for selection decisions,* NFER - Nelson, Windsor

Bolling, R. (1983) 'The tyranny of special interest', *Harvard Business Review,* 61 (2), 90-91

Bolman, L.G. and Deal, T.E. (1984) *Modern Approaches to Understanding and Managing Organisations,* Jossey-Bass, London

Bolton, R. (1979) *People Skills,* Prentice-Hall, Englewood Cliffs, New Jersey

Boshear, W.C. and Albrecht, K.G. *Understanding People: Models and Concepts,* University Associates, La Jolla, California

Boulding, K.E. (1963) 'The organisation as a party to conflict' in *Conflict and defence,* Harper and Row, 145-165

Bower, J.L. (1983) 'Managing for efficiency, managing for equity' *Harvard Business Review,* 61 (4), 83-90

Bridges, E.M. (1982) 'Research on the School Administrator: the state of the Art 1967-1980' *Educational Administration Quarterly* 18(3), 12-33

Buckley, J. (1985) *The training of secondary school heads in Western Europe*, NFER-Nelson, Windsor

Burlingame, M. (1979) 'Some neglected dimensions in the study of educational administration' *Educational Administration Quarterly*, 15 (1) 1-18

Burns, M. (1978) *Leadership*, Harper and Row, London

Bush, T. et al. (eds) 1980 *Approaches to School Management*, Harper and Row, London

Butten, L. (1976) *Developmental Group Work with Adolescents*, Hodder and Stroughton, London

Campbell, R.F. and Gregg, R.T. (eds,) (1957) *Administrative Behaviour in Education*, Harper, New York

Carkhuff, R.R. (1969) *Helping and Human Relations: A Primer for lay and professional helpers*, Holt, Rinehart and Winston, New York

Carroll, D.T. (1983) 'A disappointing search for excellence' *Harvard Business Review*, 61(6), 78-88

Cheng, J.L. and McKinley, W. (1983) 'Toward an Integration of Organisation Research and Practice: A Contingency Study of Bureaucratic Control and Performance in Scientific Settings', *Administrative Science Quarterly*, 28, 85-100

Clutterbuck, D. (1979) 'R & D under Management's Microscope', *International Management*

CMND 8836 (1983) *Teaching Quality*, HMSO, London

Cohen, M.D., March, J.G. and Olsen, J.P. (1972) 'A garbage can model of organisational change' *Administrative Science Quarterly*, 17(1) 1-25

Coldicott, J. (1985) 'Organisational Causes of Stress on the Individual Teacher' *Educational Management and Administration*, 13(1), 90-93

Conway, J.A. (1984) 'The Myth, Mystery and Mastery of Participative Decision Making in Education' *Educational Administration Quarterly*, 70(3), 11-40

Conway, J.A. (1978) 'Power and Participatory Decision Making in Selected English Schools' *The Journal of Educational Administration*, XVI (1), 80-96

Cooper, C.L. (1981a) *Coping with Stress at Work*, Gower, Farnborough

Cooper, C.L. (ed.) (1981b) *Psychology and Management*, Macmillan, London

Craig, D.P. (1978) *Hip pocket guide to planning and evaluation - a suggested approach*, University Associates, La Jolla, California

BIBLIOGRAPHY

Creighton, H. (1983) 'Analysing Policy development in curriculum innovation: a suggested approach' *Journal of Educational Administration* XXI (2), 121-136

Danzier, K. (1976) *Interpersonal Communication,* Pergaman Press, London

Davey, D.M. and McDonnell, P. (1975) *How to Interview,* British Institute of Management, London

Davis, K. (1977) 'Management Communication and the Grapevine' in Porter, L.W. and Roberts, K.V. (eds.) *Communication in Organisations*

Davis, J.H. (1969) *Group Performance,* Addision-Wesley, Reading, Massachusetts

de Bono, E. (1979) *The Happiness Purpose,* Penguin, Harmondsworth

Dennison, W.F. (1985a) 'Flexible Structures and Secondary Schools' *Educational Management and Administration* 13(1), 29-36

Dennision, W.F. (1985b) *Managing the Contracting School,* Heinemann, London

Dennision, W.F. (1983) 'Reconciling the Irreconcilable: Declining Secondary School Rolls and the Organisation of the System', *Oxford Review of Education,* 9 (2), 79-89

DES (1972) *Teacher Education and Training,* HMSO, London

DES (1982) *Education 5 to 9,* HMSO, London

DES (1983a) *Circular 3/83: The Inservice Teacher Training Grants Scheme,* HMSO, London

DES (1983b) *Curriculum 11-16: towards a statement of entitlement: curricular reappraisal in action,* HMSO, London

DES (1985a) *Better Schools,* HMSO, London

DES (1985b) *Science 5-16: a statement of policy,* HMSO, London

Deutsch, M. (1972) 'Productive and Destructive Conflict', in Thames, J.M. and Bennis, W.G. (eds.) *Management of Change and Conflict,* Penguin, Harmondsworth

Dewe, P.J. (1985) 'Coping with work stress: an investigation of teacher's actions' *Research in Education,* 33, 27-40

Dollard, J. (1939) *Frustration and Aggression,*Yale University Press, New Haven

Douglas, A. (1957) 'The peaceful settlement of industrial and intergroup disputes' *Journal of Conflict Resolution,* 1, 67-81

Drucker, P.F. (1974) *Management Tasks, Responsibilities, Practices,* Heinemann, London

Drucker, P.F. (1970) *The Effective Executive,* Pan Books, London

Drucker, P.F. (1955) *The Practice of Management,* Heinemann, London

Dubin, P. *Human Relations in Administration,* Prentice Hall, Englewood Cliffs, New Jersey

Dunham, J. (1984) *Stress in Teaching,* Croom-Helm, London

Dwyer, J.F.H. (1984) *Preparation for Secondary Headship,* Whitley Bay High School Resources Centre

Eilon, S. (1984) 'Analyzing the Art of the Possible' *The Times Higher Educational Supplement,* 13/9/84

Elliott, J. (1983) 'School focused INSET and research into teacher education' *Cambridge Journal of Education,* 13(2), 19-31

Emmerson, R.M. (1962) 'Power dependence relations, *American Sociological Review,* 27, 31-41

Esp, D (1983) 'Training Approaches in Various European Countries - An Overview' in Hegarty, S. (ed.) *Training for Management in Schools*

Etzioni, A. (1966) *A gradualist strategy at work in studies of social change,* Holt, Reinhart and Winston, New York

Etzioni, A. (1964) *Modern Organisations,* Prentice-Hall, Englewood Cliffs, New Jersey

Everard, H.B. (1984) *Management in Comprehensive Schools: What can be learned from industry,* Centre for the study of the Comprehensive School, York

Eysenck, H. (1953) *Uses and Abuses of Psychology,* Penguin, Harmondsworth

Fast, J. (1970) *Body Language,* Evans, New York

Fayol, H. (1949) *General and Industrial Management,* Pitman, London

Festinger, L. (ed.) (1964) *Conflict, Decision and Dissonance,* Stanford University Press, Stanford

F.E.U./PICKUP (1984) *Exploiting Experience,* HMSO, London

Fiedler, F.E. (1967) *A Theory of Leadership Effectiveness,* University of Illinois Press, Illinois

Fielder, F.E. (1958) *Leader attitudes and group effectiveness,* University of Illinois Press, Illinois

Finlayson, D.S. (1973) 'The goal structure of teachers in comprehensive schools', *Educational Research,* 15, 188-194

Francis, D and Young, D. (1979) *Improving Work Groups: a practical manual for team building,* University Associates, La Jolla, California

French, B. (1985) 'Stress in Educational Management - Underlying Factors?' *Educational Management and Administration,* 13 (2), 94-98

French, W.L. (1978) *The Personal Management Process,* Houghton Mifflin, New York

French, J.R.P. and Raven, B. (1959) 'The bases of social power' in Cartwright, D. *Studies in Social Power,* Institute of Social Research, University of Michigan

Friedlander, F. (1983) 'Patterns of Individual and Organisational Learning' in S. Srivista (ed.), *The Executive Mind*

Frieson, D., Holdaway, E.A. and Rice, A.W. (1983) 'Satisfaction of school principals with their work' *Educational Administration Quarterly,* 19 (3), 35-39

Glatter, R. (1972) *Management Development for the Education Profession,* Harrap, London

Goffman, E. (1965) *Behaviour in Public Places,* Free Press, New York

Goffman, E. (1971) *Relations in Public: Microstudies of the Public Order,* Penguin, Harmondsworth

Goffman, E. (1969) *The presentation of Self in Everyday Life,* Doubleday, New York

Goldsmith, W. and Clutterbuck, D. (1984) *The Winning Streak,* Weidenfield and Nicholson, London

Gomberg, W. (1966) 'The trouble with Democratic Management' *Transaction* 3(5), 30-35

Gouldner, A.W. (1955) *Wildcat Strike,* Routledge and Kegan Paul, London

Gouldner, A.W. (1958) 'Cosmopolitans and Locals: Towards an analysis of latent social roles' *Administrative Science Quarterly* 2, 280-306 and 444-480

Gray, H.L. (1982) *The management of educational institutions: theory, research and consultancy,* Falmer Press, Lewes

Greenfield, T.B. (1975) 'Theory about organisation: A New Perspective and its implications for Schools' in Hughes, M.G. (ed.) *Administering Education: International Challenge* Åthlone Press, University of London, London

Gronn, P.C. (1983) 'Talk as the Work: The Accomplishment of School Administration' *Administrative Science Quarterly,* 28, 1-21

Gronn, P.C. (1982) 'Neo-Taylorism in Educational Administration?' *Educational Administration Quarterly,* 18(4), 17-35

Gross, N. et al (1971) *Implementing Organisational Innovations: a Sociological Analysis of Planned Educational Change,* Basic Books, New York

Hackett, P. (1978) *Interview Skills Training,* Institute of Personnel Management, London

Hall, D.T. and Nougaim, K.E. (1968) 'An Examination of Maslow's Need Hierarchy in an Organisational Setting' *Organisational Behaviour and Human Performance,* 3, 12-35

Hall, R.H. (1963) 'Interorganisation structural variation - application of the bureaucratic model' *Administrative Science Quarterly,* 7, 295-308

Halpin, A.W. (1966) *Theory and Research in Administration,* Macmillan, New York

Halpin, W.W. and Croft, D.B. (1963) *The Organisational climate of schools,* Mid Western Administration Centre, Chicago

Handy, C.B. (1985, Third edition) *Understanding Organisations,* Penguin, Harmondsworth

Handy, C.B. (1984a) 'Educating for Management outside Business' in Goodlad, S. (ed.) *Education for the Professions,* SRHE & NFER -Nelson, Guildford, Surrey

Handy, C.B. (1984b) *Taken for granted? Understanding Schools as Organisations,* Longmans, York

Hanson, E.M. (1979) 'School Management and Contingency Theory - an emerging perspective' *Educational Administration Quarterly,* 15(2), 98-116

Hanson, E.M. and Brown, M.E. (1977) 'A contingency view of problem-solving in schools: a case analysis' *Educational Administration Quarterly,* 13(2), 71-91

Hargreaves, D. (1980) 'The Occupational Culture of Teachers' in Woods, P. *Teacher Strategies,* Croom Helm, London

Harris, T.A. (1978) *I'm OK - You're OK: a practical guide to transactional analysis* Avon Books, New York

Hawley, K.E. and Nichols, M.L. (1982) 'A Contextual Approach to Modeling the Decision to Participate in a "Political" Issue' *Administrative Science Quarterly,* 27, 105-119

Hegarty, S. (ed.) *Training for Management in Schools,* NFER-Nelson, Windsor

Herzberg, F.W. (1966) *Work and the Nature of Man,* Staples Press, London

Hilsum, S. and Strong, C.R. (1978) *The Secondary Teachers Day,* NFER, Windsor

H.M.I. (1984) *Education Observed,* HMSO, London

Hodgkinson, C. (1983) *The Philosophy of Leadership,* Basil Blackwell, Oxford

Hollingsworth, A.T. and Hoyer, D.T. (1985) 'Training: How Supervisors can Shape Behaviour' *Personnel Journal* 54(5) 86-88

Honey, P. (1976) *Face to Face: Practical Guide to Interactive Skills,* Institute of Personnel Management, London

BIBLIOGRAPHY

Honey, P. and Mumford, A. (1983) *Using your Learning Styles,* Honey, Maidenhead

Hoy, W.K. and Sousa, D.A. (1984) 'Delegation: The Neglected Aspects of Participation in Decision Making' *The Alberta Journal of Educational Research,* XXX(4), 320-331

Hughes, M.G. (1984) *Educational Administration: Pure or Applied,* Studies in Educational Administration, CCEA, Armidale, New South Wales

Hughes, M.G. (1977) 'Consensus and Conflict about the Role of the Secondary School Head' *British Journal of Educational Studies,* 25(1), 32-49

Hunter, C. and Heighway, P. (1980) 'Morale, Motivation and Management in Middle Schools' in T. Bush et al. (eds.) *Approaches to School Management*

Hurst, P. (1982) 'Ideas into action: development and the acceptance of innovations' *International Journal of Educational Development,* 1(3), 79-102

Ichheiser, G. (1970) *Appearance and Realities: Misunderstanding in human relations,* Jossey-Bass, London

Jackson, J.M. (1977) 'The organisation and its communication problems', in Porter, L.W. and Roberts, K.H. (eds.), *Communication in Organisations*

Janis, I.L. and Mann, L. (1977), *Decision Making: A Psychological Analysis of Conflict, Choice and Commitment,* Free Press, New York

John, D. (1980) *Leadership in Schools,* Heinemann, London

Jones, J.E. (1981) 'The Organisational Universe' in *Annual Handbook for Group Facilities* University Associates, La Jolla, California

Jongeward, D. (1976) *Everybody wins: Transectional analysis applied to organisations,* Addison-Wesley, Reading, Massachusetts

Kast, F. and Rosenweig, J. (eds.) (1973) *Contingency Views of Organisation and Management,* Science Research Associates, Chicago

Katz, R. (1982) 'Effects of Group Longevity on Project Communication and Performance' *Administrative Science Quarterly,* 27, 81-104

Katz, R.L. (1955) 'Skills of an effective administrator', Harvard Business Review, 33(1) 33-42

Katz, D. and Kahn, R.L. (1978, Second edition) *The Social Psychology of Organisation,* Wiley, London

Klinger, E. and McNelly, F.W. (1969). 'Fantasy Need Achievement and Performance: A Role Analysis' *Psychological Review,* 76, 574-591

Knowles, M.S. (ed.) (1984) *Andragogy in Action,* McGraw-Hill, London

Kolb, D.A. (1983) *Experiental Learning: Experience as the Source of Learning and Development*, Prentice-Hall, Englewood Cliffs, New Jersey

Koontz, H., O'Donnell, C. and Weihrich, H. (1980) *Management*, McGraw-Hill, London

Lam, Y.L.J. (1985) 'Exploring the Principles of Androgogy: Some Comparisions of University and Community College Learning Experiences' *The Canadian Journal of Higher Education*, XV(1), 39-52

Landers, T. and Myers, J. (1980) 'Organisational and Administrative Theory' in Bush, T. etal. (eds.) *Approaches to School Management*

Larson, R.L. (1982) 'Planning in Garbage Cans: Notes from the field', *Journal of Educational Administration* xx(1), 44-60

Latham, G.P. and Yukl, G.A. (1975) 'A Review of the Research on the Application of Goal Settings in Organisations', *Academy of Management Journal*, 18, 824-845

Lawler, E.E. (1973) *Motivation in Work Organisations*, Brooks-Cole, Monterey, California

Lawrence, P. and Lorsch, J. (1969) *Organisation and Environment: Managing Differentiation and Interaction*, Irwin, Homewood, Illinois

Leithwood, K. (1986) *Preparing Principals for School Improvement*, Croom-Helm, London

Lewin, K. (1947) 'Frontiers in group dynamics: method and reality in social science; social equilibria and social change', *Human Relations*, 1(1), 5-41

Lewin, K., Lippett, R. and White R.K. (1939) 'Patterns of agressive behaviour in experimentally erected social climates', *Journal of Social Psychology*, 10, 271-279

Likert, R. (1967) *The Human Organisation*, McGraw-Hill, London

Likert, R. (1961) *New Patterns of Management*, McGraw-Hill, London

Litwak, E. and Hylton, L. (1962) 'Interorganisational analysis; a hypothesis on co-ordinating agencies, *Administrative Science Quarterly*, 6, 395-420

Locke, E.A. (1976) 'The Nature and Courses of Job-Satisfaction' in Dunnette, M.D. (ed.) *Handbook of Industrial and Organisational Psychology*, Rand McNally, New York

Locke, E.A. (1969) 'What is job-satisfaction?' *Organisational Behaviour and Human Performance*, 4, 309-336

Lowther, M.A. and Stark, J.S. (1984) 'Perceptions of work-related conditions among teachers, and persons in other occupations' *The Journal of Educational Research*, 77(5), 277-282

Luft, J. (1969) *Group processes: an introduction to group dynamics* Mayfield, Palo Alto, California

Luft, J. (1969) 'Johari Window: An experience in self-disclosure and feedback' in Pfeiffer, J.W. and Jones, J.E. (eds.), *A handbook of structured experiences for human relations training*, University Associates, La Jolla, California

Lutz, F.W. (1982) 'Tightening up Loose Coupling in Organisations of Higher Education' *Administrative Science Quarterly*, 27, 653-669

Lutz, F.W. and Ramsey, M.A. (1973) 'Non-directive cuts as ritualistic indicators in educational organisation' *Education and Urban Society*, 5, 345-365

Maier, N.F.R. (1976) *The Appraisal Interview: Three Basic Approaches*, University Associates, La Jolla, California

Main, A. (1984) *Educational Staff Development*, Croom-Helm, London

Mann, R.D. (1959) 'A Review of the Relationships between Personality and Performance in Small Groups', *Psychological Bulletin*, 56, 241-2

Mant, A. *Leaders we deserve*, Martin Robertson, Oxford

March, J.G. and Cohen, M.D. (1974) *Leadership and Ambiguity*, McGraw Hill, London

March, J.G. (1981) 'Footnotes to Organisational Change'. *Administrative Science Quarterly*, 26, 563-577

Martin, W.J. and Willower, D.J. (1981) 'The Managerial Behaviour of High School Principals' *Educational Administration Quarterly*, 17(1), 69-90

Maslach, C. and Jackson, S. (1981) 'The Measurement of Experienced Burnout' *Journal of Occupational Behaviour*, 2, 99-113

Maslow, A.H. (1959) *Motivation and Personality*, Harper, New York

Mayo, E. (1933) *The Human Problems of an Industrial Civilisation*, Macmillan, New York

McCaskey, M.B. (1974) 'A Contingency Approach to Planning: Planning with Goals and Planning without Goals' *Academy of Management Journal* 17(2), 283-286

McClelland, D.C. (1961) *The Achieving Society*, Van Norstrand, New York

McCormick, E.J. and Ilgen, D. (1981, Seventh edition) *Industrial Psychology*, Allen and Unwin, London

McGregor, D.G. (1960) *The Human Side of Enterprise,* McGraw-Hill, London

McKenzie, R.F. (1973) *State School,* Penguin, Harmondsworth

McLeary, L.E. (1968) 'Communications in Large Secondary School' *Bulletin of Association of Secondary School Principals,* 52, 325

McMahon, A. et.al. (1984) *Guidelines for review and internal development in schools: secondary school handbook,* Longmans, York

Merton, R.K. (1957) 'The Role Set: Problems in Sociological Theory' *British Journal of Sociology,* 8(2) 106-120

Meyer, M.W. (ed.) (1978) *Environments and Organisations,* Jossey-Bass, London

Miles, M.B. (ed.) (1964) *Innovation in Education,* Columbia University Teachers College Press, New York

Miller, G.A. (1968) *The Psychology of Communication,* Penguin, Harmondsworth

Miner, J.B. and Dachler, H.P. (1973) 'Personnel Attitudes and Motivation' *Annual Review of Psychology,* 24, 379-422

Mintzberg, H. (1979) *The Structuring of Organisations,* Prentice-Hall, Englewood Cliffs, New Jersey

Mintzberg, H. (1973) *The Nature of Managerial Work,* Harper and Row, London

Miskel, C.G. (1984) 'Effects of principal succession on school coupling and effectiveness', *Research in Educational Administration and Supervision,* 4(2), 23-36

Miskel, C.G. (1982) 'Motivation in Educational Organisations', *Educational Administration Quarterly,* 18(3), 65-88

Miskel, C.G., Feverly, R. and Stewart, J. (1979) 'Organisational Structures and processes, perceived school effectiveness, loyalty and job-satisfaction', *Educational Administration Quarterly,* 15(3), 97-118

Moeller G.H. and Charters, W.W. (1966) 'Relation of Bureaucratation to sense of Power among Teachers', *Administrative Science Quarterly,* 10, 444-465

Morgan, C. et al. (1983) *The selection of secondary school headteachers,* Open University Press, Milton Keynes

Morley, I.E. (1981) 'Bargaining in Negotiation' in Cooper, C.L. (ed.) *Psychology and Management*

Morris, D. (1977) *Manwatching. A field guide to human behaviour,* Jonathan Cape, London

Mosak, H.H. (1971) 'Life Style' in Kelly, A.N. (ed.) *Techniques for Behaviour Change,* C.C.Thames, Springfield

BIBLIOGRAPHY

Mouton, J.S. and Blake, R.R. (1984) *Synergogy: A new strategy for Education, Training and Development,* Jossey-Bass, London

MSC - Manpower Services Commission, *Management Self Development: A practical Manual for managers and trainers,* Sheffield

Musgrove, F. (1971) *Patterns of Power and Authority in English Education,* Methuen, London

Muth, R. (1984) 'Towards an Integrative Theory of Power and Educational Organisations', *Educational Administration Quarterly,* 20(2), 25-42

Mykleton, R.J. (1985) 'Work stress and satisfaction of Comprehensive School Teachers: An Interview Study', *Scandinavian Journal of Educational Research,* 29(2), 57-71

Nias, J. (1980) 'Leadership styles and job-satisfaction in Primary Schools' in Bush, T. et al. (eds.), *Approaches to School Management*

Nixon, K. (1974) 'Customer Contact Skills - an assessment of effective approaches', *Industrial and Commercial Training,* 6(1), 26

NUT (1981) *A fair way forward: NUT memorandum on appointment promotion and career development,* London

Nyberg, D. (1981) *Power over power,* Cornell University Press, Cornell

OECD (1982) *Inservice Education,* Paris

Olmosk, K.E. (1972) 'Seven Pure Strategies of Change' in Pfeiffer, J.W. and Jones J.E. (eds.) *The 1972 Annual Handbook for group facilitors,* University Associates, La Jolla, California

Olsen, T.P. (1982) 'School -Based In-Service Education: Model or Utopia' *British Journal of Inservice Education',* 8(2), 73-79

Packwood, T. (1977) 'The School as a Hierarchy' *Educational Administration,* 5(2), 1-14

Padgett, J.F. (1980) 'Managing Garbage Can Hierarchies' *Administrative Science Quarterly.* 25, 583-602

Paisey, A. (1984) 'Trends in Educational Leadership Thought' in Harling, P. (ed.) *New directions in educational leadership,* Falmer, Lewes

Parmerlee, M.A. et al. (1982) 'Correlates of Whistle-blowers' Perceptions of Organisational Retaliation' *Administrative Science Quarterly,* 27, 17-34

Pastor, M.C. and Erlandson, D.A (1982) 'A study of higher order needs strength and job satisfaction in secondary public school teachers' *Journal of Educational Administration,* XX(2), 172-185

Pedler, M. et al (1978) *A managers guide to self-development,* McGraw-Hill, London

Perls, F.S., Hefferline, R.F. and Goodman, P. (1972) *Gestalt Therapy: Excitement and Growth in the Human Personality,* Souvenir Press, London

Peters, T.J. and Waterman, R.H. (1982) *In Search of Excellence: Lessons from America's Best-Run Companies,* Harper & Row, London

Pettigrew, A.M. (1972) *The Policies of Organisational Decision-making,* Tavistock Publications, London

Pfeffer, J. (1981) *Power in Organisations,* Pitman, London

Pfeffer, J. and Salancik, G.R. (1978) *The External Control of Organisation: A Resource Dependence Perspective,* Harper & Row, New York

Pocock, J.G.A. (1973) *Politics, Language and Time,* Methuen, London

Pondy, L.R. (1983) 'Union of Rationality and Intuition in Management Actions' in Srivasta, S. (ed.) *The Executive Mind: New Insights on Managerial Thought and Action,* Jossey-Bass, London

Pondy, L.R. (1967) 'Organisation Conflict, Concepts and Models' in Thomas, J.M. and Bennis, W.G. *Management of Change and Conflict,* Penguin, Harmondsworth

Porter, L.W. (1963) 'Job attitudes in management', *Journal of Applied Psychology,* 4

Porter, L.W. and Roberts, K.H. (eds.) (1977) *Communication in Organisations,* Penguin, Harmondsworth

Poster, C. (1982) *Community Education: its Development and Management,* Heinemann, London

Poster, C. (1976) *School Decisionmaking: Educational Management in Secondary Schools,* Heinemann, London

Prebble, T.K. (1978) 'Goal dissensus and educational change' *The Journal of Educational Administration,* XVI (1), 7-18

Pugh, D.S. and Hickson, D.J. (1976) *Organisation Structure in its Context: Aston Programme 1,* Saxon House, Farnborough

Quinn, J.B. (1982) 'Managing Strategic Change' in Tushman, M.L. and Moore, W.L. (eds.), *Readings in the Management of Innovation,* Pitman, Boston

Raven, J. (1977) *Education, Values and Society,* Lewis, London

Rawlinson, J.G. (1978) *Creative Thinking and Brainstorming,* British Institute of Management, London

Reddin, W.J. (1970) *Managerial Effectiveness,* McGraw-Hill, London

Reich, C.A. (1971) *The Greening of America,* Penguin, Harmondsworth

Revans, R.W. (1980) *Action Learning,* Blend and Briggs, London

Rodgers, E. and Shoemaker, F.F. (1971) *Communications of Innovations: A Cross-Cultural Approach,* Free Press, New York

Roger, E.M. and Agarawal-Rogers, R. (1976) *Communication in Organisations,* Free Press, New York

Schein, E. (1971) 'The individual, the organisation and the career: A conceptual scheme', *Journal of Applied Behavioural Science,* 7, 401-426

Schilit, W.K. and Locke, E.A. (1982) 'A Study of Upward Influence in Organisations', *Administrative Science Quarterly,* 27, 304-316

Schools Council (1968) *Enquiry 1: Young School Leavers,* HMSO, London

Schmuck, R.A. (1974) *The Creativity of the School,* CERI, Paris

Schmuck, R.A. and Miles, M.B. (1971) *Organisational Development in Schools,* University Associates, La Jolla, California

Schwab, R.L. and Iwanicki, E.F. (1982) 'Perceived Role Conflict, Role Ambiguity and Teacher Burnout' *Educational Administration Quarterly,* 18(1), 60-74

Scott, B. and Edwards, B. (1972) 'Appraisals and Appraisal Interviewing', *Notes for managers: 18,* The Industrial Society, London

Sergiovani, T.J. (1967) 'Factors which affect satisfaction and dissatisfaction of teachers' *The Journal of Educational Administration,* V(1), 66-82

Shenton, K. and Dennison, W.F. (1978) 'Professional autonomy versus educational effectiveness: The example of a split-site comprehensive school' *The Irish Journal of Education,* 12(1 & 2), 36-49

Shiman, D.A. and Lieberman, A. (1974) 'A New-model for School Change' *Educational Forum* 38(4), 443

Silverman, D. (1970) *The Theory of Organisation,* Heinemann, London

Simon, H.A. (1964) *Administrative Behaviour: A study of decision-making processes in administrative organisation,* Free Press, New York

Simon, H.A. (1957) *The New Science of Management Decision,* Harper Row, New York

Smith, A.G. (1966) 'Communication and Status' in *The Dynamics of a Research Centre,* Eugene Centre for Advanced Study of Educational Administration, Eugene

Smith, D.F. (1982) 'Teacher Participation /Consultation in Decision Making in some of the 11-16 Secondary Schools of Cleveland' Unpublished B.Phil Dissertation, University of Newcastle-upon-Tyne

Sousa, D.A. and Hoy, W.K. (1981) 'Bureaucratic Structures in Schools: A refinement and synthesis in measurement' *Educational Administration Quarterly,* 17(4), 21-39

Southworth, G.W. (1984)' Development of Staff In Primary Schools (some ideas and implications)' *British Journal of Inservice Education,* 10(3), 6-15 ·

Sperry, L. and Hess, L.R. (1974) *Contact Counselling: Communications Skills for People in Organisations,* Addison-Wesley, Reading, Massachusetts

Srivasta, S. (ed.) (1983) *The Executive Mind: New Insights on Managerial Thought and Action,* Jossey-Bass, London

Stewart, R. (1982) *Choices for the Manager,* McGraw-Hill, Maidenhead

Stewart, R. (1967) *The Reality of Management,* Pan Books, London

Stewart, V. and Stewart, A. (1977) *Practical Performance and Appraisal,* Gower, Farnborough

Stodgill, R.M. (1974) *Handbook of Leadership,* Free Press, New York

Stodgill, R.M. (1948) 'Personal Factors Associated with Leadership: A Survey of the Literature' *Journal of Psychology,* 25, 35-71

Stodgill, R.M. and Coons, E. (1957) *Leader Behaviour: Its Description and Measurement,* Ohio State University, Ohio

Strauss, A. et al. (1963) 'The hospital and its negotiated order' in Friedson, E. (ed.) *The Hospital in Modern Society,* Macmillan, New York

Tannenbaum, R. and Schmidt, W.H. (1958) 'How to Choose a Leadership Pattern', *Harvard Business Review,* 36(2), 95-101

Taylor, A. and Sluckin, W. (1982, Second edition) *Introducing Psychology,* Penguin, Harmondsworth

Toffler, A. (1973) *Future shock,* Pan Books, London

Tolman, E.C. (1932) *Purposeful Behaviour in Animals and Men,* Appleton-Century-Crofts, New York

Torrington, D. and Weightman, J. (1982) 'Technical atrophy in middle management' *Journal of General Management,* 7,(4), 5-17

Trethowan, D. (1983) *Management in Schools - Target Setting,* Education for Industrial Society, London

Turner, C. and Clift, P. (1985) *A First Review and Register of School and College Based Teacher Appraisal Scheme,* Open University Press, Milton Keynes

Vernon, M.D. (1969) *Human Motivation,* Cambridge University Press, Cambridge

Vroom, V.H. (1964) *Work and Motivation,* Wiley, New York

Wailin, E. and Berg, G. (1983) 'Research into the School as an Organisation III. Organisational Development in schools or developing the school as an organisation?' *Scandinavian Journal of Educational Research,* 27, 35-47

Warwick, D. (1983) *Management in Schools - Staff Appraisal*, Education for Industrial Society, London

Weber, M. (1947) *The Theory of Social and Economic Organisation*, Free Press, New York

Weick, K.E. (1979, second edition) *The Social Psychology of Organising*, Addison-Wesley: Reading, Massachusetts

Weick, K.E. (1976) 'Educational organisations as loosely coupled systems' *Administrative Science Quarterly*, 21, 1-19

Whitaker, P. (1980) *Selection Interviewing*, Industrial Society, London

Wildavsky, A. (1972) 'The self-evaluating organisation' *Public Administration Review*, 32, 509-520

Willsmer, R.L. (1984, 2nd edition) *The Basic Arts of Marketing*, Business Books, London

Willower, D.J. (1982) 'School Organisations: Perspectives in Juxtaposition', *Educational Administration Quarterly*, 18(3), 89-110

Wilmot, W.N. (1975) *Dyadic Communication - a Transactional Perspective*, Addison Wesly, Reading, Massachussetts

Woodcock M. and Francis, D. (1982) *The Unblocked Manager: a practical guide to self-development*, Gower, Farnborough

Wragg, E.C. (1984) *Classroom teaching skills: the research findings of the Teacher Education Project*, Croom-Helm, London

Wright, P.L. and Taylor, D.S. (1984) *Improving Leadership Performance*, Prentice Hall International; London

Yukl, G. (1975) 'Towards a Behavioural Theory of Leadership' in Houghton, V. et.al. (eds.), *Management in Education - The Management of Organisations and Individuals*, Open University Press, Milton Keynes

INDEX

AUTHOR INDEX

AUTHOR INDEX

Edwards, B. 167
Eilon, S. 24
Elliott, J. 177
Emmerson, R.M. 74
Etzioni, A. 40, 110
Everard, H.B. 113, 119
Eysenck, H. 136

Fast, J. 143
Fayol, H. 58, 105
Feather, N.T. 47
Festinger, L. 106
Fiedler, F.E. 35, 38, 40, 70
Finlayson, D.S. 93, 97
Francis, D. 113, 181
French, B. 112
French, W.L. 167
French, J.R.P. 74
Friedlander, F. 184
Frieson, D. 44

Goffman, E. 63, 123, 138
Goldsmith, W. 33, 96
Gomberg, W. 42
Goodman, P. 122
Gouldner, A.W. 86, 87
Greenfield, T.B. 103
Gregg, R.T. 21
Gronn, P.C. 16

Hacket,, P. 138
Hall, D.T. 46
Hall, R.H. 56
Halpin, A.W. 43, 94, 113
Handy, C.B. 13, 18, 24, 32, 34, 38, 48, 94, 98, 157
Hanson, E.M. 68
Hargreaves, D. 173
Harris, T.A. 130

Hawley, K.E. 75
Hefferline, R.F. 122
Hagarty, S. 1
Heightway, P. 169
Herzberg, F. 43, 44, 49
Hess, C.R. 117, 136
Hickson, D.J. 56
Hilsum, S. 50
Hodgkinson, C. 51, 52
Holdaway, E.A. 44
Hollingworth, A.T. 3
Honey, P. 26, 30, 134, 141
Hoy, W.K. 57, 59, 85
Hoyer, D.T. 3
Hughes, M.G. 17, 21
Hunter, C. 169
Hurst, P. 80
Hylton, L. 87

Ichheiser, G. 124
Ilger, D. 48
Iwanicki, E.F. 109, 111

Jackson, J.M. 145, 173
Jackson, J. 107
Janis, I.L. 90
John, D. 159
Jongeward, D. 124, 132

Kahn, R.L. 34, 45, 95
Katz, D.24, 34, 45, 95
Klinger, E. 47
Knowles, M.S. 29
Kolb, D.A. 28
Koontz, H. 45

Landers, T. 32, 39
Larson, R.L. 103, 104
Lam, Y.L.J. 130

211